BAD
PSYCHOLOGY

BAD PSYCHOLOGY

How Forensic Psychology Left Science Behind

ROBERT A. FORDE

Jessica Kingsley *Publishers*
London and Philadelphia

First published in 2018
by Jessica Kingsley Publishers
73 Collier Street
London N1 9BE, UK
and
400 Market Street, Suite 400
Philadelphia, PA 19106, USA

www.jkp.com

Library of Congress Cataloging in Publication Data
A CIP catalog record for this book is available from the Library of Congress

British Library Cataloguing in Publication Data
A CIP catalogue record for this book is available from the British Library

ISBN 978 1 78592 230 5
eISBN 978 1 78450 505 9

Printed and bound in Great Britain

For all those psychologists who work hard,
often against considerable odds,
and sometimes outright persecution,
to provide an evidence-based service.

ACKNOWLEDGEMENTS

No book is the product of one person's efforts. Directly or indirectly, we are all influenced by others who therefore contribute to what we achieve. A glance at the bibliography at the end of this book will reveal the names of scores of people who have influenced me by the quality of their work. I would like to mention two colleagues in particular: Dr Brian Stollery, who was my supervisor at the University of Bristol when I did my master's degree, and Professor Tony Beech, who was my doctoral supervisor at the University of Birmingham. I did both of these degrees late in life; both supervisors were younger than I, but rose to the challenge admirably.

I would also like to thank Graham Taylor, who on the basis of his long experience in the publishing industry advised me on publishers to approach, and how to pique their interest. Thanks also go to the staff of Jessica Kingsley Publishers, without whom the book would never have reached publication.

Lastly, and most importantly, I would like to thank my family for their encouragement and forbearance. The latter applies particularly to my wife, Pam, who married a widower late in life and then became a grass widow herself for three years while he did his doctorate and another year while he wrote a book. I thank her also for her frank criticism of the early drafts and her ability to convey the expectations of the 'general reader', as she is not a psychologist. One in the family is enough.

CONTENTS

– 1 –

WHO DOES HE THINK HE IS?

My reason for writing this book is to challenge some widely held but erroneous views in psychology. These views are costing taxpayers a great deal of money and blighting many lives. Because I am a forensic psychologist most of the examples I use come from that field, but some of the conclusions may also challenge views held in other fields of psychology. I aim to show why they are erroneous, and that there are alternatives. This is not a popular position to take, almost by definition.

There is a particular reason why I have come to the views that I now hold. During much of the 1980s and 1990s I was not working in psychology at all. I had previously worked in HM Prison Service (as it was then called in England and Wales) for eight years, but left in 1978. At least in part, I left because of frustration that psychologists were not being used properly. In many prisons they were not being used at all, and it often seemed that no one (including the psychologists themselves) knew what they should be doing. In 1999 I returned to psychological work, and to the criminal justice sector, and found that a great deal had changed. Far from being underused, psychologists now seemed to be ruling the roost. They were running various 'programmes' intended to change the behaviour of prisoners and reduce their risk of reoffending. They were also closely engaged in assessing the risk that parole applicants might pose to the public if release was granted. Other professionals were often surprisingly deferential to the psychologists, many of whom were inexperienced and still in training.

Initially I was delighted to see that psychologists appeared to have found their role within prisons. I even recommended their programmes in some cases with which I dealt. Then doubts began to creep in. For one thing, I was not happy simply to be told that offending behaviour programmes were effective; a responsible professional wants to see the evidence, and my prison service colleagues were disturbingly unable to refer me to it. They had rules to follow, and that is what they did. They didn't appear to know what the evidence was, but would hide behind statements declaring in effect that whatever it was, it was good enough for the Home Office (and later the Ministry of Justice) so that was that. The scientific evidence was contained in research papers published in academic journals, and I began to read them with a sense of steadily mounting dismay. It was abundantly clear that much of the evidence was of very poor quality, and that the effectiveness of these programmes had never been established according to good scientific standards. Having been a reviewer for an academic journal, and subsequently forensic editor of another, which means having to advise on whether articles are up to publishable standard or not, I knew a bit about this. There were similar problems with psychological methods of risk assessment. Ministry of Justice psychologists (and sometimes probation officers) were routinely giving evidence before the Parole Board and laying claim to levels of accuracy which were frankly absurd. The academic literature made it clear that the prediction of reoffending was only about 70 per cent accurate. That's it: 70 per cent is as good as it gets. This is not a high figure, but it is even less impressive when you remember that you can get 50 per cent accuracy by tossing a coin! What's more, this figure refers to making predictions about groups of people. Predictions about individuals are much more likely to be wide of the mark.

To begin with I was very nervous about questioning any of this. After all, the people who had accepted this evidence, no matter how weak it seemed to me, were highly qualified and experienced. Many of the front-line staff were trainees, but those who ran the service and told them what to do often had years of experience behind them, and many had doctoral degrees. Part of obtaining a doctorate is the study of advanced research methods; surely these people must know their stuff? Surely they could not be wrong?

Reading more of the academic literature made it clear that they were not only wrong, but disastrously and irretrievably wrong. Public policy in this area had taken a wrong turning some years ago, and had departed from the scientific evidence on which it was supposed to be based.[1] It also became clear that the public had been needlessly endangered as a result, and equally that many low-risk prisoners had been refused parole when it would have been perfectly safe to release them. All because of 'expert' evidence which was not worth the paper it was printed on: expensive evidence, which provided a livelihood for what I have come to think of as the 'offending behaviour industry'. As the American writer Upton Sinclair used to say, 'It is difficult to get a man to understand something, when his salary depends on his not understanding it.'[2] Therefore, if the evidence threatens our employment, the evidence must be wrong.

So much for a rational stance based upon the evidence. The more I studied what was going on, the more it seemed that what was preventing many of my colleagues from seeing the evidence clearly was not some conscious (and therefore corrupt) attachment to money or career goals. It was not an attack of some kind of irrationality, and it was certainly not lack of intelligence.

---

1   The practice of psychology in criminal justice policy has been influenced by the so-called 'New Public Management' school of thought, according to Professor Brian Thomas-Peter (2006) and Professors Towl and Crichton (2016). This emphasises outcomes (rather than inputs), targets and competition.

2   Sinclair, U. (1935) *I, Candidate for Governor: And How I Got Licked.* University of California Press, 1994, p.109.

It was the fact that psychologists, like those whom they study, are human beings. As a profession, we often forget this, and implicitly assume that our judgements about other people are not subject to the same flaws as *their* judgements are. In fact, there is abundant and increasing evidence that psychologists' judgements are subject to exactly the same weaknesses as everyone else's. The difference is that we are often put in a position to affect people's lives profoundly by the judgements that we make. This is true in educational psychology and clinical psychology, where decisions can affect people's entitlement to services. In forensic psychology, it can affect people's entitlement to liberty. In some non-British jurisdictions it can affect their entitlement to life itself. It seemed that there was nothing for it but to challenge the prevailing orthodoxy, and that is what I began to do, especially when giving evidence in parole hearings. Very often a prison psychologist would report on the same prisoner, but come to a very different view of his suitability for parole. Partly, this was because prison psychologists have a standardised training so that they always write their reports in the same way. This tends to produce a formulaic report in which pretty much the same recommendations are always made. Importantly, because it never occurred to them that their conclusions might be challenged, very little evidence was ever given to support the claims that were made. For example, if someone had committed a particular kind of offence it was routine that a particular kind of offending behaviour programme would be recommended for him. My own reports were not based on official training, but were much more like an academic paper. They contained references to the published research literature so that readers could see how my opinion had been reached, and what scientific evidence there was for it. Professionals in both the Ministry of Justice and the Parole Board found this very challenging, and there has been an aggressive response.

Unlike some people who have challenged an entrenched and allegedly scientific point of view, I have not received death threats.[3] I have, however, received verbal abuse, been subject to slanderous allegations, and encountered attempts to discredit my work, put me out of business or have me declared unfit to practise my profession. One attempt even involved lawyers paid at the taxpayers' expense to make representations to the British Psychological Society to have me removed from one of their committees. All these attempts failed, which says something in itself; but in a profession that is supposed to be guided by the scientific evidence one might expect a more rational response. One might reasonably expect to be challenged to defend one's position with reference to the evidence, or perhaps be invited to a discussion or debate in order to resolve the differences. None of these has occurred, which is odd if the practitioners concerned are convinced that their position is sound.

People who challenge a point of view that is widely accepted within their profession should be prepared not only to express their views, but also to explain why they are qualified to do so. I am not referring simply to relevant academic and professional qualifications (although I do hold them) but to the reasons why they adopted their view when many others in their profession have not. What makes them particularly fit to express a divergent point of view? Why should anyone listen to them? The views which they are challenging have been accepted by hundreds of their professional colleagues, especially those acting for criminal justice services, and acted upon for decades. Who do the critics think they are? These are reasonable questions, and no one undertaking a challenge like this should duck them.

First, I should point out that I am far from the only one to express these views. Many who agree with me are among

---

3 For example, Alice Dreger, who challenged widely accepted anthropological dogma and gender stereotypes in her book *Galileo's Middle Finger* (Dreger 2015).

the foremost international researchers on the planet.[4] Similar views are regularly expressed by independent psychologists in parole hearings throughout the UK. By 'independent' I mean psychologists who are in private practice, often sole practitioners, and who are therefore not constrained by departmental requirements like their colleagues in the Ministry of Justice. According to the British Psychological Society, only about a third of registered forensic psychologists work for that Ministry,[5] so it is not the sole arbiter of good practice in this field. Furthermore, many of its psychologists are still in training, and many leave without ever qualifying. They are not therefore the most experienced or most highly qualified members of the profession. The situation in other countries may be different, and the profession is not always divided up into the same specialisms. In the United States, for example, there is no separate specialism of forensic psychology. American forensic psychologists tend to be clinical psychologists who have specialised in forensic work, but there is no accepted definition of 'forensic psychologist' there.

Over the last 40-plus years, since graduating in 1969, I have worked in a variety of fields, starting as a prison psychologist in the Home Office (there was no Ministry of Justice then) and later moving to the Home Office in London as a senior research officer. After that came periods of working in education, business, and staff selection and training for the private prison sector. There was also a period of keeping house while my wife went out to work, and some work as a writer. This adds up to

---

4   For example, Rice and Harris 'The size and sign of treatment effects in sex offender treatment' (2003). They showed that most of the studies claiming effectiveness for sex offender treatments were seriously flawed. Where the flaws have been avoided, no treatment effect is found, as was confirmed by Schmucker and Lösel (2015).

5   This was the approximate figure given by the BPS when I was a member of its Forensic Division Committee from 2013 to 2016.

over 40 years' experience of a wide and varied range of work, both inside and outside the psychological profession.

When it comes to knowledge of good psychological practice, I was for four years a member of the British Psychological Society's Investigatory Committee. This investigated complaints of misconduct against psychologists as there was no statutory regulatory body at the time. We handed that duty over to the legally established regulator, the Health Professions Council (now the Health and Care Professions Council), in 2009. From 2015 to 2017 I was a member of a working party established by the British Psychological Society to draw up revised professional practice guidelines for the profession as a whole.

My contention is not that psychology in general, or forensic psychology in particular, has no value. Far from it. I firmly believe that it could help us avoid many policy mistakes and take better decisions. On the other hand, the further we get from the scientific evidence the worse our judgement becomes. There are many reasons why we drift away from the evidence, but the fact that we have done so in forensic psychology has resulted in a generation of bad policy decisions and damaged many individuals. It is common to find that people have a cavalier attitude to the lives of offenders or prisoners. However, some of these policies may have resulted in *increased risk* on the part of released offenders, and the public should certainly care about that. Professionals should care about it anyway, as humanitarian values are enshrined in their professional codes of practice.

In the following chapters I aim to show what has gone wrong, what we can do about it, and how we might prevent it from continuing.

2

HOW PSYCHOLOGISTS WORK

Psychologists generally work as consultants of one kind or another. That is, they are usually invited into a situation to sort out a problem. Even those who work routinely in one place, such as clinical psychologists in one of the health services, can be regarded as consultants to the individual patients with whom they work. Generally speaking, the patient has a problem and needs help in solving it. In other situations, psychologists may be consultants to an organisation rather than an individual. This is usually the case with occupational psychologists (usually called organisational psychologists in America), who work in business settings. Some of their work may be with individuals, but typically they are called in by the organisation in order to help it improve one of its tasks, such as staff selection or training.

In prison settings, psychologists are usually permanently employed in the organisation, and may fulfil a variety of roles. In UK prisons, and those of many other countries, the task is largely to run (or train others to run) offending behaviour programmes for prisoners. These are mostly group work programmes intended to challenge and try to change the attitudes and beliefs that are supposed to give rise to offending behaviour. This approach is based very much upon the use of group work in clinical psychology over many years. In theory, actions are preceded by thoughts, feelings and habitual reactions to situations. In theory, if we can change these thoughts, feelings and habitual reactions we can change the way the person behaves after release from prison. In theory.

Whatever role they take in an organisation, and in whatever setting, psychologists tend to work in the same sort of way. There are stages which their work has to pass through, and these form a generally recognised model of psychologists' ideal working practice. There is nothing controversial about this, and when working on the British Psychological Society's Professional Practice Guidelines Group we adopted this five stage model:

1. Assessment

2. Formulation

3. Intervention

4. Evaluation

5. Communication.

Sometimes these are presented in the form of a wheel or circle, so that after Communication the psychologist moves on to Assessment again and the cycle repeats. In more cynical moments, I am tempted to think that psychologists spend a lot of their time going around in circles, but of course the cycle diagram does not represent this. It is meant to imply that the process is continuous, with the psychologist's actions being continually revised in the light of progress. Ideally, this is perhaps how it should work. In this chapter I will examine each stage in turn and then consider legal regulation, which has a lot to do with how professional standards are maintained. Finally, there will be a short section describing the structure of this book, and how the subsequent chapters split the subject matter between them.

ASSESSMENT

Most people are probably familiar with the idea of psychological tests, especially IQ tests. This is not the place to go into that subject in detail, although there will be some consideration of it later on. Psychological tests can certainly be helpful in accomplishing some kinds of task. For example, there is no doubt that they can be helpful in staff selection procedures,[1] and can save organisations a great deal of money by making these procedures more effective.

Two key concepts in the field of assessment and testing are reliability and validity. Reliability means the extent to which a test consistently measures the same thing, be it an aspect of personality, ability, a person's attitudes or some other characteristic. There are different kinds of reliability. Test-retest reliability is a measure of the test's ability to obtain the same result if it is carried out at two different times (say, one month apart). Inter-rater reliability is a measure of its ability to obtain the same result if it is carried out by two different assessors; if this is poor, then it is measuring the assessor's behaviour as much as the client's. There are other kinds of reliability, but for those not interested in the detail the general concept is probably information enough:[2] a test is reliable if it consistently measures the same thing. Reliability can be measured mathematically; it does not have to be perfect (and it never is) but there are generally recognised levels of reliability that assessment techniques should reach.

Validity is the extent to which the test measures what it is intended to measure. A test cannot be valid if it is not also reliable. That is, it cannot consistently measure the *right* thing if it does not consistently measure the *same* thing. A test could perhaps be highly reliable, but if it was intended to measure IQ and it was actually measuring anxiety it would not be a lot of use as an indicator of ability. The validity of a measure

---

1   Among many examples, see Robertson, Bartram and Callinan (2002).

2   And for those who are interested, a good basic text such as that by Kline (2000) will explain the whole subject of psychological assessments and how they are developed.

is assessed in a variety of ways, including seeing whether it predicts relevant behaviour, finding out how it relates to other measures of similar characteristics, and whether items on the test cover the full range of the characteristic in which we are interested. Again, the basic concept is simple: a test is valid if it measures what it is supposed to measure. As with reliability, validity can be measured mathematically and is never perfect. In fact, we wouldn't want perfect validity in the sense of having one measure correlate perfectly with another. If two measures correlate perfectly, then one of them is redundant!

Any form of assessment (and not just a traditional pencil and paper test) must be both valid and reliable, or it is useless. Indeed, this applies to all forms of measurement, whether psychological or not. Modern measures of validity and reliability are highly mathematical and require a great deal of data. Assessment measures are not normally marketed until validity and reliability have been established through an extensive programme of research.[3] But 'assessment' covers more than the assessment of an individual's characteristics. It may include that, particularly where a psychologist is working with a client on a one-to-one basis. However, in this more general context it refers to the assessment of the problem which has been brought to the psychologist. As mentioned above, this may be an organisational problem or perhaps a problem within a family. For a criminal profiler it might even be an assessment of patterns of crimes committed by someone who has not yet been identified. It is common that psychologists working with offenders are required

---

3   Unfortunately, this is not invariably the case, especially where some of the older assessment methods are concerned. Once a test has gone into production and is being marketed to practitioners, defects in its reliability and validity are often played down. There is a parallel here with the behaviour of pharmaceutical companies (Goldacre 2012). It costs money to publish tests (as it does to publish books) and publishers obviously want to get the costs back. Furthermore, if a test becomes very popular it can be a real money spinner. I have dealt with this problem elsewhere (Forde 2017).

to assess their 'criminogenic' needs. In other words, they are asked to assess the presence and severity of various factors in the offender's life which are known to be associated with the risk of further criminal behaviour. This assumes that (a) we know what these factors are, and (b) we have a means of measuring them in some way. As will be seen later, these assumptions are very often unwarranted. Because of this, the methods of assessment used are often both unreliable and invalid.

Not all so-called 'psychological tests' have good reliability and validity, and some are distinctly dubious, but most of these would not be regarded as mainstream. Some would not be regarded by psychologists as tests at all. Paradoxically, perhaps, one of the best-known 'psychological tests' (actually designed by the psychiatrist and Freudian psychoanalyst Hermann Rorschach[4]) is the Rorschach inkblot test, in which people are shown various patches of coloured ink and asked to say what they think they represent. Despite many attempts to improve this test to the point where its reliability and validity match that of more conventional tests, it remains very controversial. It is very rarely used in the UK, and is the subject of much controversy elsewhere.[5] It is, however, still widely used in North America and in Continental Europe.

FORMULATION

Formulation refers to the process by which psychologists, having assessed the problem, integrate all the information they have acquired to come to an understanding of what is going on.

---

4   See https://en.wikipedia.org/wiki/Hermann_Rorschach.

5   For a short criticism of the Rorschach Test, see Forde (2003). In their book examining the topic more comprehensively, Wood et al. (2003) posed the question, 'What's wrong with the Rorschach?' and the answer appeared to be 'almost everything'.

For example, an occupational psychologist (organisational psychologist in America) may gather information about an organisation's staff selection procedure and find that it is selecting employees who tend to drop out of the initial job training. That immediately suggests a possible solution, although finding job candidates with the right qualities to last out through the training may present the psychologist with further problems, not least, finding out what these qualities are and how to measure them. In a clinical situation, a psychologist may find that an anxious client perceives a great many threats in life which are not really there, and therapy may then be directed towards modifying these perceptions. The whole process is a bit like one of those 'join the dots' puzzles, in which one has to join up a set of dots to reveal a picture. The dots are the results of our assessments, and joining them up is the process of formulation. The problem is, we can usually be sure that some of the dots are missing, but we may not know which ones. Indeed, it may be that some of the dots which we can see shouldn't be there. We join up the dots to produce a picture of a lumbering camel, when we were hoping for a sleek racehorse.

It will be obvious that correct formulation of a problem must depend upon good (reliable and valid) assessment procedures. If occupational psychologists have no information about those who drop out of training, then they won't be able to understand the causes of the problem. If the clinical psychologist has no effective means of assessing the client's perceptions, then modifying them and assessing the results when one has done so is going to be a tall order. It is clear from this that assessment is basic to formulation, and if it is faulty this pulls the rug out from under any further step in the process.

However, effective formulation is not only dependent upon effective assessment. Formulation requires that psychologists should be able to combine the various types of information which they have collected to create an accurate overview of the problem. In order to do this, they must be able to make objective judgements about the accuracy and utility of the information. More than this, they must be able to weigh the various factors about which they have collected the information. For example, in forensic psychology there are a number of checklists for assessing a person's risk of violence. These are not tests in the traditional sense, and are often referred to as 'instruments' or 'tools'. Typically these contain 20 items, each one scored for presence or absence of a particular characteristic, such as impulsiveness or drug abuse. But it is no use just having 20 scores: psychologists must be able to combine them in a way that reflects their varying importance. Is a substance abuse problem more or less important than an employment problem? Is a diagnosis of personality disorder more or less important than lack of insight into one's mental health problems, or are they different aspects of the same thing? 'Ordinary' people are probably not able to make this kind of judgement, but what about psychologists? Do they really have powers greater than those of anyone else when it comes to weighing the relative importance of such factors and combining them accordingly? Much psychological practice is based on the premise that they do. Unfortunately for the profession, much psychological research suggests that they do not.

INTERVENTION

Intervention refers to the action taken by psychologists on the basis of their formulation. For clinical psychologists this will probably be some form of treatment, for forensic psychologists it may be some kind of offending behaviour programme, for educational psychologists it might be advising that a child should be given special educational help, while occupational psychologists might find themselves recommending and designing a way of adapting organisational practices to the needs of intellectually disabled employees, and so on. Whatever the intervention is called, it is essentially a way of trying to achieve change (and preferably improvement) in the problem situation.

Obviously, both assessment and formulation will contribute greatly to the effectiveness of any intervention. They will be crucial in determining how appropriate the choice of intervention is, not to mention the exact way of applying it in the individual case. However, failures in intervention clearly cannot all be attributed to failures in assessment and formulation. The assessment and formulation stages may have been completed successfully, but that will not help if the intervention itself is of no value: that is, if the clinical treatment is not effective, the offending behaviour programme doesn't reduce risk, or the new staff selection programme recruits just as many people who drop out from training as the old one. In that case, one must question whether the intervention is any good. The story is told of a patient who had undergone a psychoanalysis with Sigmund Freud, who ended up wailing, 'Doctor, I understand all my complexes, my strange dreams, and all the problems of my upbringing, so why do I still have all the symptoms?' We must hope to do better than that.

Within my own field of forensic psychology, with which this book is primarily concerned, organisations have constructed policies, and individuals have built careers, on the idea that forensic interventions (mostly, offending behaviour programmes) are effective. The scientific evidence suggests that much of this money has been wasted, and that the judgements of those responsible have been influenced by factors similar to those that affect 'ordinary' people's judgement. In particular, the scientific evidence does not support the use of offending behaviour programmes based on so-called 'cognitive-behavioural' techniques. These programmes have nonetheless become common throughout the Western world and large amounts of public money have been spent on them, despite the lack of scientific support for them. If these assertions are shocking, rest assured that they are not without foundation: I will return to them in greater detail and describe the scientific evidence later in this book.

EVALUATION AND RESEARCH

The term 'evaluation' is probably self-explanatory, and in an individual case refers to the process of measuring what the intervention has achieved. There is also a more general sense in which psychologists typically use the term, and that refers to how well a particular kind of intervention does across the board. In the first sense, we might ask how much improvement there has been in a client after a particular treatment for a mental health problem; in the more general sense, we might ask whether that particular treatment works for anyone at all. Equally, a treatment could be effective in general, but may not be effective in an individual case. Sometimes this may reflect the severity of the problem, but it could also reflect the appropriateness of the choice of treatment; perhaps there is another treatment which would work better with this individual. The more general type of evaluation is carried out by means of research, and all psychologists are supposed to be trained in proven research techniques. This should enable them to make sound judgements about research findings, whether they have found them through their own work or whether they have read about them in the academic literature.

In individual cases, determining whether an intervention has been effective or not may be very difficult. Apart from anything else, psychologists often have to rely on the client's self-report, which can be influenced by a number of factors. For example, someone in therapy may not wish to offend the therapist by complaining that their problem is no better. Since the measure of effectiveness is often the client's subjective distress, which no one else can experience, who can argue? Our occupational psychologist who was trying to avoid selecting dropouts may be in a better position, since clearly it is easy to know whether someone has dropped out of training or not, but the nature of the problem is different. The occupational psychologist is not interested in which specific individuals drop out, only in the overall numbers.

Forensic psychologists are more like clinical psychologists in this respect. In individual cases, they may be asked how someone has responded to a programme, or how serious an offender's risk is. But this is actually very difficult to determine. Many forensic psychologists have been asked to assess a prisoner's response to offending behaviour programmes, but, as I shall show, we do not have any valid method of doing this. The real test can only come when the prisoner is released and has the chance to reoffend, but even if he does not this may be nothing to do with the programme. Psychologists who are very enthusiastic about these programmes will still admit that many factors may affect a person's chances of a repeat offence.

When it comes to 'across the board' effectiveness there are well-established methods of measuring this. These were mostly pioneered in medicine, but have just as much application to psychological and other interventions. Their basic principle is that we compare treated with untreated groups of people. In the case of medicine, there may be a treatment already available and the test is whether a new treatment is any better. In that case the comparison will be between a group treated in the traditional way ('treatment as usual') and a group treated with the new technique.[6] With offending behaviour programmes there is usually no equivalent of treatment as usual ('treatment

---

6   See Goldacre (2008).

as usual' is usually 'no treatment at all') and the comparison is between groups of offenders who have or have not undergone the offending behaviour programme in question. However, it is crucial to bear in mind that a simple comparison between two groups proves nothing. What is important is that those groups should be similar in every way apart from whether they have done the programme or not. As I hope to show in later chapters, this crucial requirement has been lacking in most evaluations of offending behaviour programmes. Where the requirement has been met no treatment effect has been found, and, more disturbingly, when evaluated according to strict scientific standards some treatments actually appear to *increase* risk.

COMMUNICATION

In this context, communication refers both to communicating findings to a client, and communicating with colleagues. In forensic settings, the first will include such things as disclosing the results of a risk assessment or a post-programme report to an offender. The second will include publishing the results of research or presenting case studies, perhaps in the form of written articles or presentations at conferences.

At the risk of stating the obvious, communication is a two-way process. This applies to both of the communication scenarios outlined above. In the case of offenders, they must be able to comment on reports made about them, if only to correct inaccuracies. In practice, they may want to do much more than this: it is not unusual for offenders in prison to query how an assessment has been arrived at. In some cases they are quite right to do so, as inferences may be drawn from quite trivial incidents to the offender's detriment. Despite this, I have known cases in which offenders who could not speak English were reported on without the help of an interpreter, who could have explained the report to the offender and relayed the offender's feedback to the psychologist. Similar considerations apply to the profoundly deaf, and signers may be equally crucial to communication in their cases. When it comes to communication with colleagues, one would expect that any group of professionals would communicate with others, both within their field and outside it. In practice, many forensic psychologists working in the criminal justice system, at least in the UK, appear isolated and unwilling to discuss work with colleagues outside. In particular, they have appeared unwilling to discuss the effectiveness of many of their practices. I hope this book will be able to show why.

UK REGULATION

Psychologists in the UK, like most professions, are now legally regulated. In America they have been legally licensed for many years, and psychologists have to be licensed in the state in which they work (and licensed separately in each state if they work in more than one). The UK legal regulation was only introduced in 2009 and is carried out by the Health and Care Professions Council (HCPC). Before that there was a voluntary system of regulation run by the British Psychological Society (BPS), whose Investigatory Committee used to consider complaints of misconduct made against its members. It had no legal power to stop people practising, although it could take away the recognised title of 'Chartered Psychologist' which would have deterred many people from employing them. It was (and is) illegal to call yourself a Chartered Psychologist if you are not. Although the BPS pressed the government for some years to introduce legal regulation, the system they ended up with was not of their choosing. They had hoped for an independent body, rather like the General Medical Council for medical practitioners. Instead, they were forced by the government to join with various ancillary medical professions who are regulated by the HCPC, despite the fact that most psychologists do not work in health settings.

The HCPC can strike registered psychologists off the register and make it illegal for them to practise. They can also impose lesser sanctions. In theory, this makes it a powerful body, but in practice it appears to be very reluctant to act. If a clinical psychologist has sex with a patient, they will almost certainly be struck off. Another reason for being struck off is committing a crime, including that of defrauding clients. However, it is clear from my own experience and that of a number of colleagues, that mere bad practice or incompetence are not sufficient to incur even a minor sanction. Many of us have taken complaints against colleagues for such things as 'assessing' people without ever meeting them (how could that possibly work?), exhibiting gross unfamiliarity with the scientific research literature (which provides the evidence upon which our work is supposed to be based[7]), for writing reports which include derogatory and abusive comments about other psychologists,[8] and for 'assessing' non-English speakers without using an interpreter.[9] Not a single one of these complaints has ever been upheld. In one case, the HCPC defended their decision on the basis that the accused psychologist's conduct was not objected to by her employer. In effect, this means that bad practice can be excused on the basis of the Nuremberg defence, 'We were only obeying orders.' It also means that the task of maintaining professional standards is handed over to the employer, who may ignore any failings that make their business easier. Thus, the employer can often be part

7   Rule 3.4 of the HCPC's Standards of Conduct, Performance and Ethics states: 'You must keep up to date with and follow the law, our guidance and other requirements relevant to your practice.' See: www.hpc-uk.org/publications/standards/index.asp?id=38.

8   Ibid., Rule 9.

9   Ibid., Rule 2.4 and the HCPC's Standards of Proficiency: Practitioner Psychologists, Rule 8.12. See: www.hpc-uk.org/publications/standards/index.asp?id=198.

of the problem. The logic of 'policing' a profession by ignoring most of the professional offences committed by its members is elusive.

THE STRUCTURE OF THIS BOOK

These, then, are the problem areas which I believe the profession faces. The chapters that follow will each take one of these areas in turn and review the evidence upon which the criticisms are based. For the sake of clarity, Chapters 3 and 4 split assessment between them, Chapter 3 being concerned with the assessment of treatment needs and Chapter 4 with the assessment of criminal risk. Chapters 5, 6, 7 and 8 deal with formulation, intervention, evaluation and communication respectively. Chapter 9 describes the parole process as it takes place in the UK and most of the Western world. Chapter 10 describes some of the flaws that have been shown to affect human judgement, some of them quite surprising, and why these apply to psychologists as well as anyone else. Chapter 11 briefly describes the biology that appears to lie beneath some of our difficulties in accepting unwelcome evidence. Chapter 12 again considers each of the five stages outlined in this one, with suggestions for how practice could be improved in each of them. Finally, Chapter 13 summarises the main conclusions.

3

TREATMENT NEEDS ASSESSMENT

Who Needs It?

'The trouble is, they just keep going on and on at you until you tell them what they want to hear.' This quotation, from a life sentence prisoner, illustrates one of the unintended consequences of some kinds of assessment. Of course, professional psychologists would not dream of badgering people until they got the answer they wanted, would they? Unfortunately, it was professional psychologists who were doing precisely that, or at least the trainees whose work they were supervising and approving. Clearly, any results obtained by such methods must reflect the characteristics of the assessor as much as the person being assessed. In that case, both reliability (consistently measuring the same thing) and validity (consistently measuring the *right* thing) must both be compromised.

If assessment methods must be valid to be any use at all, and must be reliable if they are to be valid, then obviously reliability and validity are key to their success. However, it is most unusual for an assessment method to be equally valid for all people in all situations. It is also true that different kinds of assessment need to be carried out, even within the one field of forensic psychology. In this field, assessments tend to fall into two main areas: assessment of criminogenic (or 'treatment') needs, and risk assessment.[1] Treatment needs analysis is concerned with deciding what needs to be changed to reduce a person's tendency to commit crimes, and these assessments are linked to decisions about 'treatment' (usually, offending behaviour programmes). Risk assessment attempts to assess the level of risk at any given time, which may be after some 'treatment', and is usually linked to some kind of decision about the level of security that an offender requires. Risk assessment is very important in decisions about parole and supervision.

The first problem is knowing what to call these assessment methods. They are often referred to as 'instruments', but this suggests things like microscopes and spectrometers and seems to convey an air of scientific precision that is completely unwarranted. Words like 'schedule' or 'checklist' are sometimes used in the titles of the scales themselves. For want of anything better, when referring to these assessments in general, I will refer to them as 'tools'.

CAN WE ASSESS TREATMENT NEEDS?

When I first began producing risk assessment reports on prisoners in 2001 many of the sex offenders' dossiers[2] included something called a 'Progress in Treatment Report' (PIT). As the name suggests, this was a report by a prison psychologist detailing the

---

1   These are the main areas of strictly forensic assessment. They are not, of course, the only kinds of assessment to be carried out with offenders, who may have other needs. For example, an offender may have mental health needs which require treatment, but are not directly to do with risk.

2   When considering a prisoner for possible parole, those involved with the decision receive a dossier of papers concerning the case. These may include reports by uniformed staff, work supervisors, teachers, prison governors, prison psychologists, probation officers and others, as well as details of previous criminal history (especially the offence leading to the current sentence) and family background. A dossier can easily run to over 200 pages of A4 paper.

'treatment' programmes which the prisoner had undergone, and assessing the degree to which he had benefited from them. If he had been through several programmes there might well be several such PIT reports. An interesting feature of PIT reports was a disclaimer on the front cover stating that, although some benefit from 'treatment' (offending behaviour programmes) could generally be 'assumed' (an interesting choice of word), it was not possible to state how much benefit had been derived in any particular case. This was an extraordinary admission in the context of a system that was claiming great benefits for offending behaviour programmes. In effect, it was saying that, whatever a Progress in Treatment Report might be, it could not be a report on an individual's progress in treatment. As an independent forensic psychologist in private practice, retained by lawyers acting for a prisoner, part of my job was to point out flaws in the psychological reports produced by the Ministry of Justice. I began pointing out the nonsensical nature of this disclaimer, with its implication that PIT reports were of no value; coincidentally or not, PIT reports soon stopped appearing. That is, they stopped appearing under that name. Instead, something called a 'Structured Assessment of Risk and Need – Treatment Needs Analysis' (SARN-TNA) started appearing in files relating to sex offender cases. This was essentially a special use of the Structured Assessment of Risk and Need (SARN), the standard tool used by the Ministry of Justice to assess the treatment needs of sex offenders. The SARN-TNA purported to be an assessment of those treatment needs which still remained after treatment, but it was essentially the PIT report under another title. The SARN was used by the Ministry of Justice to assess supposed treatment need and level of risk in sex offenders. It could be repeated at various times, such as before and after participation in a sex offender programme, and before important decision points such as parole hearings. It was also used by the probation service, which ran programmes for ex-prisoners after release.

For convenience, I will refer to both uses of the assessment as the SARN as they are essentially the same thing.

The SARN was based on structured interviews with the offender, which would seek to establish what his thoughts, feelings and actions had been before, during and after his offences. These would then be used as the basis of discussion and written exercises as part of the 'treatment' programme.[3] The problem with this is that, despite being devised by psychologists, it ignores almost everything that psychological research has told us.

First, interviews have limited value for eliciting the sort of information required. This is why they are generally not recommended for selecting staff, although they used to be the standard method of doing so[4] and are still widely used. They simply aren't very effective, because people can dissimulate in interviews, and are keen to put forward their best side. Also, any interview is an interaction between the interviewer and the interviewee. Even without being aware of it, interviewers can leak information and convey expectations to the interviewee, who may be equally unaware of absorbing them. As if that were not enough, interviews give a great deal of scope for the assessment to be influenced by the prejudices of the interviewer, and even experienced psychologists and probation officers often have beliefs which owe more to folklore than to science.[5]

---

3   Prison psychologists often refer to 'treatment' when talking about offending behaviour programmes, such as the Sex Offender Treatment Programme. I have adopted that terminology because it is widely used, but in principle I think it is unwise because the term 'treatment' implies the presence of a disorder and has spurious medical or clinical psychological overtones. What offending behaviour programmes actually do is tackle well-established behaviour patterns, not mental disorders. It is therefore more similar to what we would generally call 'training' rather than 'treatment'.

4   Amongst many others, see Pulakos (2005).

5   Classic demonstrations of this are: Meehl (1954), Meehl (1973) and Quinsey et al. (2006).

Second, much of the information relates to events that occurred a long time ago. In many of the lifer cases with which I have dealt, prisoners are being asked to give details of their thoughts, feelings and actions about something that occurred more than 20 years earlier. It doesn't take a psychologist to understand that this is a pretty futile exercise.[6] Psychologists who use the SARN point out that it is not simply an unstructured interview of the kind that we know to be ineffective. It is a 'structured professional judgement' (SPJ), in which a number of items thought to be related to risk are each assessed in turn. SPJs are in general superior to unstructured clinical interviews. Many a prison psychologist has written in a report that the SARN is acceptable because it is an SPJ and this means it is accurate. Several are indeed known to be more accurate than clinical judgement alone, because they have been properly researched and shown to be so. The trouble is that although SPJs are *in general* more accurate than unstructured interviews, it does not automatically follow that *every* SPJ is accurate. That would be like saying that some edible items are good for us, therefore all edible items are good for us. Some are poisonous. Nonetheless, studies have been published showing that the SARN has reasonable, though not outstanding, interrater reliability.[7] That is, different assessors generally get similar answers when assessing the same people. This is not proof that these are the *right* answers, and the SARN allows the interviewer considerable room for interpretation of the material that the offender has produced.

---

6   Although it is in fact a psychologist who has done most of the work in this area. Elizabeth Loftus (1997) has demonstrated how memories can be altered, even after they have been laid down, and how completely false memories can be engendered in people. Even after false memories have been revealed as false to the person concerned, and the process fully explained, they can still persist. Memories have great staying power, but not necessarily in their original form.

7   For example, Webster *et al.* (2006).

So what evidence is there that the SARN in its various forms can tell us anything about an offender's treatment needs and how he has progressed in treatment? Surely, if the assessment is conducted before and after treatment, and scores on the various measures of treatment need have diminished afterwards, isn't that evidence of improvement? Unfortunately not. The ultimate aim of treatment is to reduce reoffending, not to reduce scores on a particular assessment tool. Although pre-treatment SARN scores do relate to subsequent risk of reconviction for a sexual offence, research shows that its measures of improvement post-treatment do not.[8] Indeed, even pre-treatment SARN scores add little or nothing to a risk estimate derived from a few simple facts in the offender's previous criminal history.[9] It might be objected (and the Ministry did) that the SARN is not a risk assessment tool, but an assessment of treatment need. There are two answers to this. First, if meeting treatment needs does not reduce risk, then it cannot possibly be regarded as treatment; risk reduction is the entire point of treatment for sex offenders. Second, compliance with treatment programmes is often considered when life sentence prisoners are applying for parole, and risk to the public is a prime consideration in this process. Keeping people in prison on the basis of a supposed treatment need unrelated to risk to the public would be unlawful, at least in the UK. Prisoners whose release had been delayed on that account could therefore sue for damages.[10]

---

8   See Tully, Browne and Craig (2014).

9   See Wakeling et al. (2011).

10   There is a strong suspicion in some quarters that resistance to the evidence about ineffective risk assessment and treatment is partly motivated by fear of lawsuits. This is, of course, very difficult to prove, but at least in England the authorities have not hesitated to use lawyers to try to suppress dissent from their point of view. Since neither the authorities nor their lawyers know anything about assessment and treatment, one must presume that they have been instructed by their in-house psychologists.

The Ministry of Justice appeared to have difficulty with the research finding that supposed improvements in treatment, as measured by the SARN, were unrelated to risk. They took retaliatory action against one of the researchers (who was also a practitioner psychologist who worked for them under a private contract). The Ministry withdrew the psychologist's accreditation for conducting the SARN assessment. This was a major attack on this psychologist's business, which partly consisted of conducting such assessments on behalf of the Ministry. Without the accreditation, this whole area of work had to be abandoned. The other authors of the research were not attacked, presumably because they were academics who did not do this work. The retaliatory action was remarkable when one considers that the Ministry of Justice had itself funded the research and approved in advance the research methods used. It appeared that the researcher was being punished for finding the 'wrong' answer. This breathtaking hypocrisy brought a lawsuit from the researcher concerned. The Ministry won the case in the UK, but would probably have lost at the European Court, which would have been the researcher's next move. No doubt for entirely unrelated reasons, the Ministry of Justice announced in 2016 that the SARN was no longer to be used as a measure of individual improvement in treatment. In any case, it would have been impossible to keep the episode quiet, and the Ministry's position was clearly untenable. The SARN can still be used as a pre-treatment assessment, but even this is indefensible if it is officially not a risk assessment, and if changes between pre- and post-treatment assessments do not mean anything. What function could a pre-treatment assessment have in isolation from anything else? We already have simple statistical predictors, which can predict repeat offending with about 70 per cent accuracy on the basis of a few verifiable facts about an offender's history.

FAKING IT

As mentioned earlier, a test or assessment that is reliable is still no good unless it is also valid. That is, it must measure what it is supposed to measure, and clearly the SARN did not measure improvement in treatment. That is not surprising, if you consider that it is based on self-report from offenders (who may have their own agendas), filtered through the personal prejudices of the assessor. But the SARN has another major problem with validity: it can be faked. What is more, it can be faked easily and undetectably, as a prisoner explained to me.[11] The reason is that the SARN is based ultimately on the self-report of the offender. For example, it examines the extent to which sex is a major preoccupation for someone; it asks for details of 'deviant'[12] sexual fantasies which he may have, and other things which only the person being assessed can know. In order to appear much improved after treatment, all he has to do is report a few things on the pre-test assessment which he knows will get him a higher score: nothing too outrageous, but perhaps some kinky fantasies, or an obsession with pornography. On the post-test assessment he simply tells the truth, so that by comparison with the pre-test assessment he will appear much improved.[13]

---

11 I acknowledge that this evidence is purely anecdotal. However, I received it from a prisoner serving a life sentence for a sexual murder. In this context, he is an expert.

12 The term 'deviant' is not a scientific term, although it is frequently used by psychologists working in this area. Indeed, it is pejorative and moralistic by its very nature, and moralising is not the business of science. This is not to say that all activities are equally acceptable, just that it is not the business of science to say or imply which ones should be and which ones not. The acceptability of activities, including sexual activities, is culturally and legally determined. For example, homosexual behaviour is still outlawed in many countries of the world, although not in the 'enlightened' West. We tend to forget that until only about 50 years ago it was the same here.

13 It may be surprising that a prisoner would want to make himself appear worse than he really is, but the point of this is to show that he is, in the jargon, 'engaging with treatment' as evidenced by his supposed improvement.

'The beauty of it is,' said my informant, 'that you don't have to tell lies and then try to remember them: on the second occasion you are just telling the truth.'

Although this example relates to the SARN used in the UK, it could apply to any pre-treatment assessment used anywhere which is based on similar methods. This illustrates a problem that exists in psychological science but not in the physical sciences: our subject matter is people, and they have minds of their own. They also communicate with one another, so that prisoners participating in a treatment programme are free to tell others what to expect, and how to fake the assessment. All in all, it is not surprising that the SARN is not an accurate measure of change during treatment. The only surprising thing is that any psychologist could have thought it would be.

Despite the disproportionate publicity they receive, sex offenders make up a tiny proportion of all offenders, and about 10 per cent of the prison population, so the SARN is not relevant to most of them. However, the offending behaviour industry has programmes for the others as well, and assessments intended to measure how much they need them.

VIOLENT OFFENDERS

Sex offenders tend to get most of the publicity, and in the past they got the lion's share of the offending behaviour programmes too. The situation has equalised somewhat in recent years. Violent offenders also have a set of programmes intended to reduce their propensity for offending. In the UK and many other jurisdictions, there is a tradition of dividing violent offences into 'instrumental' and other kinds. Instrumental violence

---

Prison staff and parole boards often seem to be more impressed by those who have shown evidence of improvement than they are by those who don't appear to need it and were therefore clearly low in risk to begin with.

does not represent genuine anger on the part of the offender, but is inflicted upon victims to ensure their cooperation. The bank robber who fires a shotgun into the ceiling and screams at everyone to 'do as you're told and nobody gets hurt' is an example. He isn't genuinely angry at the customers, he just wants them to stay out of the way and not impede the robbery. People who are put in this category are likely to be offered an offending behaviour programme that attempts to change their attitudes to crime by emphasising its impact on other people and other undesirable consequences.

Other crimes of violence are thought of as being related to genuine anger on the part of the perpetrator, and not coolly thought out in advance. These crimes can still be highly varied: they range from fairly minor assaults on people to brutal murders, and may be motivated by fear, loss of face, loss or potential loss of a partner, or a host of other things. Nonetheless, they may have in common the fact that they reflect poor regulation of emotions. Programmes to tackle this kind of offending include such things as teaching people to recognise their emotions, teaching relaxation techniques to bring emotions under control, and recognising the 'triggers' which set their emotional behaviour off in the first place. They may also teach techniques intended to help people break the train of thought which is often assumed to exist, whereby offenders ruminate on some wrong which they feel has been done to them and increase the intensity of their emotion rather than getting it under control. These techniques may encourage them to look at the other person's point of view, and question whether they have really been wronged in the way that they imagine. Programmes for domestic abusers may include many of these techniques, but apply them in the context of a personal relationship. There is often some overlap, because research shows that men who are domestically violent are very often violent in other circumstances as well.

Although I have read a great many prison psychological reports I have yet to find any standardised way of assessing the supposed treatment needs of violent offenders. In general they seem to be assigned to one of the categories outlined above, and sometimes more than one. Since each category is associated with a particular kind of programme, a recommendation for that programme is pretty much automatic. As with programmes for sex offenders, there is an assumption that treatment will be individualised to some extent during the programme itself. That is, the practitioners running the programme will try to tailor it to the individual needs of those taking part. Inevitably, there are limits to this, as the programmes are essentially provided on a 'one size fits all' basis, but that is not the concern of the assessor. Some practitioners appear to use the HCR-20 as a means of assessing treatment needs, but this is totally invalid. We will hear more of the HCR-20 in the next chapter, which deals with risk assessment, because the HCR-20 is actually a risk assessment tool. It is not designed to be a treatment needs assessment, nor is it easy to see how it could be used as that.

Another feature which is conspicuous by its absence from treatment needs assessment, at least in the UK, is an assessment of mental health needs. Most forensic psychologists in this country are neither qualified nor experienced in the field of mental health. In the United States many similar assessments are carried out by assistants with master's degrees (rather than the doctorates required of qualified practitioners), so the situation appears to be similar. This is regrettable, because it is universally agreed that mental health problems are rife among the offender population in general, and the prison population in particular, and for some it may be a significant contributor to their criminal behaviour. This is a fact which is often glossed over by mental health advocacy groups, who rightly stress that those with mental health problems are more likely to be the victims of crime than the perpetrators. Unfortunately, the same could be said of all of us; the fact is that mental health difficulties are indeed a problem in certain kinds of offending,[14] and it would no doubt strike the average citizen as strange not to include these in an assessment of treatment needs. This is a topic to which we shall return, as it is relevant to both risk assessment and interventions in the forensic field.

TEACHING THEM HOW TO THINK

It is very common for offenders of all kinds to be invited to participate in 'cognitive skills' programmes. The notion behind these is that many offenders are deficient in thinking skills, and in particular tend to be very impulsive, prone to acting in the heat of the moment without considering what happens next.[15] Cognitive skills programmes are intended to train them in looking at problems from every angle and thinking things through before they act, and to consider the possible consequences. They are also considered to provide a grounding in clear-thinking skills for offenders who will later go on to do other kinds of programme, such as those targeting sexual or violent offending. They may also challenge the rationalisations that offenders often have for their crimes, such as, 'I only steal from businesses, and they have plenty of money.' They are not treatment programmes in the sense of trying to treat a mental disorder, but they are certainly training programmes that aim to inculcate new ways of thinking. In the UK this is frequently phrased in terms of giving offenders a wider range of choices in how they approach situations, in the hope that they will learn to make better choices

---

14   See Mitchison *et al.* (1994), Kingston *et al.* (2011) and Fazel *et al.* (2015), among many others.

15   This is so widely found that it is not regarded as controversial (Quinsey *et al.* 2006; Shine and Hobson 1997; Vitacco, Neumann and Jackson 2005).

in future.[16] A recommendation for the Enhanced Thinking Skills (ETS) programme, which used to be the standard cognitive skills training programme in UK prisons, was for some years decided on the basis of a few questions about a prisoner's thinking skills and how important they were in his offending. These questions were included in a standard assessment interview conducted as part of the Offender Assessment System, known as OASys.[17] OASys assessments are conducted when someone enters prison, and may be repeated at intervals throughout the sentence.

From the point of view of cognitive skills assessment it was disappointing when a study found that the thinking skills items on the OASys assessment were very unreliable, although some of the other items were more reliably scored.[18] This may be particularly important when one remembers that good thinking skills are considered to be essential before embarking on one of the more specialised offending behaviour programmes. But again, what is most surprising is that anyone would have expected reliability in a situation where so much depends upon the subjective opinion of the interviewer. In general, however, the most difficult assessment to make with offenders is not an assessment of their supposed treatment needs. Broadly, it is easy to see what they are doing wrong; it is putting it right that is the difficult bit, but that is for a later chapter on problems with intervention.

---

16 See Thomas and Jackson (2003).

17 Government services appear to be obsessed with acronyms. This one is pronounced 'oasis', like the proverbial island of serenity in the middle of the desert. Given the disputes which occur between assessors and prisoners over their OASys assessments, the image is hardly appropriate.

18 See Morton (2009). It is fair to point out that the cognitive skills training programmes and the OASys assessment have both been changed since then, but my understanding is that the advisability of the new cognitive skills programme, the Thinking Skills Programme (TSP), is still decided on these few items.

TREATMENT NEEDS ASSESSMENT: IMPLICATIONS

The truth is that psychologists, despite all their professional skills, are not able to assess characteristics of people reliably and validly. The reason for this hinges on what psychologists' professional skills actually are. One colleague, while training psychological assistants in testing techniques, was told that one of them wanted to become a psychologist in order to 'help people'. His reply was pretty blunt, 'If you want to help people, train as a social worker.' Of course, he didn't mean psychologists can't be useful and help solve problems. His intention was to stress that psychologists have developed certain techniques (including those that the assistant was being trained in) and that this is where their primary professional skills actually lie. The idea that a psychologist necessarily has some special expertise in dealing with people in a personal sense is less certain. Some of them do, but the same could be said for lots of people working in other fields. Many people who have management or leadership roles, many teachers, many medical practitioners and a host of others involved in activities that have social significance may be very helpful to people at a personal level. More to the point, psychologists are not immune from those emotional considerations that affect how empathic we are to others, or how seriously we can take their concerns.

What psychologists learn in the course of their professional training is mainly a set of techniques, as with any profession. They know (or should know) a great deal about experimental design and assessing the results; they should know a great deal about how psychological tests are constructed and how the results should be applied; they should know how to assess the reliability and validity of a measure. Of course, some psychologists (especially those who train as therapists) may claim specialised interpersonal skills, but they are still subject to the same biases as other human beings. They do not have supernatural powers, they cannot see into people's minds and they cannot predict with any great accuracy what someone's behaviour will be in some hypothetical future situation. As we will see with risk assessment, a simple statistical predictor based on a few objective facts about someone will outperform a psychologist's personal judgement with ease, even when it is allegedly based on 200 pages of information in a parole dossier. Furthermore, if a psychologist uses 'clinical judgement' in an attempt to adjust the statistical prediction and improve accuracy, it invariably gets worse.

If this is hard to accept, think about a firm of structural engineers who are asked to assess the safety of a bridge. What would we expect them to do? The stakes are pretty high if a railway or a road passes over that bridge and we want to avoid a heap of shattered vehicles and people in the valley below. I suggest that the engineers would be very unlikely to cast their eyes over the bridge and decide whether or not it looks okay. Even if traffic appears to be travelling over it safely at the moment, this does not preclude the possibility of a fatal collapse tomorrow. Nor does it tell the engineers much about the ability of the bridge to continue being safe. I suggest that they would take a number of measurements. Not being a structural engineer myself I can only guess at these, but perhaps they would include measures of how much the bridge deflects as weight passes over it; perhaps they would examine whether rainwater drains off the bridge adequately, to avoid a buildup of moisture in the brickwork. Perhaps they would examine the bridge pier foundations for cracks. The point is that they would use the professional techniques which they have learned, and which they know from previous cases to be related to the risk of bridges collapsing. They would not rely on gut feeling or appearances. Neither should psychologists.

We have seen that reliability (essentially, consistency in measurement) can be established in a psychological tool, so part of the question can be answered positively. Validity (measuring what the tool claims to measure) is often more difficult to establish. However, since we are very often interested in predicting behaviour, it is predictive validity that is of paramount importance. This too can be established mathematically and objectively. That is, if we have something like a personality test, and wish to predict whether someone will successfully complete a training course if selected for a job, it is relatively easy to find whether the personality test does this. On the first occasion, we may simply have to let everyone through and see who sticks with the course and who does not. But on subsequent occasions we have the data already available, and the more we use the test the more evidence we have of how useful it is. So, both reliability and validity can be established.

What cannot be regarded as a valid psychological skill is the ability to 'sum people up' and use the result to predict anything and everything they are going to do in the future.[19] This applies not only to interview-based assessment, but also to an assessment of someone's personality arrived at by any other means, including validated psychological tests, *unless they have been shown to predict reliably the outcomes in which we are interested.* For example, there is no point in having an assessment of psychopathic characteristics unless we can translate the resulting score into a meaningful prediction about something else, such as the likelihood of committing a violent offence. We cannot simply say that a person gets a high score for psychopathic characteristics and this necessarily or even probably means that he will do X, Y or Z, if it has never been shown that the supposed relationship between psychopathic characteristics and X, Y or Z

---

19 Nonetheless, lawyers persist in requesting a 'full psychological assessment', when there is really no such thing. My response has always been: 'What question do you need answering?' Questions which might be answerable could include: 'Does this person have the intellectual capacity to understand legal proceedings?', or 'Is this person so suggestible that they might have confessed falsely?'

actually exists. It is far too easy to create a narrative that suits us, which convinces us that we know how the person 'ticks', but which ultimately has nothing useful to tell us. The sad thing is that we have known this for more than half a century,[20] but many psychologists still appear unaware of it today. This is despite the fact that many attempts to assess treatment needs, and reductions in them through treatment, have been shown to be useless.

If we cannot assess treatment needs, and the degree to which they have changed, what are the implications for treatment? The implications are not good. It must be obvious that in order to conduct any valid form of treatment for anything, we must first be able to identify the disorder which needs treating. Therefore, if we cannot identify treatment needs it must be equally clear that we cannot prescribe any valid form of treatment, *even if one exists*. A physician who is completely unable to identify what is wrong with a patient is in a very poor position to treat the condition; there might be a variety of treatments available, and all of them might be valid treatments for some disorders but not for this one. Again, if we cannot assess progress during treatment, then how do we know when there has been enough? Clearly, it is a waste of resources to carry on treating someone who does not need any more treatment. Conceivably, it could be counter-productive, if only because he could turn against it.

I have presented good quality evidence demonstrating that we cannot validly assess treatment needs, nor changes in them. Indeed, I have suggested that the whole concept of 'treatment' is rather dubious in the context of learned behaviour patterns, and will return to this topic. Treatment in the context of mental health problems is another matter. It is generally accepted that mental

20 Paul Meehl (1954) gave a convincing and well-written demonstration of this; much has been discovered since, but has only confirmed what he wrote all those years ago.

health problems are extremely common in the prison population,[21] and in some cases these may be related to a person's offending, although often indirectly.[22] For example, many people with mental health problems will try to 'self-medicate' with alcohol or illegal drugs, or even both, and this may lead them to commit offences. However, in many cases prisoners should receive mental health treatment simply because they have mental health problems, not because it is related to their offending. Most offending consists of a pattern of voluntary behaviour which may be partly a result of genetics, partly a result of seriously flawed upbringing and partly a result of social learning. This may require retraining of some kind, but it is not a mental health problem in itself, and the notion of 'treatment', let alone 'treatment need', is of dubious relevance.

---

21   See, for example, Coid et al. (2003) and Kakoullis, Le Mesurier and Kingston (2010).

22   See, for example, Kingston et al. (2015).

– 4 –

RISK ASSESSMENT

Coffee Cans and Crystal Balls

Picture the scene: in the psychology department of a respected university three highly regarded and professional psychological researchers are conducting an experiment in risk assessment. On small strips of paper they solemnly write down the names of 20 risk factors (drug use, violence history, etc.) taken from each of four widely used violence risk assessment tools. They then put all the strips of paper in a large empty coffee can and stir. No, they are not making up some bizarre new beverage because of a coffee shortage. Remember that each of these four assessment tools has already been researched extensively. Each has been validated and shown to predict reconvictions for violence (not always very well, perhaps, but certainly at much better than the chance level[1]). The researchers then go on to draw out 13 slips of paper at random, making four new assessment 'pseudo-scales', each composed of a random mix of supposed risk factors. They add a 14th item, 'total number of previous convictions' because all of the four published scales had contained such an item. They then test out these pseudo-scales, using data from criminals whose reconviction rate is known. How good are the pseudo-scales? What would we expect to happen? All will be revealed later in this chapter.

---

1   The assessment tools were the Psychopathy Checklist-Revised (PCL-R), the Level of Service Inventory-Revised (LSI-R), the Violence Risk Assessment Guide (VRAG) and the General Statistical Information on Recidivism (GSIR). See Kroner, Mills and Reddon (2005).

FORETELLING THE FUTURE

The assessment of supposed treatment needs was covered in the previous chapter. Obviously, the purpose of that kind of assessment is to try to identify characteristics of a person that are amenable to change, and after treatment to see what changes have actually taken place. There is nothing in treatment needs assessment that directly concerns the future. Risk assessment is different. It is not concerned with whether things can be changed, or whether treatment needs are being met. It is simply concerned with the level of risk posed by an offender at the time of the assessment. Essentially, it tries to answer the question, 'Will he do it again?'

There are two main kinds of risk assessment tool. The first is the statistical (or 'actuarial') predictor and the second is the structured professional judgement (SPJ), which we have already met. The term 'actuarial' has been cheekily borrowed from the insurance industry, which uses statistics about accident risk and so on to determine how much money to bet on a given individual. However, psychologists often base their 'actuarial' predictions on relatively small samples, sometimes only a few hundred. Insurance company actuaries typically use samples in the hundreds of thousands. Small samples are notorious for producing effects that are difficult to replicate. In other words, it may have worked once but that doesn't mean it will work again on a different group of people. The widely used Risk Matrix 2000 was based on a sample of around 30,000, which is larger than most. It was mentioned earlier that the SARN adds little or nothing to the prediction of repeat offending over and above a prediction scheme based on a few simple figures. This scheme is the Risk Matrix 2000, a statistical predictor used in the UK. It exists in three forms, respectively intended to predict repeat sex offending, violent offending or either. It is included along with the SARN in prison-based risk assessments for sex offenders. An important difference between the two is that the Risk Matrix 2000 (like all statistical predictors) can only take into account 'static' risk factors, that is, factors which cannot be changed through treatment or any other intervention. These include the offender's total number of previous convictions, the number for the specific type of offence in which we are interested (sexual or violent) and other measures of past behaviour. The only static risk factor which can change is age, but that is not within our control. Statistical predictors normally take age into account, but often not sufficiently. For example, the Risk Matrix 2000 only takes age into account up to the age of 35. This means that if our offender is 50, 60 or 70 the Risk Matrix 2000 still treats him as if he is 35.[2] In fact, criminal risk reduces enormously with age,[3] so any risk assessment tool which fails to take this into account (which routinely happens) will exaggerate risk in older offenders.[4]

The problem with age and static predictors is an example of a wider problem: that of using predictors with cases which are not similar to the original group of people used to develop the tool (the 'construction sample'). The way that these prediction tools are constructed is to take a large group of the offenders in

2   The Static-99 prediction scheme, rather similar to the Risk Matrix 2000 but more widely used in North America, used to stop correcting for age at 25, which was insupportable when it was known that risk reduced massively after this age. A new version, the Static-99R, now takes age into account up to 60.

3   This has been demonstrated for sexual offenders (Barbaree, Blanchard and Langton 2003), violent offenders (Mokros et al. 2010), offenders in general (Sampson and Laub 2003), and even highly psychopathic offenders (Porter, Birt and Boer 2001), generally agreed to be the most dangerous of all.

4   The situation is actually quite complicated. Several studies have shown that recidivism rates for different kinds of offenders all reduce with age, but not necessarily all at the same rate. For example, rapists appear to age out of offending much earlier than child abusers (Craig 2008; Hanson 2001). This research is not in any way controversial. Nonetheless, I have sat through many a parole hearing in which a prison colleague has argued (in effect) that a prisoner must be high in risk now because he was high in risk 20 years ago. Of course, he was high in risk back then. We know that because he committed the offence.

question (e.g. sex offenders) who were released some years ago and then see what has happened to them in the meantime. From this, rules for scoring can be developed. For example, if people with more than three previous convictions were more likely to be reconvicted after release, they might be given a higher score for this. If the original group of offenders consisted entirely of male offenders serving fixed terms (as the Risk Matrix 2000 development group did, for example) then the scoring system can only validly be used with other male offenders serving fixed terms. A scoring system would have to be developed separately for use with other kinds of offenders, such as women or those on life sentences. Life sentences are only given for extremely serious offences, and to use a risk assessment system based on the histories of relatively minor offenders makes little sense. Furthermore, we have already seen that age reduces risk, and most lifers are getting on a bit by the time they are being considered for release.[5] Despite this, the Risk Matrix 2000 is routinely used with life sentence prisoners, who were not represented at all in the construction sample used to develop it. Similar considerations apply to the Static-99, widely used in America, which has been shown to be less reliable with some groups than others.[6] In 2015 the Canadian Supreme Court issued a judgement that assessors must take adequate account of cultural differences when using five popular risk assessment tools with indigenous peoples. They considered that the applicability of these tools to such peoples

---

5   It is commonly not understood that a life sentence in the UK does indeed mean life. It does not, however, normally mean life without the possibility of parole. When someone gets a life sentence, a minimum term (commonly known as the 'tariff') is set before which he cannot be released. After that, it is up to the Parole Board to decide whether or not his risk is sufficiently low for release to be granted. In a sample of lifers which I collected in 2012–2013 (Forde 2014), the average age was 48, the average tariff 13 years, but the men were on average seven years past tariff without having been released yet. The longest serving prisoner in this group had been in prison for 41 years.

6   See Varela et al.(2013) and Helmus et al. (2012).

had not been adequately demonstrated.[7] The tools included the Static-99 and the PCL-R measure of psychopathic traits, whose limitations will be discussed in a later section of this chapter.

It is thought that one reason for the higher reliability of statistical predictors is that their scoring systems avoid human judgement. Most of the items that enter into the scoring consist of relatively simple and objective pieces of information, such as age and number of previous convictions. There is not much room for prejudice or bias to enter into this. However, not all of the items used are as free from judgement as this: for example, one Static-99 item increases an offender's score if he has committed an offence against a stranger. But what is a 'stranger'? Is it someone the offender has never met before, and that he has literally leapt upon out of the blue? Is it someone he has known for an hour, or a day? This results in some discrepancies in scoring and lower reliability as a result. For example, it has been found that reliability of scoring with the Static-99 tool is lower with high-scoring individuals.[8] That is, if someone is given a low score by one assessor he will probably be given a similar low score by another. However, if he is given a high score, another assessor may give him a similar one, may give him one that is substantially lower. This is very worrying in circumstances where a high score may be used to deprive someone of liberty or extend his term of imprisonment – or maybe where a low score could help end it. It is not obvious why the discrepancy arises, and why it is not uniform across all scores. Possibly, some individuals (or their offences) are seen as more unpleasant or frightening than others, and those assessors who are more susceptible to this give higher scores. This would be in keeping with what we know about human judgement, as will be seen later.

---

7   For a discussion of the issues this raises for Canadian practice, see Shepherd and Lewis-Fernandez (2016).

8   See Rice *et al.* (2014).

IMPROVING THE FUTURE

So, if statistical predictors are less than perfect, can their predictions be improved? In everyday practice it is commonplace to see statements about risk which 'adjust' the score derived from a statistical predictor. For example, a probation officer may write something along the lines of 'Mr X's score on the Risk Matrix 2000 places him in the Medium Risk group, but given the evidence of serious risk outlined above I would adjust this to High Risk.' Probation officers generally are not as highly statistically trained as psychologists are (or ought to be), so they may be forgiven for making this error. Psychologists who hear such a statement and fail to correct it may not. Yet they do the same thing themselves: it is routine for prisoners to be told that they do not meet the high risk criteria for inclusion in an offending behaviour programme, but the psychologist has recommended them anyway on grounds of 'clinical override'. That is, the psychologist has decided the risk is higher than the risk assessment says it is. The problem with adjusting a statistical score like this is that it makes prediction *worse*.[9] Always. The reason is very simple: combining a more accurate risk assessment with a less accurate one reduces accuracy to the level of the poorer. Clinical judgement has long been known to predict reconviction at approximately the chance level, like tossing a coin.[10] Therefore, if we use clinical judgement (or personal prejudice) to adjust a statistical prediction we might as well toss a coin, which would be a lot cheaper but a lot less accurate.

---

9   See Krauss (2004), Campbell and DeClue (2010) and Hanson and Morton-Bourgon (2009) on adjusting actuarial risk estimates. On the issue of 'clinical overrides' specifically, see Gore (2007).

10   See for example Meehl (1954) and Quinsey and Maguire (1986).

CLINICAL JUDGEMENT BY THE BACK DOOR

Clinical judgement is a factor in structured professional judgements (SPJs) mentioned earlier in the context of the SARN. The SARN is an assessment of supposed treatment needs, but SPJs are very widely used in risk assessment as well. Examples are the Sexual Violence Risk-20 (SVR-20) for sex offence risk, the Historical, Clinical and Risk Management-20 (HCR-20) for violence offence risk, and the Spousal Abuse Risk Assessment (SARA) for assessing the risk of domestic violence. The idea behind these is that they present a series or checklist of items (for no very good reason, always 20). Ideally, each of these should be related to risk and this fact should have been established by good quality research. It is not always so: many of the 20 items on some scales have been chosen on the basis of some sort of distillation of clinical wisdom from a number of sources. The professional judgement comes in when deciding which of these 20 items is present in the case that the assessor is examining, and how to combine them. For example, an offender may exhibit a history of employment problems, or substance abuse, or perhaps be impulsive. Typically, the assessor will be asked to rate the presence or absence of each item on a three-point scale, according to whether it is definitely present, partially or possibly present, or definitely absent. This does suggest a numerical scoring scheme, but the authors of such tools do not generally encourage this. They suggest that the assessor should somehow use professional judgement to combine all of these ratings into an overall assessment,[11] while suggesting that numerical scoring may be used for research purposes. There is an immediate problem here, for this means that research that converts these ratings to numerical scores (and that means most of it, as research must represent everything numerically) can only be used as evidence for the utility of the numerical

---

11 See, for example, the manual for the SVR-20 (Boer *et al.* 1997), page 35.

scoring system. It is no use recommending that an assessment tool should be used in one way, and then claiming support for it from research that has used it in another.

This is not the only problem. Proponents of this sort of risk assessment stress the advantages of incorporating clinical judgement in risk assessment. They point out that statistical predictors are mechanistic, and based on group data, so they make predictions which have very wide margins of error when used with individuals;[12] this is certainly true. Neither is there any provision for giving extra weight to one risk factor if it happens to be overwhelmingly important, e.g. a statement by the offender that he would like to commit a sexual murder. The difficulty here is that this is not necessarily any more reliable than a statement by the offender that he is full of remorse for what he has done (which may well be true) and will never commit any offence again. Offenders say a great many things in different circumstances and different moods, and often mean them at the time. However, they are not necessarily a good guide to future behaviour. A story from my own experience may illustrate this point.

Many years ago, when working in Wandsworth Prison in London, I received a request from the medical officer to carry out an IQ assessment on a prisoner. Such assessments were routine in pre-trial cases when there was a question about a defendant's capacity to stand trial or understand court proceedings. For this reason I was surprised when the prisoner told me that he was near the end of his sentence and would soon be released. Testing his IQ at this point seemed to have no purpose, and I began to wonder what was going on. When I asked the medical officer why he wanted an IQ test done on someone who was about

---

12   See Hart (2005) and Hart, Michie and Cooke (2007); the latter concluded that statistical risk assessment instruments 'cannot be used to estimate an individual's risk for future violence with any reasonable degree of certainty and should be used with great caution or not at all'.

to be released I was told he 'wanted the man put away', that is, committed to a psychiatric hospital. It transpired that the reason for this was that the man had made a threat against a prison officer. Had I known the reason in advance I should certainly have refused to conduct the test, but it was standard practice at the time for medical officers to request the assessment without giving a reason. As it happened, the prisoner's IQ was well within the normal range, so there was no support from the assessment for any kind of psychiatric diagnosis. He was released on time and no attack against the prison officer in question was ever carried out. It is possible that the prison authorities were oversensitive at the time because an attack on a prison officer had been made some months earlier. This was a drive-by shooting, in which someone in a car discharged a shotgun at an officer outside the prison. He had his regulation issue thick winter coat on at the time, which absorbed most of the shotgun pellets. That incident had not been preceded by any threat, and the two incidents show that threats and actual attacks may not be much related to each other. Indeed, one might argue that people seriously planning to commit a crime are most unlikely to announce the fact in advance. Threats are more an expression of frustration and anger at the time they are made than a statement of intent.

This is precisely the problem with clinical judgement: it appears to be swayed too easily by personal experience, folklore and short-term considerations to which the assessor attaches too much weight.[13] This is why insurance companies do not use personal judgement to decide how much customers should pay. They use statistical predictors, and charge younger people more for their motor insurance (for example) because records show that younger people pose a greater risk of accidents. They do not depart from these assessments on the basis of personal statements by people who know these young people

---

13 For a masterly, and very readable, exposition of this problem see 'Why I do not attend case conferences' (Meehl 1973).

well, because they know that such information does not predict reliably. No doubt some very careful young people are penalised in this way because of the irresponsible behaviour of their peers, but that is not the companies' concern. They need to make a judgement about financial risk based on the group as a whole; they are not making predictions about individuals. This underlines the fact that risk is a statistical concept by its very nature. It is meaningless to demand (as parole panels often do) an assessment of a single prisoner's individual risk. There is no such thing, and there could not be. Even if we decide that someone poses a high risk because of his character or history, we can only do that validly if we know that the particular character or history is indicative of high risk. In turn, we can only do *that* if the research is available to show it. Otherwise we are back to clinical judgement, and we might as well toss a coin. This is one of the fundamental problems with SPJs. They try to treat risk as if it were an individual personality characteristic of some sort, rather than a statistical judgement about a group. There is a good reason why insurance companies use statistical information to calculate risk and not SPJs.

This is not to say that SPJs are useless. As previously stated, studies show that they have a level of accuracy that is better than clinical judgement, though usually not quite as good as statistical predictors.[14] However, this still leaves statistical predictors ahead, despite their limitations. One of the defences of SPJs which is sometimes made is that, because of their use of clinical judgement in deciding which risk factors are present, they enable better decisions to be made about *managing* risk (for example, if a prisoner is paroled). It is also suggested that, in a similar way, these assessments can help by identifying areas in need of treatment. Unfortunately, this argument is logically faulty. If indeed SPJs enabled better decisions to be made about treatment and risk management then this should enhance the

---

14   See Hanson and Morton-Bourgon (2009) and DeClue (2013).

accuracy of their predictions and they should do better than statistical predictors which rely on static, historical evidence alone. The evidence is that they do not do as well.

One of the basic principles of SPJs is that the items on them relate to the risk of reconviction for the kind of offence in question. For example, the HCR-20 is supposed to be an assessment of the risk of violent reconviction, so the items on it should all be related to the risk of violence. Unfortunately, this appears too optimistic. In an important British study[15] by Professor Jeremy Coid and his colleagues it was shown that, of the 20 items in the HCR-20, only seven were associated with the risk of violent offending (including robbery). The other 13 items variously predicted theft, drug-related offending, or in some cases reconviction in general. The study also showed that the most reliably predictive items were those in the Historical section, which contains 'static' items about the offender's history, and these do not change. Once again, it seems, the evidence is that those factors least amenable to alteration are the best predictors. A similar result came from an American study[16] in which a team of academics rated the three sections of the HCR-20 for the subjectivity involved in its scoring. They found that the more subjective the scoring, the less predictive of reconviction for violence that section was. Again, the most accurate predictor was the Historical section, the one least prone to subjective bias. There were similar results for the SVR-20, a risk assessment tool for sex offenders produced by the same research team, and for the PCL-R assessment of psychopathic characteristics.

But before going on, a word about that coffee can. You will remember that the researchers selected at random items from four different popular risk assessment tools, and combined them

---

15   See Coid *et al.* (2011). This was part of the Prisoner Cohort Study, a long-term study of hundreds of prisoners which was funded by the Ministry of Justice and led to a number of other papers besides this.

16   See Rufino, Boccaccini and Guy (2011).

to form four new pseudo-scales. They had initially compared the four published scales and found that none predicted these prisoners' violent reconvictions better than any other,[17] despite having rather different theoretical bases. They then took the four random 'risk assessment pseudo-scales' which they had created artificially and risk-assessed each of their 1614 cases using these. The results were very disappointing for those who had spent years developing the four published scales, because each of the four random pseudo-scales (despite having fewer items) predicted violent reconviction just as well as the four published ones. The authors concluded that the theoretical bases for the published scales could not be valid. Instead, they were simply recording a number of facts that were related to criminal risk, and the more that applied to a particular man the higher his risk was. This was perhaps particularly disappointing for the author of the Psychopathy Checklist-Revised, because that measure was supposed to be a measure of personality and not simply criminal risk. Unfortunately, this was not the end of its problems, and an account of it is appropriate here because it is so widely used as a measure of violence risk. Indeed, I have known many cases in which parole panels have refused to take a decision until a man has had a PCL-R assessment carried out, in order to assist them in assessing his risk. So how well does it really do as a measure of risk?

THE PSYCHOPATHY CHECKLIST-REVISED (PCL-R)

Psychopaths are great value if you are a lazy TV scriptwriter. Although very rare in reality, these vicious predators without conscience create instant drama. Real life is rather less dramatic,

---

17 The instruments were the Psychopathy Checklist-Revised (PCL-R), the Level of Service Inventory-Revised (LSI-R), the Violence Risk Assessment Guide (VRAG) and the General Statistical Information on Recidivism (GSIR). See Kroner et al. (2005).

although offenders who are diagnosed as psychopaths have sometimes committed dramatically violent offences. There has been much argument about the whole concept since it was first put forward in the 1940s.[18] When I was a prison psychologist in the early 1970s a new assessment tool was being researched which appeared to show great promise. This was the Psychopathy Checklist, the brainchild of a Canadian researcher called Robert Hare. Professor Hare had intended to do some research on psychopaths, but had found that there was no clear definition of what psychopathy actually was, and considerable disagreement about who qualified as a psychopath. He concluded that what was needed was a standardised method of rating people for psychopathic traits, and much of his working life thereafter was devoted to developing one.[19]

Hare began by studying the classic accounts of psychopathy, and eventually selected a number of traits that he felt any measure of psychopathy should include. In his view, psychopaths were not a separate class of human beings; rather, they exhibited a series of traits that are found in many people to a greater or lesser extent. Those diagnosed as psychopaths simply had more of these traits, and to a greater extent. In other words, one could visualise people as lying at some point on a *scale* of psychopathic traits: psychopaths were not a distinct group, different in kind from other human beings, just further along the scale. The Psychopathy Checklist was developed in the light of further research; and a further development, the Psychopathy Checklist-Revised, appeared in 1991. From the assessor's point of view it is very similar to the HCR-20 and other risk assessment tools. That is, it has 20 items and each is rated on a three-point

18 Much of it has been republished since. See Cleckley (1976) and McCord and McCord (1964) for some of the classic accounts.

19 Robert Hare has produced a very readable account of his work for the general reader (Hare 1999), and co-written another dealing with noncriminal psychopaths (Babiak and Hare 2007).

scale according to whether the assessor judges a particular characteristic to be present, partially/possibly present or absent. These characteristics include manipulativeness, lack of empathy, a parasitic lifestyle and irresponsibility. They also include some criminal characteristics, such as a history of juvenile delinquency and a wide range of different kinds of offences. However, an important difference between the PCL-R and the HCR-20 and its stablemates is that the PCL-R is not strictly speaking a risk assessment tool. Indeed, Hare makes this point explicitly, 'Properly used, the PCL-R provides a reliable and valid assessment of an important clinical construct—psychopathy. *Strictly speaking, that is all it does.*'[20] Hare made it clear that he originally viewed the PCL-R as a tool for research, which would enable people to conduct research into psychopathy and be sure that they were all using the same definition of the condition and classifying the same people as psychopaths (that is, their measure of psychopathy would be reliable and valid). He did *not* see it as a risk assessment tool.

However, Professor Hare soon came under a lot of pressure to produce a commercially published version of the PCL-R so that it could be used as a means of assessing psychopathy in individuals about whom judicial decisions had to be made. That is, psychologists (and some others) wanted to use it to assess individual offenders for psychopathic traits because they believed it would help them assess the risk that these individuals posed. Hare eventually gave in to this pressure and allowed the publication of the PCL-R, which swiftly moved from being a personality measure to a purported risk assessment measure. It also became commercially highly successful, having been translated into many languages and marketed all over the world. Indeed, it is now so widely used that some researchers have expressed the anxiety that it is regarded as the very definition of psychopathy, a situation that is highly undesirable because

---

20   Hare (2003), p.15, emphasis in original.

it implies there is nothing left to learn about the concept.[21] A major problem is the inclusion of a number of items in the PCL-R that are not personality characteristics but measures of previous criminal behaviour. It turns out that these are the items most highly predictive of future criminal behaviour, especially violence. The difficulty here is that it leads to a circular definition, so we say someone has done terrible things because he's a psychopath, and we know he's a psychopath because he's done terrible things.

This is bad enough, but it gets worse. For one thing, although the PCL-R appears reasonably reliable across different assessors when they are all members of the same research team, the same is not true when PCL-R assessments are done 'in the field', that is, by practising forensic psychologists serving courts and prisons. It seems that reliability is much higher for those items concerned with the offender's criminal record (static, historical and unchangeable items once again)[22] than it is for those items reflecting the traditional personality characteristics of the psychopath, such as lack of empathy and manipulativeness. Perhaps even more worryingly, it has been found that the PCL-R scores obtained for defendants in trials may be biased according to whether the assessor has been hired by the defence or the prosecution.[23] This is less of a concern in the UK, where the PCL-R is unlikely to appear in trial evidence, although it may do in parole hearing evidence. In the United States it may be very important, because the PCL-R may be cited as evidence of psychopathy in death penalty evaluations, where the jury has to decide whether someone is sentenced to death, or life without parole. Such considerations have caused some PCL-R researchers, and even Hare himself, to question whether it may

---

21 See Skeem and Cooke (2010) and Skeem et al. (2011).

22 See Rufino et al. (2011) and Murrie, Boccaccini, Caperton, and Rufino (2012).

23 See Murrie et al. (2009).

contribute to injustices and human rights violations.[24] Finally, it has been shown that assessors' ratings of offenders may be influenced by the personality characteristics of the assessors themselves.[25] Clearly, an assessment which partly reflects the personality of the person conducting it cannot be of much value, and may potentially be highly misleading. Small wonder that one review concluded the PCL-R was not fit for use in clinical assessment at all.[26]

Why does this matter? It matters because the PCL-R assessment can have a major impact on someone's life. It can result in parole being delayed or refused, because it can result in inflated estimates of risk. Indeed, this is particularly likely because one of the items used in many other risk assessment tools (including our old friends the HCR-20 and the SVR-20) is the individual's PCL-R score. Another reason for inflated risk assessments is that the only part of the PCL-R that is actually predictive of violent recidivism is the part based on previous criminal history. Since other risk assessment tools are also largely based on previous criminal history, an offender can be judged high in risk because he gets high scores on both tools. Of course he does: they are both measuring the same thing! Finally, there are a number of myths associated with measures of psychopathy, of which the PCL-R is the most popular. Perhaps the most pernicious of these is that psychopaths who go through treatment programmes actually get worse. There was some research many years ago that appeared to show this, but it turns out that it was seriously flawed. A proper review of the evidence has since shown that this is not true.[27] All in all, the PCL-R is nowhere near as impressive as it originally seemed.

---

24   See Hare (1998), Zinger and Forth (1998) and Walsh and Walsh (2006).

25   See Miller *et al.* (2011).

26   See Thomas-Peter and Jones (2006).

27   See D'Silva, Duggan and McCarthy (2004).

LIMITS TO RISK ASSESSMENT

It was pointed out in Chapter 1 that there are inherent limits to the accuracy of prediction. The research project by Professor Coid mentioned earlier found that most items in the HCR-20 risk assessment tool were not predictive of violence. The researchers considered risk assessment scales other than the HCR-20, but the results were much the same. They then combined the predictive items from each of the scales in the hope that prediction would be better once the less useful items had been culled. However, the result was still much the same. It appeared that, no matter what they did, it was impossible to improve the accuracy of prediction beyond about 70 per cent. But it is obvious that there must be a limit, simply because we cannot foretell the future. To quote an example which I often use, we might know that someone is likely to respond violently if we insult his mother, but how can we possibly know whether he will at some point in the future encounter someone who is unwise enough to do this?

In my experience, parole panels (who are very often the keenest consumers of risk assessments) are very reluctant to hear this. They want certainty, and are not about to be told that they cannot have what they want. This is not simply because they want to avoid serious mistakes (although of course they do). It is also because they have the natural desire of educated and reasonable people to be part of a system which is constructive. They want prison to be more than simply warehousing. After I had given evidence about the limited usefulness of risk assessment tools and offending behaviour programmes to a parole panel, the judge who was chairing it said to me sadly, 'If you are right, then all we are doing is waiting for prisoners to get older and less impulsive.' Unfortunately, that is exactly what we are doing. One of the interesting results of my own doctoral research was that parole panels throughout the Western world pay little or no attention to genuine risk factors in any case.[28]

---

28   See Forde (2014).

RISK ASSESSMENT: IMPLICATIONS

The coffee can experiment has serious implications for risk assessment. The researchers got as good a prediction with their randomly assembled pseudo-scales as they did with the original, carefully constructed, risk assessment tools. One of these carefully constructed tools was the PCL-R, which was intended to be a measure of the personality dimension of psychopathy, and not simply a risk assessment tool. The fact remains that years and years of behavioural research have gone into constructing risk assessment tools, and they all work to some extent. What is clear, however, is that they are not really measuring anything about an individual. Risk is a statistical concept, not a personality characteristic. How risky people are at a given stage in their lives, and what type of risk they pose, depends on a wide range of things, most of which are short term and not known to us. This is why attempts to improve upon statistical predictions by incorporating professional judgement do not work. In effect, they are an attempt to inject the professional's 'knowledge' of the individual into the equation. But even if that knowledge is valid, it is a knowledge of the person's personality. Personality has surprisingly little to do with risk.

Injecting clinical judgement into the equation only makes things worse. Since we know that unstructured professional judgement about risk is as accurate as tossing a coin, it *must* make prediction worse. This is a mathematical certainty, and even if it were not, the research evidence proves it. Therefore, if the assessment of risk factors depends partly upon professional judgement, and knowledge of the offender's personality and individual characteristics, let's just toss a coin. Apart from anything else, it's a great deal cheaper.

So, given its limitations, is there any point in risk assessment at all? A barrister with whom I dealt professionally thought there was none. Essentially, she claimed that people got an impression of an offender, and thereafter interpreted the evidence to fit that impression. As we shall see in the later chapter on heuristics and biases, there is considerable evidence for this. Nonetheless, I would suggest that there is one use for risk assessment, if it is objective and free of clinical judgement: it may help to allocate resources to cases if we can put people into a small number of risk categories. We cannot tell what an individual's risk is, but we can tell with some accuracy if one category is more risky than another. For example, we might settle on three categories, such as high, medium and low risk. We could then allocate more intensive supervision to the categories judged higher in risk, or perhaps put more stringent conditions on their parole. This would at least be a recognition of the essentially statistical nature of risk. What we should definitely not do is allow the assessment of risk to depend upon personal opinion or folklore masquerading as professional judgement, nor upon bogus assessment of alleged unmet treatment needs.

It has been made clear that we can predict with about 70 per cent accuracy overall whether someone is going to repeat a violent or sexual offence. Statistical predictors appear unable to do better than this, and nor do structured professional judgements. Indeed, they often do worse, even if we try to create new scales by choosing the most predictive items from the old ones. This works about as well as choosing items from them at random. Almost certainly, this is because of the nature of offending. To take an example, it is universally found that impulsiveness is one of the features of offenders, but we need to be clear what we mean by that. To say that someone is impulsive does not necessarily mean that he is prone to 'off the wall' actions that just come from nowhere. What it normally means is that he is very prone to reacting to the situation that he is in at the moment, and not taking more long-term considerations into account. In other words, this type of behaviour is very much determined by the situation in which he finds himself. We cannot predict what situations he will get into, because we do not have a crystal ball. Therefore, our ability to predict his actions will be severely limited.

There is another problem, which is that most attempts at predicting (say) sexual offences have tended to treat them all as if they were the same. That is, we tend to use the same instruments when trying to predict rape, indecent exposure, offences against children, incest and offences that are dependent on aspects of the legal system, such as the age of consent, which differs widely between countries. A different problem is that the principal risk posed by rapists is actually not one of further sexual offending but of further violent offending. Incest offenders have an extremely low reconviction rate, possibly because they are unlikely to be returned to the family situation in which the original offences occurred. They are less likely to have an enduring sexual interest in children than those who commit offences against children outside the family, and are therefore less likely to seek child victims out. These risks are clearly all different, and the use of just one instrument to predict all of them is self-evidently overoptimistic.[29] Furthermore, what these risk assessment tools actually predict is repetition. No consideration is given by any of them to the severity of any repeat offence. This is important because in general a high rate of offending is associated with less serious offences. This doesn't seem to have been investigated with respect to sexual offending, although one study did contain a hint that offenders labelled High Risk by the Risk Matrix 2000 were not those who carried out the most severe repeat offences.[30]

---

29 For evidence about the different risks posed by different types of sex offenders, see Hanson (2001), Campbell (2004) and Craig (2008).

30 See Grubin (2011). To be clear, the total number of participants was reasonably large (1,223), but the number of serious re-offences was extremely small. Serious re-offences are so rare that one would need an extremely large sample of offenders to study this adequately. The study found that the Low and Medium Risk groups combined got longer sentences when reconvicted than the High and Very High Risk groups combined. Of course,

Unfortunately, the numbers were not high enough to be reliable, but it would be a worthwhile research topic for someone.

It appears that the main pressures upon practitioners which drive them to make unrealistic claims for risk assessment are commercial and political. Political pressures are fairly obvious: politicians are very keen to avoid embarrassing headlines in the tabloid newspapers. For some years, there seems to have been a competition amongst political parties to see who can be toughest when dealing with criminals. This certainly leads to pressure on parole panels and others involved in the decision-making process. Despite the fact that crime has been falling for decades, the publicity around a few notorious cases has driven up public awareness (and fear) of crime. Politicians feel they have to respond to that, so the political pressure is pretty obvious. But what about commercial pressures? Does the commercial marketing of some risk assessment scales have any bearing on how widely used they become, a decision that ought to be based on purely scientific considerations? This is an important topic, and one which I have written about elsewhere.[31] Essentially, the answer that I came to was 'Yes'. During a training course which I attended in the use of one assessment tool, its author described it as his 'pension plan'. He was joking, of course, but there is a serious point. If it had become apparent, on the basis of scientific evidence, that the tool was of no use, would he have abandoned his 'pension plan'? We cannot know, but given the clear evidence that professionals are not especially objective in their assessment of professional issues we have some reason to doubt it.

The book chapter that I wrote on this topic considered the PCL-R psychopathy assessment and the Meyers-Briggs Type Indicator (MBTI). The Meyers-Briggs claims to be the most trusted personality assessment in the world, according to its publisher's

---

it is possible that the Low Risk people got longer sentences because they had more previous offences, so the question is still open.

31   See Forde (2017).

website.[32] If so, this reflects very badly on the state of personality assessment. The flaws in the MBTI have been apparent for many years, and have often been the subject of criticism in both academic and business journals.[33] It violates most of the basic principles that govern assessment tool construction, including the establishment of good reliability and validity. The MBTI is not widely used in forensic psychology (at least in the UK) but I mention it to show that the problems are not confined to my own specialism.

Turning to risk assessment in forensic settings, it is quite apparent that the commercial success of many instruments has caused them to be over-applied. Although most of them have some validity, this does not necessarily mean that they are valid for all people in all circumstances. However, in the UK, and I have reason to believe in other countries as well, they tend to be treated as if they were. For example, there is no risk assessment tool whose use has ever been tested on life sentence prisoners. That is, we don't know whether these tools work with life sentence prisoners or not, even though they may work well enough with those on short sentences. Yet I have sat through literally hundreds of lifer parole hearings in which extensive reports have been presented backing up an assessor's use of the HCR-20, the SVR-20, or indeed the Risk Matrix 2000, none of which has been validated for use with these prisoners. The authors of these instruments tend to promote the idea that they can be used with anyone. That is an interesting proposition, but unless it is backed up with actual scientific evidence it remains just an idea. Unfortunately, given that they have gained money and professional prestige on the back of these tools, there is reason to think that they could be a tad biased.

This is not all the fault of test publishers, who like any other publisher need to see a return on their investment. It is partly the fact that the easy availability of such tools makes them too easy

---

32 See CPP Inc. (2009).

33 For example, Krznarik (2013) in *Fortune* magazine: the MBTI has been popular in HR departments for decades.

for the professional to adopt. Indeed, I myself have often used the HCR-20 or SVR-20 because this assessment had already been carried out on the client in question, and I needed to see whether I would come to the same answer as a colleague using the same assessment tool. Familiarity in this case does not breed contempt, but over-use. It is the same for parole panels. The constant use of the same tools and the presentation of results in evidence makes them feel at home with these things. In many reports I have tried to present the evidence against the use of most of these tools, but it is routinely ignored. This appears to be, not because the parole panel thinks I am wrong, but because if they don't use one of these tools they don't know what else to do. As far as UK lifers are concerned, the reconviction rate for violence is so low that use of a structured professional judgement like the HCR-20 with all its out of date detail is hardly worth the bother. It would be more honest to tell parole panels that we simply do not know how risky someone is. My own practice has been to stress the inadequacy of risk assessment, and to list those *known* risk factors and *known* protective factors which are present in a given case. In many cases the result has been a statement along the lines of, 'There are no factors present in this case which are known to be evidence of *current* risk.' One stresses the word 'current' because obviously there must have been risk at some time in the past. But again, risk is not a personality characteristic, and circumstances change; in particular, people get older and risk reduces on that count alone. It is doubtful whether any commercially produced risk assessment tool can really do better than this.

— 5 —

FORMULATION

When 'I Don't Know' Is the Correct Answer,
All Other Answers Are Wrong

As we saw earlier, formulation is the process by which psychologists combine and integrate all the information they have gleaned from various sources, to come to an understanding of the problem that they have to solve. In forensic psychology there are two main types of problem about which formulations are made: formulations about how patterns of criminal behaviour have arisen (usually concerning the choice of treatment or offending behaviour programme), and formulations about risk (usually concerning decisions about the security category of prison someone needs, parole, supervision and/or monitoring).[1] Both types can be carried out on offenders who are in prison or in the community. Naturally, if formulation is to mean anything, there must be some reliable method of combining all the information that has been collected. There is good reason to doubt whether such a method exists.

UNBRIDLED OPTIMISM

In 2005 I attended a conference sponsored by the Home Office for England and Wales, in which a variety of professionals

---

1   See, for example, Towl and Crichton (1996).

presented lectures and led discussions about a proposed new policy on so-called 'dangerous and severe personality disorder'.[2] The rationale was that *some* serious offences (by no means all of them) are committed by people who have such disorders, and we should be considering methods of treatment to reduce their risk. At the time it was also seriously being suggested that it might be possible to commit people with dangerous and severe personality disorders to secure units for preventative treatment even though they had not yet committed any offence. Thankfully, the latter suggestion seemed to fall by the wayside after some practitioners pointed out a few salient statistical facts. In particular, we pointed out that, although it might in principle be possible to identify groups of people with serious personality disorders, most of them would never commit an offence. Even though we could identify a very disordered group of people whose *average* risk was high, almost certainly most of them would never become criminals. In order to prevent one single major offence we might easily have to lock up dozens or even hundreds of innocent people. This was reminiscent of the film *Minority Report*, in which some people with the gift of precognition could see into the future and witness people committing crimes before they actually did, so they could then be safely put away and the foreseen crimes prevented. The politicians and authorities were strenuously reminded that this film was a science-fiction story, if not outright fantasy. They were also reminded that no effective treatment for personality disorder had yet been devised.[3]

---

2   International Conference on the Management and Treatment of Dangerous Offenders, 28–30 September 2005, University of York.

3   That was in 2005. As I write this in 2016 some special regimes which claim to be therapeutic have been established in the UK, e.g. Whitemoor Prison. It is not yet clear whether their treatments work, or quite how we should judge their effectiveness. However, a number of studies do suggest that psychotherapy brings about some improvement in personality disorders, while not necessarily solving all the problems (Livesley 2012; Perry, Banon and Ianni 1999).

One of the speakers at this conference was Professor Stephen Hart, an internationally respected and highly experienced Canadian psychologist. Hart is also one of the co-authors of the HCR-20, SVR-20 and SARA risk assessments mentioned in the previous chapter. It is therefore safe to assume that he is not opposed to risk assessment in principle. Even so, the general tone of his presentation may be judged from the title of its second section: 'A Few Small Concerns, or, Even Scientific Cowboys Need to Bridle Their Optimism'. The gist of this section was that the pressure to identify and neutralise dangerous individuals was not driven by any scientific knowledge of how to do so, but by social and political pressures – especially the latter, as politicians wanted to be seen to respond to public concerns. According to Hart, one result was pressure on practitioners to over-diagnose mental disorders and overstate their ability to predict violence. In other words, they were being pressed to tell politicians what they wanted to hear.[4] He also argued that the relationship between mental disorders and violence was very hard to establish.[5] For example, not all psychopaths are violent, and not all violent people are psychopaths. Hart criticised statistical predictors precisely because they are based on groups but applied to individuals. He pointed out that every prediction is made

---

4   Politicians seem to be especially prone to this. This may be why they over-interpret military information to justify entering wars of dubious legality.

5   It is often stated by advocates for those with mental health problems that they are more likely to be the victims than the perpetrators of violence. Whilst this is true, it is true of everyone, and not just those with mental health problems. It seems to be quoted in an effort to suggest that those with mental health problems commit no more violence than anyone else, which is a logical error. In fact, some mental disorders are indeed associated with a raised risk of violence. For example, a diagnosis of a recognised personality disorder is a risk factor for violence (Quinsey et al. 2006), and violence rates amongst those suffering from depression are appreciably higher than in the general population (Fazel et al. 2015). However, it is fair to say that the vast majority of people with mental disorders do not commit crimes of violence, or any other kind.

with a certain margin for error on either side. These margins are relatively small when making predictions about groups, e.g. '60 per cent of this group will reoffend', but very wide indeed when making predictions about whether a particular individual will reoffend. Hart backed up his arguments with some very clear examples, casting doubt on the whole business of risk formulation by statistical means.[6] Of course, although Hart has been heavily involved in developing structured professional judgements, the fact that statistical methods have limited accuracy does not necessarily mean that SPJs are any better.

As for understanding the causal relationship between mental disorder and violence, Hart thought that had simply been kicked into the long grass because it was too difficult. At the time that may have been true, but since then efforts have been made to develop therapeutic regimes for personality-disordered individuals, and this necessarily means attempting a formulation that suggests some form of treatment. Hart stated in 2005 that most violent offenders would qualify for a diagnosis of some form of mental disorder but that it was very difficult or even impossible to demonstrate reliable improvement in such disorders. This is almost certainly still true today, especially if one includes personality disorders. In prison populations, it is estimated that at least half would qualify for a diagnosis of antisocial personality disorder alone,[7] and some other personality disorders are overrepresented in the prison population when compared with the population outside the walls. The situation is complicated by the fact that many with mental health problems may qualify for more than one diagnosis at the same time, and also by the fact that the reliability of diagnosis is quite poor. This is

---

6   Hart and two colleagues later presented these arguments in a published
     paper (Hart *et al.* 2007).

7   Fazel and Danesh (2002) found a figure of 47 per cent in their paper, itself
     based on an amalgamation of 62 previous research studies. Some individual
     studies have found a substantially higher proportion.

partly because symptoms rarely fit one-to-one with textbook definitions: for example, there is reasonable agreement between practitioners on whether someone suffers from a personality disorder or not, but if they decide that a personality disorder is present there is much less agreement about which one it is.[8] It is also partly because people change over time, so they may seem to have one personality disorder today, but a different one in six months' time. This matters more in some countries than others: in countries with insurance-based medical systems such as the USA it is often necessary to specify a disorder before treatment can be funded. Attempts have been made to systematise the diagnosis of personality disorders, but improvements have been moderate.[9]

But before we can treat, we must formulate. This is easier said than done, as integrating different kinds of information together is not straightforward. For example, how does one integrate a client's numerical results on pencil and paper tests with written or spoken family background information? They are two quite different kinds of information and it isn't obvious how they can be combined. Neither is it obvious how either of these (or some

---

8   Different classification systems don't even agree on how many there are or which ones exist. The widely used World Health Organization (WHO) classification system for personality disorders lists nine different types, but allows others to be diagnosed as 'not otherwise specified' or 'mixed'. The other widely used system (and not just in the USA) is the American Psychiatric Association (APA) DSM-5, which recognises 10 different types, and does not allow a diagnosis of personality disorder 'not otherwise specified'. To complicate the issue further, schizotypal disorder is regarded as a personality disorder under the APA system, but a schizophrenia-spectrum disorder under the WHO system. There are real problems in pigeonholing patients when you can't even agree which pigeonholes to put them in!

9   In particular, an SPJ has been developed to try to make diagnosis more reliable. This is the International Personality Disorder Examination (Loranger 1997). It comes with two sets of questions, one to suit DSM-5 categories of disorder, and another for those recognised by the ICD-10. This leads to improved agreement between practitioners, but it is still a long way short of total agreement.

combination we may eventually arrive at) can be integrated with, say, information about a client's previous criminal history, or drug use, or employment problems. The significance, if any, of each piece of information may be quite obscure even before we consider how these various factors might interact with each other. Or might not. It is hard to imagine a situation more likely to provide openings for the influence of common prejudices, outdated points of view and outright folklore. It is possible for a psychologist to examine all of this information and come up with a plausible-sounding narrative which seems to make sense of it, but it is rarely possible to test the usefulness of that narrative in making real-life decisions. It is not surprising that clinical judgement about risk is no better than tossing a coin. This problem is, of course, one of the difficulties with SPJs: they not only require the assessment of clinical characteristics in an individual, they also require the resultant ratings to be combined into an overall risk assessment. Human brains are not computers, not even those of psychologists, and calculating and combining large amounts of information is not something at which they excel.

Risk is one thing, but understanding which treatment programmes might benefit someone is another. Surely a clinical formulation can direct us to the right sort of intervention? Again, the evidence for this is elusive. The SARN is an example of a structured assessment procedure that was supposed to clarify treatment need and assess improvement during treatment, yet it could do neither. Furthermore, the concept of 'clinical override' is used to justify putting someone on a programme even when he does not satisfy the criteria for entry. A clinical judgement is made that he needs the programme whatever the objective assessment says. Yet treatment need must equate to risk if it is to be valid (or even lawful, if someone's freedom depends upon undertaking it) and we know that clinical 'adjustment' of statistical risk estimates makes prediction worse. In short, allowing personal judgement into the equation does not improve the outcome.

The suggestion that relatively amateurish judgements are being made in the guise of professional expertise may seem harsh, or even insulting, but perhaps one or two examples can illustrate the problem. In a case that I dealt with some time ago, a man who had served 20 years for murder was applying for parole. He was in his 50s, but many years earlier in his teens he had committed two minor sexual offences against other boys of a similar age. He had been sexually abused himself in a children's home, and explained these offences by saying 'it was the only experience I had, and at that age I thought that's what you did; I soon learned better'. There was no particular reason to doubt this; he had not continued with this pattern of behaviour, and had married successfully. Some years later he committed the murder at the same location where the sex offences had been committed. The murder was premeditated, and the victim was lured to the spot so that he could be attacked there. The prison psychologist's formulation included a suggestion that the location had some special significance for the prisoner because the sexual offences had previously taken place there. There was some sort of sinister Freudian implication that this needed to be investigated fully, although there was actually no evidence for this, other than the coincidence of the location. I thought it much more likely that the man knew the area and had chosen it because it was relatively secluded and a criminal act unlikely to be observed, because it hadn't been when he had committed the sex offences. When I asked him a very open question about why he had chosen it he said it was because it was out of the way and he was not likely to be seen there. The moral of this, I think, is that it is very easy to attribute great significance to irrelevancies and make them part of our clinical narrative when they do not merit it.

An example of folklore is a statement that I have frequently seen in the dossiers of parole applicants with a history of alcohol or drug abuse. The form of the statement varies, but the gist is that alcohol and drugs only 'disinhibit' behaviour and do not cause it. In other words, the substance abuse might cause the offender to act upon impulses which are normally held in check, but the nature of these impulses is the 'real' problem. Therefore, the argument goes, it is not enough to deal with the substance abuse problem; we must also change the attitudes and beliefs that allegedly underlie the offending behaviour. Part of the formulation therefore consists of assessing the nature of these 'cognitive distortions'.[10] To the best of my knowledge, there is no evidence for this kind of formulation. I can only assume that practitioners who subscribe to it have never dealt with anyone who was actually in a state of extreme intoxication at the time, however many they may have seen in the calm surroundings of an office. I have, and can vouch for the fact that someone who is high on alcohol or drugs, and particularly some mixture of the two, is capable of the most extreme 'cognitive distortions' which they would not adopt if they were not intoxicated. Indeed, with some combinations people can become quite delusional. This is obvious when you consider that hallucinogenic drugs are taken precisely to obtain such experiences. The reason for the effects is almost certainly that memory and perception are very seriously interfered with. You will not have seen what this looks like if your worst experience of intoxication is seeing someone sociably tipsy at a party, and if you have only seen offenders with a substance abuse problem when they are not actually intoxicated.

Again, an example from a parole applicant may serve to illustrate the point. In this case the man had a history of depression and was feeling suicidal when he committed a totally irrational murder. He owned a double-barrelled shotgun and

---

10 'Unacceptable ideas' in the opinion of the assessor. This field is full of jargon.

one evening he decided to go off into the woods near where he lived and shoot himself. However, as he was scared of the idea as well, he decided to get his courage up by drinking. He drank an enormous amount. He also took some prescription tranquilisers to calm himself down. He then staggered off into the woods with a full bottle of spirits just to help things along.[11] He drank the whole of this, and the police later found the empty bottle in their search for evidence. His wanderings led him to the edge of an industrial establishment, where one of the staff was visible through a window, talking on the telephone. For some unaccountable reason he concluded that this man was a foreign spy, caught in the act of relaying confidential information to his masters. Instead of shooting himself he shot the 'spy' with both barrels. To suggest that he was merely 'disinhibited' and we needed to treat the 'cognitive distortions' which caused him to see people as foreign spies would obviously be absurd. This is an extreme example, and intentionally so because it shows up the point so clearly. There is no reason to think that less extreme examples make the clinical formulation about disinhibition and cognitive distortions any more valid. Intoxication obviously affects judgement, and the stronger it is the more it does so, but this does not mean that altering 'cognitive distortions' in substance abusers is more important than dealing with the substance abuse.

---

11 It is extraordinary how much alcohol some people can imbibe and still walk, but in some cases this may be an effect of the other things with which the alcohol has been mixed. A very relevant point in such cases is that we have very little understanding of the effects of combining alcohol and drugs in various proportions, including prescription drugs. Since these combinations could potentially cause permanent brain damage, it is not likely that we will ever be able to research these effects in human beings. There is a good reason why the notes accompanying many prescription drugs contain warnings not to mix them with alcohol.

A NARROW VISION

These examples underline the fact that in coming to our formulation we are forced to rely on a lot of information coming from the client. In some cases we may be able to corroborate the information from other sources, but often we cannot.[12] For example, it is an article of faith amongst some of those involved in treatment programmes for sex offenders that such people fantasise about their crimes before committing them, often with the help of pornography, and use these fantasies to obtain sexual gratification through masturbation. In other words, they rehearse their offences mentally before going out to commit them in reality. This may be true in a few cases, but I have listened to scores of sex offenders complain that colleagues involved in 'treatment' are pressing them to admit that they have indulged in this pattern of behaviour when it is not true.[13] Furthermore, they may be told that they have to make these admissions in order to be allowed to undertake the 'treatment', which includes discussion of their actions, thoughts and feelings connected to their offences. Without completing the treatment they will be deemed not to have reduced their risk and will be unlikely to get parole. Some have even told me that they have given in to this pressure and eventually made up some story

---

12   I'm not suggesting that all clients lie to us routinely, but clients often put a particular interpretation on facts because they don't want to face up to them. This can be for reasons of shame or guilt, but it might simply be that these facts are incompatible with their image of themselves. In the forensic field, of course, we are often dealing with people who feel all of these things, not to mention the fact that they may have committed undiscovered offences which they would prefer not to reveal! Not that most offenders are especially dishonest about these things: having spent many years dealing with them I have often been surprised at what they *will* admit.

13   At least two studies suggest that 'contact' sexual offenders (as opposed to those who view illegal pornography) have a poor ability to create fantasies for themselves (Elliott *et al.* 2009; Sheldon and Howitt 2008). In other words, an inability to imagine a particular sexual situation may lead to them going out to find it in reality.

to suit the psychologists' prejudices. This is particularly sad, because it is psychologists who have shown how this kind of pressure can result in false admissions being made.[14] Many of my prison-based colleagues appear not to be aware of this work, or if they are do not see how it applies to them.

A similarly blinkered approach is often taken when dealing with discrepancies in people's stories. It is not uncommon for the offender's view of what happened during the offence to be different from that of the police or the victim. It is, however, very common that the police and victims are assumed by people working in the criminal justice system to be totally truthful and accurate. Therefore, if there is a discrepancy they tend to assume that the offender is trying to disguise the truth. I have frequently seen in reports by prison psychologists statements to the effect that there was a discrepancy between the victim's account and the prisoner's, and they do not see why the victim would lie. Again, it is psychologists studying memory who have shown that this simplistic view is unwarranted. People may have different recollections of the same event, but it does not follow that either of them is lying. I am particularly doubtful when neither version of the event seems to make a lot of sense, which is often the case. Offences, particularly violent ones, often involve high states of emotion in both the offender and the victim. It is precisely in these states that memories are most likely to be incomplete or distorted.[15]

Assuming that the offender is being deliberately untruthful tends to lead to a further logical error: he is assumed to be manipulative. Being manipulative is a very serious allegation for a prisoner. Not only does it mean that anything he does is assumed to have an ulterior motive, it may also earn him

---

14 See Gisli Gudjonsson's classic book *The Psychology of Interrogations and Confessions* (Gudjonsson 2003).

15 For a readable account of what we know about memory, written by experts in the field, see 'Memory' (Baddeley, Eysenck and Anderson 2014).

points on the PCL-R psychopathy scale, item 5 of which rates him for being 'conning and manipulative'. In fact, there may be another explanation if a prisoner is an inconsistent historian. An interview is not simply a process where a dispassionate observer puts someone else under a microscope like a specimen. It is a social process. Each participant can influence what the other says and remembers. This is why in high-stakes investigative interviews suspects can end up confessing to something they have not done. Perhaps because I have dealt with a number of such cases, it occurred to me that something similar could be going on with some prisoners when being assessed. An assessment interview is an investigative interview of a kind, especially in the forensic context, and there can be pressures (even very subtle ones) to make certain admissions. There is a test of interrogative suggestibility, the Gudjonsson Suggestibility Scale,[16] which psychologists sometimes use in false confession cases. I have used it in connection with a number of cases where defendants claimed to have made false confessions in police interviews, and am satisfied that a number of wrongful convictions have been avoided through its use. Using it with allegedly manipulative prisoners was a novelty, but in several cases prisoners who were supposed to be manipulative, and had certainly given different stories to different interviewers, turned out to be highly suggestible. The likelihood was that they were influenced by different interviewers to give different accounts of themselves. Again, prison-based colleagues were either unfamiliar with Gudjonsson's work, or did not see that it could have applications outside of the police interview. It doesn't have to be this way. I have given talks on this subject to medical staff in training, who have been able to see the applications to their own

16   Gudjonsson is unusual in that he is not only a clinical and forensic psychologist but was previously a police detective. Perhaps this is why he was aware of the problem. The Gudjonsson Suggestibility Scale (Gudjonsson 1997) tests specifically for suggestibility in investigative interviews, and is not related to other kinds, such as hypnotic suggestibility.

clinical interviews immediately. It appears to be psychologists who have the problem in applying this psychological research to themselves.

THE CAUSES OF CRIMINAL BEHAVIOUR

In a general sense, we can claim to know quite a lot about the causes of crime, or at least the histories of those who become criminals. Generally, they tend to be characterised by domestic instability during childhood and often by abuse of various kinds.[17] Some of this instability may be due to the fact that their parents were criminals, but not always. In many cases, they start offending and abusing substances at an early age and become involved in juvenile delinquency before going on to more serious crimes. Many also become involved with social agencies and children's homes before going on to probation and prison services as an adult. There are probably also wider sociological and economic influences, such as economic inequality.[18] In the case of any individual crime, no one would imagine that these wider societal influences could be quantified exactly. We can demonstrate that they contribute something to a delinquent group as a whole, but one could not say that a specific individual got drunk and assaulted a companion because of economic inequality. There is a parallel here with making risk assessments in individual cases using instruments that are only accurate with large groups of people. However, many professionals seem happy to state that it was a person's upbringing that caused his criminal behaviour later, when in reality the causal link may be more complicated than we realise.

---

17 For a very readable first-hand account of a criminogenic upbringing I recommend *Redeemable: A Memoir of Darkness and Hope* (James 2016).

18 See *The Spirit Level: Why Equality is Better for Everyone* (Wilkinson and Pickett 2009) and The Equality Trust (www.equalitytrust.org.uk).

Take the issue of substance abuse. There is no doubt at all that many criminals drink to excess and take illegal drugs, and have done so from an early age. In some cases, some of their crimes have been committed while intoxicated. But suppose we know that a criminal's father committed similar crimes for which he was also imprisoned, and was an alcoholic and beat him up regularly. Does this lead us to suspect a genetic contribution to the son's substance abuse and criminality? Does it suggest that an upbringing characterised by neglect and parental absence fails to establish ground rules for acceptable behaviour? Does it suggest that being the victim of violence during childhood may lead to a personality disorder? If it does, how important is the personality disorder in the development of a criminal lifestyle? The correct answer to all of these questions is simply that we do not know. And, as the title of this chapter states, when 'I don't know' is the correct answer, all other answers are wrong.[19]

One of the problems in evaluating information like this is that practitioners tend to have great confidence in their perceptions and judgements about people. Indeed, overconfidence in one's judgement appears to be a basic human characteristic. For example, most people believe themselves to be better than average car drivers, which clearly must be wrong.[20] However, we have known for a very long time that clinical judgement about cases was not very predictive of what a client would actually do in a given situation; what's more, getting more information does not improve accuracy.[21] This is probably why unstructured clinical judgement about future risk is as good as a coin-toss.

---

19 This is a very simple truth, which I first heard articulated by Dr Joel Dvoskin, a forensic psychologist and former president of the American Psychological Association's Division 41 (the forensic psychology division).

20 See 'Are we all less risky and more skilful than our fellow drivers?' (Svenson 1981).

21 The classic study of clinical judgement is by Oskamp (1965), but for more general discussions of overconfidence see Chapter 17 of *Irrationality* (Sutherland 2009) and 'Part 3: Overconfidence' in Kahneman (2011).

There are also other reasons for this. Amongst other things, human beings tend to over-interpret information. As mentioned earlier, trying to formulate a clinical picture of someone is rather like trying to complete one of those 'join the dots' picture puzzles, but one in which some of the dots are missing. In general, however, we tend to fill in the gaps with what we know, or think we know, and become convinced that our view is a valid one. We also tend to convince ourselves that something which is 'obvious' in hindsight was actually clear to us beforehand, and we misremember the fact that we got it wrong.

Professionals are not immune to these effects, for the simple reason that they are human beings, and it has been shown that these errors occur in a wide variety of different occupations. Indeed, Daniel Kahneman, the psychologist who was able to show this, won the Nobel Prize for doing so.[22] There isn't a Nobel Prize for psychology; he won it for Economics, specifically for demonstrating that financial judgements were not made on the rational basis that had been assumed for approximately 250 years. Instead, they were characterised by the same sorts of biases as other judgements, and to date Kahneman has discovered over 150 such biases. Many of these he terms 'heuristics', that is, rules of thumb and automatic responses which are applied to situations when they may not be appropriate. There is no reason to suppose that psychological and other expert judgements are any more rational. Indeed, specifically in the forensic psychology field, some attention is belatedly being paid to the possibility that they are not.[23]

The process of joining up too few dots and making a whole picture (or 'adding two and two and making five') is not confined to psychology. It happens in every field where insufficient information exists, which is most of them. A very

---

22 See Kahneman (2011).

23 See especially Neal and Grisso (2014), who have considered how the work of Kahneman and others can be applied to forensic psychological assessment.

good example is that of high-tension electric power lines. All electrical currents generate electrical and magnetic fields around them, and when a piece of research suggested that these might impact on human health the newspapers naturally took it up as a major scare story.[24] Other pieces of research then surfaced, linking power lines to cancer, leukaemia and depression (and a host of other things). What is most interesting to me about this is not that a needless scare story developed. We know that most people are not scientifically sophisticated, and that the press will play up any possible scare story because it sells newspapers. We also know that some people appear predisposed to believe conspiracy theories, especially about government cover-ups. What I find interesting is that scientists began to develop theories about *how* power lines might affect human health. For example, it was hypothesised that air molecules around power lines might become electrically charged, and that when inhaled this might cause lung cancer. Note that there was no actual evidence for either of these hypothetical possibilities. After many years of research, and millions of taxpayers' dollars, the American Physical Society concluded that none of these scare stories had any scientific basis.[25] What appeared to have happened was that some statistical 'hotspots'[26] had thrown up illusory relationships between ill health and power lines, and imagination filled in the gaps.

Having mentioned scientific sophistication, it is worth pointing out that science normally develops by testing ideas out against evidence. When we have tested and verified enough

---

24 See Robert Park's excellent book *Voodoo Science* (2000).

25 See American Physical Society (2005).

26 Nothing is ever evenly distributed throughout the entire world. Just by chance, there will be more ill health of a particular kind in one place than there is in another. That will give the appearance of some kind of association between health and location, but appearance is all it is. This is sometimes referred to as a statistical hotspot. The situation may be complicated by 'bound for publication bias' which will be discussed in the next chapter.

ideas about something, we may feel we have a viable theory. But a theory is not simply a guess (that's a hypothesis): it is a working model of a process that has been tested and supported by research evidence. Eventually it may be that the evidence shows the theory to be false, or at least inadequate. That is part of the scientific process. Picking up an idea and running with it, regardless of the evidence, is not.

SOME FLAWS IN JUDGEMENT

There is not enough room here to summarise all the findings in the field of human judgement and how it can go wrong, although a later chapter will examine how the research on human judgement and decision-making may relate to psychological judgements. However, experience suggests that serious flaws do occur in professional judgements. I have seen very trivial disputes with prison staff, involving nothing more than a raised voice in a frustrating situation, being cited as evidence of continuing violence risk in prisoners who have not struck another human being for 20 years. This is despite the fact that the kinds of frustrating situations which may arise in prison are not likely to arise outside, and that there is little evidence that behaviour within prison relates strongly to behaviour after release.[27]

A relatively well-known bias which affects other judgements may also affect psychological judgement: this is 'confirmation bias'. This bias is the tendency to seek (and, of course, to find) evidence to support the opinion one has already formed. In one

---

27 One study related variables measured in the LSI-R risk assessment instrument to offending behaviour after release (Austin *et al.* 2003). The LSI-R contains eight measures of behaviour in prison, but none of them related to post-release behaviour. Another study (Mooney and Daffern 2011) found that actual violence in prison only predicted post-release violence if there had been at least three violent incidents in prison. Prisons are not in general easy places.

case with which I dealt, it was clear that a prison psychologist had decided at an early stage that a parole applicant was too dangerous to be released. Thereafter, most of her report consisted of statements about events that appeared to confirm this opinion. For example, she cited the fact that he had been involved in a dispute with his brother and punched him. As he had been 12 years old at the time, and he was now in his 50s and had served 20 years in prison after a murder conviction, it was difficult to see this incident as having much relevance to his risk. To put it the other way round, if we had seen him punch his brother at 12 years old, would we have concluded that he was a potential murderer? And that he was likely to remain potentially violent even after a murder conviction and 20 years of a life sentence? Surely not.

There is little doubt that psychological judgement can be as prone to these heuristics and biases as any other kind. However, what concerns us in this section is formulation, the process of combining all of these varying pieces of information (valid or not) into an overall picture of the problem before us. Even assuming all the information is valid, and means what we think it means, and disregarding the difficulties of combining totally different kinds of information, can we actually do this? After all, in making a parole decision about an offender we may easily have 200 pages of papers, each with several items of information. Do we psychologists honestly think that we can combine hundreds or even thousands of pieces of information to construct a picture with any validity?

This problem too has been studied. Indeed, there is a long history of doing so, going back at least as far as George Miller's classic 1956 study whimsically entitled 'The magical number seven, plus or minus two'.[28] Miller discussed the research on human processing of information (there was already quite a lot

---

28   See Miller (1956).

even in 1956) and suggested there were inherent limits on the ability of the human brain to do this. What's more, the huge amount of research done in the intervening 60 years has not done anything to invalidate Miller's work; rather, it has given us more detail about the ways in which biases and errors occur. According to Miller, human beings appeared to be capable of handling about seven pieces of information at a time, rather less than the several thousand found in a typical prison dossier, or even the 20 items found in a typical risk assessment schedule. This was not the whole story: he proposed that information handling capacity could be increased by a process called 'recoding'. Recoding means combining information into 'chunks', each of which can then function as one of the seven or so items to be processed. For example, if I were to say a string of random letters of the alphabet and then ask you to repeat them back to me, you would probably remember only a few. However, if I chose random words instead of random letters you would probably remember about the same number of words in this task as you did letters in the previous one. Those words might contain dozens of letters between them, so your capacity to recall the letters might appear to have increased enormously. Miller recounted a number of experiments involving artificially created methods of recoding, demonstrating that it did indeed occur. Something similar may be happening when we deliberately over-train emergency workers such as firefighters. In the middle of an emergency they must act far too fast for the taking of coolly calculated decisions. The fact that they have been very highly and repetitively trained means that they don't have to. Commonly such people will say of an emergency, 'I didn't have to think; the training took over', or something similar. There is, however, one drawback: the ability to act fast in the situations comes at a cost. This cost is simply that when these people meet a situation that was not covered by the training they tend to make important errors. This may be because they recognise the problem and have to revert to slow calculated decision-making, but it can also be because they treat the situation as they would the most similar situation that their training did cover. This may be wrong.[29]

The evidence is clear that psychologists cannot be immune from this sort of error, simply because they are human beings. Faced with large amounts of information they will have to recode it or it will be overwhelming. The likelihood is that they will fall back on paths with which they are familiar, as we all do. Psychologists are not usually dealing with emergency situations, and it would be rare that someone might die as a result of their mistakes, but their life can certainly be dramatically affected.

FORMULATION: IMPLICATIONS

By now it should be clear that psychologists have been overoptimistic about some of the tasks that they claim to perform. In particular, they have applied risk assessment procedures that work well with groups, but applied them to individuals as if they were just as accurate in that case. This is quite simply untrue, and has resulted in a great many unjustifiable decisions being taken about those individuals. In particular, it has resulted in grossly inflated risk estimates for some prisoners, particularly older lifers, many of whom have spent far longer in prison than they should have done. This is particularly unfortunate in the UK, where life sentence prisoners are supposed to be paroled when their minimum term has expired, unless there is continuing evidence of risk. The fact that much of this 'evidence' is invalid should be disturbing; many people may not be very concerned about the personal impact upon prisoners, but they should at least be concerned about the unnecessary expenditure of hundreds of thousands of pounds, dollars and euros that continuing imprisonment costs us all.

---

29 For a discussion of this, and many real-life examples, see Reason (1990).

Chapter 9 will deal more extensively with the research on human decision-making. In the meantime, there is certainly evidence that psychologists have failed to apply this research to themselves, although they have been ready enough to criticise the decision-making processes of 'ordinary' people. This is not to say that psychologists have any special defects in self-awareness that other people do not have. The point is that other people do indeed have them, and psychologists are not exempt. For example, they have assumed that they can assimilate a 200-page dossier crammed with thousands of items of information, interpret it correctly (despite not knowing what the implications of each item may or may not be), and integrate these thousands of items of information to produce a coherent and valid result. Given that human beings have limited information-processing capacity, can psychologists really undertake to combine into a single judgement the vast amounts of information that they are typically given to study? No. No one can do this, and no psychologist who knew anything about human information processing would think that any human being could do it. There are three main reasons for this. First, we cannot hold thousands of items of information in mind at any given time. Second, even if we could, we still would not be able to calculate how they interacted with each other in millions of complex ways to produce the result of interest. Third, we do not know the significance (if any) that most of the information has. When our cognitive system which processes this information is put under strain, it tends to revert to the simplest decision, which is to leave things as they are, an effect termed 'mental depletion'. Information overload is built into our methods of assessment because we insist on having every possible piece of information. This is despite the fact that psychologists themselves are the people who have shown that we cannot process it.

It isn't just the amount of information that matters. Other factors, including physical ones, can put the cognitive system under strain. One of these is fatigue. If we have to keep on making similar decisions one after the other we tend to become tired and our blood sugar level falls. This also leads to mental depletion. One study of Israeli parole panels showed that this had a measurable effect on parole decisions. The researchers found that parole panels became less inclined to grant parole as the day went on, but that after a break for refreshment they were once again more inclined to grant parole and less inclined to maintain the status quo (that is, to leave the parole applicant in prison). None of this had anything to do with the level of risk the person might genuinely pose, nor the arrangements made for supervision in the community. Needless to say, the idea that parole decisions might depend in part on whether the judge had had lunch or not was seriously disputed.[30] There is no reason to think that psychologists are any better than judges at resisting mental depletion. If you want the psychologist to come to a formulation that is favourable to you, perhaps you had better make the interview appointment right after a meal.

Given that large amounts of information can only be handled by recoding them into bigger chunks, is there a risk that psychologists may inappropriately treat new situations like superficially similar ones they have met before? The earlier section on flaws in judgement mentioned the work of George Miller. This suggested that we could only successfully hold in our minds about seven pieces of information, unless they were recoded into larger chunks. In a similar way, it was suggested that such people as emergency workers are often trained to the point where they behave almost automatically. Psychologists and similar professionals are usually not involved in emergencies,

---

30 See Danziger, Levav and Avnaim-Pesso (2011). These findings were disputed by Israeli criminal justice staff, who suggested possible administrative factors accounted for the apparent effects. When Danziger *et al.* re-examined their data, these administrative factors were slight and did not account for the findings.

but they tend to perform many tasks of a similar nature during their career. It is inevitable that they will fall into relatively 'standard' ways of doing things – all the more so if they work in an organisation that lays down strict guidelines for how these tasks should be completed. Again, if they have trainee or similar status, they will not have the confidence to depart from these rules.

Several examples of the resultant problems have already been given. One more is evident in the case of a prisoner who had been given a life sentence for a single case of rape. He had committed lesser sexual offences before, but nothing as violent as this. As in other discretionary life sentence cases, the judge had decided that the man might exhibit mental abnormalities which might continue to make him a risk, and was therefore unwilling to put an exact figure on the amount of time that he should serve. During his time in prison he behaved well and appeared to relate perfectly appropriately to female prison staff. Having served over 20 years, he was transferred to an open prison where he continued to behave perfectly well with all staff, male or female. He then attended a parole hearing. Without warning, a senior prison psychologist who had never seen him arrived from the head office in London and declared that he was too dangerous to release because he had not completed the appropriate sex offender treatment programme, *and for no other reason*. He was told he would shortly be returned to closed prison, and promptly absconded. He was at large for two years, during which time he continued to behave well and committed no offences, but was eventually recaptured. Having served over 10 years more, he again was transferred to an open prison and again continued to behave perfectly well. He was then abruptly returned to closed prison on the word of a different senior prison psychologist, who declared that he had failed to give a full account of his offending behaviour and should stay in closed prison until he did so. In point of fact, he had repeatedly given comprehensive accounts of his offending behaviour. The problem was that, alone amongst prison service staff, this psychologist was unwilling to accept them. He applied for parole from closed prison, and I attended to give evidence. Part of what I said was that the psychologist was, in effect, blackmailing the prisoner into saying something that he did not want to say, because his previous accounts of his offending did not fit the 'official' line. She had essentially recommended that he should stay in closed prison conditions until he said something that she wanted to hear. I went on to say that 33 years in prison was an exceptionally long period for a single offence of rape, and that there was now no evidence of current risk. Indeed, I suggested the prison service had proved its complete inability to deal with this kind of case. The parole panel evidently agreed, as they ordered his immediate release. The point about this case, as I see it, is that the psychologist concerned was dealing with it very much on an automatic basis, as if it were like lots of other cases involving very much younger men. The fact that he was of an age where offending of all kinds is much less likely, and the fact that he had worked successfully in the community alongside female staff without incident, were simply ignored, as was the fact that a conviction for rape is predictive of later violence, not further sexual offending.

Given the findings about human decision-making, why then do we persist in a task that we know for a fact is completely impossible? Almost certainly, the pressures that have led psychologists to claim these superhuman abilities are nothing to do with the scientific research on which psychology is supposed to be based. For one thing, there is plenty of research already, and none of it suggests that these abilities are present in psychologists or anyone else. The pretence that they are can only be motivated by political, commercial and career considerations.

INTERVENTION

A Suitable Case for Treatment?

So, having carried out assessments that are seriously flawed, and combined the results using a method that is seriously flawed, what is the status of intervention? Do we have 'interventions' (treatment programmes, offending behaviour programmes, or anything else) that actually reduce the risk of future criminal behaviour in those who undergo them? Prison authorities throughout the Western world apparently think so. They have all been spending millions to fund such programmes over the last two decades. Surely there must now be enough evidence to find whether their confidence has been justified? There is, indeed, rather a lot of evidence, especially about sex offender treatment. The news is not good.

THE ORIGINS OF PRISON TREATMENT PROGRAMMES

When I joined the English prison service in 1971 it employed very few psychologists. Many of the older ones had been trained in an earlier tradition, heavily influenced by the psychoanalytic tradition founded by Freud. It was already generally accepted that these traditional 'psychodynamic' forms of psychotherapy had little effect upon offending behaviour, and there was little support for the idea that criminality was some sort of mental disorder requiring therapy. However, there was considerable academic argument about whether criminality was genetically determined or the result of environmental influences.[1] Most of us thought that it was likely to be a mixture of the two, like virtually every other kind of human behaviour.

There was another argument going on at the time, exemplified by the attacks on psychoanalysis which had been made by Hans Eysenck for some years by then.[2] The old idea that you could solve people's behavioural problems by talking them through (so-called 'talking therapy') was largely discredited, and the idea of 'behaviour modification' was on the rise. The guru of behaviour modification was B.F. Skinner, and he was not primarily interested in what was going on inside people's heads.[3] He was interested in altering behaviour. Without going into too much dry theoretical detail, the point of behaviour modification was that behaviour patterns could be changed by altering the consequences that followed them. In the jargon, behaviour could be 'reinforced', and to influence it you needed control of the reinforcers.

In everyday terms, a 'reinforcer' is similar to a 'reward'. However, it is important to note that reinforcers are operationally defined (that is, they are only reinforcers if they actually work; supposed rewards are often chosen on an intuitive basis and may not be effective, as any parent knows). Reinforcers may be positive (after performance of an act, the presentation of something that strengthens the behaviour) or negative (after performance of an

---

1   For example, Dalgard and Kringlen (1976); Hutchings and Mednick (1974). My own first published paper made a very modest contribution to this debate (Forde 1978).

2   The late Professor Hans Eysenck wrote several books in the 1960s and 1970s, such as *Sense and Nonsense in Psychology*, *Uses and Abuses of Psychology*, etc. These are out of print now, but his more recent book *Decline and Fall of the Freudian Empire* (Eysenck, 2004) details his arguments against psychoanalysis.

3   See *Science and Human Behaviour* (Skinner, 1965).

act, the removal of something which strengthens the behaviour). An example of the former is giving a hungry rat a food pellet when it presses a bar; an example of the latter is turning off an electric shock when a rat presses a bar. Negative reinforcement is often confused with punishment, but it is the precise opposite. Punishment involves *imposing* something unpleasant after an act has been performed (such as turning an electric current *on* when the rat has pressed a bar), whereas negative reinforcement is the *removal* of something unpleasant. Punishment tends not to be an effective method of inhibiting a particular kind of behaviour, unless it is paired with a reinforcement scheme designed to strengthen an alternative behaviour. Without this, its effects are usually only temporary, and may simply be disruptive. To take another child-rearing example, small children may quickly forget being told off and revert to forbidden behaviour (e.g. throwing toys around), but are much less likely to do that if something else has been reinforced instead (in this case, perhaps putting toys away in the toy cupboard).

As far as criminal behaviour was concerned this raised a major problem: we very rarely had much control of the reinforcers. We could control the consequences of behaviour in prison, at least to some extent, and that could help to make life better for staff and prisoners, but there didn't seem to be much that we could do within prison to alter what people did when they went back out into society. A number of attempts were made, but there was doubt about their effectiveness and also doubt about whether any apparent improvements were actually due to the processes which behavioural psychologists claimed. For this reason, psychologists began to consider whether they could combine the behavioural approach with what went on inside a person's head – the way in which they perceived and understood the world. After all, surely the person's behaviour must depend on how they interpret the world around them, and if we could change that perhaps behavioural change would follow?

This approach is usually termed 'cognitive-behavioural', and is the basis of most offending behaviour programmes throughout the Western world today.[4]

COGNITIVE-BEHAVIOURAL PROGRAMMES

A prisoner with whom I dealt had a history involving a number of moderately serious violent offences, and had been imprisoned several times. After the last sentence he had found religion. Not only did he find Jesus, he decided that he had to atone for his past misdeeds. One of these was an assault that he had committed upon an acquaintance, for which he had never been prosecuted. The victim had been too frightened of him to make a complaint. One reason for accepting the offender's conversion as genuine is that he decided to persuade the victim to make a complaint. Initially the man was unwilling to do so, but the offender persuaded him that he really wanted him to do this. He wanted to wipe the slate clean, and make his peace with his God. Eventually the victim made the complaint as requested, the offender pleaded guilty and received a new prison sentence which he served willingly. It is hard to envisage anyone giving clearer evidence of a change in his attitudes towards offending, and a willingness to change his behaviour and atone for past misdeeds. After all, volunteering for several years of imprisonment is a pretty convincing demonstration of sincerity. We will see later how this worked out in practice, but for now we may note that this case demonstrates great changes in attitudes and beliefs.

Cognitive psychology is concerned with the ways in which people perceive and interpret information. In the latter part of the 20th century there was an upsurge of interest in cognitive

---

4   Many if not most of these programmes were developed in Canada and the United States, but have since been adopted (and adapted) throughout the UK, Western Europe and Australasia.

processes, because it appeared that the behaviour modification approach outlined in the previous section was inadequate for many purposes. It had done well in the treatment of some uncomplicated clinical conditions, such as simple phobias, but more complex conditions were another matter. Meanwhile, an alternative tradition, ultimately traceable back to the pioneering work of Sir Frederick Bartlett,[5] had been growing. Bartlett, a professor at Cambridge University in England, had discovered that long-term memory tended to be changed after it was first laid down, and suggested that his findings implied the existence of structures within the mind which he termed 'schemata' (a plural of the Greek word 'schema', meaning a plan or outline; subsequent theorists without the benefit of his classical education have tended to refer to 'schemas'). In fact, he freely admitted that he was not the first to use the term; he seems to have adapted it from earlier writers. What Bartlett suggested was that schemas were a way of organising information in the mind, and that new information would be interpreted in the light of these schemas. Let's be clear: he did *not* say that schemas were attitudes and beliefs. He gave the name to structures which he hypothesised to *underlie* attitudes and beliefs. They were responsible for organising information in the mind, and for interpreting new information in the light of what they had already organised. In other words, schemas were not directly observable, nor were they directly reportable by the individuals in whose minds they occurred. Their existence was inferred from those processes which could be observed. Most importantly, the changeability of these schemas meant that memories could be altered even after they had initially been laid down. For example, Bartlett

---

5   See Bartlett (1932). Bartlett's studies of long-term memory were original and had a great impact. Indeed, when I first enquired about pursuing a doctorate in this area in 1969 I was told that he had said pretty much all there was to say on the subject! I don't think anyone would take that attitude now.

asked people to read a Native American folk tale and then try to reproduce it from memory. He also retested their recall at intervals – in some cases many years after the reading. He was able to show that over a long period people's memory of the tale changed. Not only that, it changed in ways that made it conform to ideas they already had from immersion in their own culture. That is, the memory was changed to fit in with the schemas that the reader already had. For example, the original folk tale contained supernatural elements to do with Native American spirit beliefs which were unfamiliar to students in Cambridge, so they were either omitted or changed to something more familiar. In some cases Bartlett was able to follow people up a decade or two later, and show that their memory of this tale had changed beyond simply the loss of some items of information. Their version of the story had lost some items but acquired new ones. There was an active process going on, not just a passive process of forgetting, like a photo fading in bright sunlight.

Unfortunately, I suspect that most of my modern fellow professionals have not read Bartlett's book. Frankly, it is not the easiest of reads, but it does repay study. I constantly see references to schemas in the writings of my colleagues, but they are always referred to as being attitudes and beliefs, not the structures underlying these things. Does it matter? Actually, it does. This is not just of theoretical interest, because it has influenced the way in which psychologists have approached offending behaviour programmes. Typically, offenders are asked about their thoughts, feelings and behaviour in the time leading up to their offence. In many cases, that offence may have been years before; in lifer cases, it may have been decades before. Given that memory is an active process of change, and given that many years have passed, how likely is it that a prisoner (no matter how cooperative he wishes to be) can have an accurate memory of these things?

There is a further problem. If we are aiming to change schemas, and according to those who run cognitive-behavioural programmes we are, what is the point of changing conscious attitudes and beliefs? These are not unconscious schemas, but a pale reflection of them. It is as if a volcanologist were to say that certain emissions of fumes and steam in a volcanically active area were indicators of an impending earthquake, and the way to prevent the earthquake was to block up the fumaroles and hot springs that emitted them. But in any case, as I shall show below, changing behaviour patterns by changing attitudes and beliefs had been tried decades before, and it didn't work then, so it is not obvious that it would now.

Cognitive-behavioural therapies have in fact been tried with some apparent success in the field of mental health, especially in the treatment of depression and anxiety.[6] However, I would suggest that there is a world of difference between an anxious or depressed person seeking help from a clinical psychologist, and a prisoner being more or less coerced into taking an offending behaviour programme to improve his chances of parole. Coercion aside, in the clinical example the person recognises a problem and wants help with it. Prisoners are often not aware of their problem, and don't particularly want to change. As one colleague put it, 'People don't suffer from antisocial personality disorder, they have a personality disorder which causes suffering to those around them.' What is more, emotional states like depression and anxiety are very different from habitual behaviour patterns like committing crimes. Emotional states influence the way that we look at the world (perhaps thinking it hopeless and remote if we are depressed, and threatening if we are anxious). There may be a connection where criminal behaviour results primarily from emotional states, as some violent behaviour may do, but there is little obvious similarity between, say, an irrational fear of spiders

---

6   See Beck and Beck (2011).

and minor theft, drug-dealing or robbery. The latter are not an emotional state but a pattern of habits.

There is a further problem, and we have known about it for more than a hundred years. All therapies or programmes that try to change behaviour involve some form of learning. We are trying to get people to stop doing what they have previously learned, and to learn something new to replace it. One of the earliest established rules of learning is that we learn best when the situation in which we acquire the new learning is similar to the situation in which we will later have to perform it. In the jargon, the more similar two situations are, the more easily learning 'transfers' from one to the other.[7] It is hard to see much similarity between being in a classroom with seven or eight other offenders (a typical situation for participants in an offending behaviour programme) and any real-life situation out on the street. To be fair, some of these programmes also involve written 'homework', diaries of thoughts and actions, and some one-to-one sessions with psychologists. However, all of this is what behaviourists like Skinner would call 'verbal behaviour': it is spoken, written and recalled in words. As Skinner pointed out many years ago,[8] verbal behaviour can be viewed in the same way as other behaviour, and is subject to the same kinds of reinforcers. An everyday example is how we train children in good manners. Children may see that their parents have produced some cake and start clamouring to be given some. Typically, the parents will prompt children to say 'please' and then reward this by giving them the cake. This is fine for encouraging children to use the correct word, but this is a very simple kind of behaviour compared with encouraging people to give a detailed correct account of something. A great many

---

7   A good account of what we know in the field of learning (and one which can be downloaded free) is given by Bransford, Brown and Cocking (2004).

8   B.F. Skinner's 1957 book *Verbal Behaviour* has been made available online free of charge by the B.F. Skinner Foundation (Skinner, 2014).

situations encourage a particular kind of verbal account, and make it much more likely to be given. This does not necessarily make it any more likely to be true, which is one reason why false confessions occur. When it comes to statements of intent, encouraging a particular description of one's ideas does not make it any more likely that one will be able to live up to these new ideas in future. And even this assumes genuine cooperation on the part of the offender. In fact, it is quite clear from the accounts of prisoners that a good deal of collaboration goes on between them to fabricate 'homework' and other written tasks. Of course, they are not likely to give these accounts to prison staff, including prison psychologists, any more than they will tell them how they fake the SARN assessment.[9]

At the beginning of this section I gave an example of someone with a violent past who had undergone major changes in his attitudes and beliefs and acquired a new religious and moral outlook on life, evidenced by a serious attempt at atonement by spending several years in prison. It is most unusual to find someone who has been through this kind of attitude change and backed it up with evidence like this. On the face of it, he should have been able to draw a line under his past and live a better life. Unfortunately, when I met him he was back in prison again, having committed a further violent offence under very similar circumstances to those in his record. Nonetheless, he maintained that his love of Jesus would keep him out of trouble in future. This illustrates the problem in a nutshell: people may genuinely change their verbally expressed attitudes and beliefs, as I believe this man did, but these are a poor guide to behaviour change, if any. Knowing *what* to do is not the same thing as being

---

9   I do not mean to imply that all prisoners fake everything all the time. Indeed, I am quite sure that they do not. However, I am surprised by the degree to which some prison colleagues willingly accept prisoners' statements about their cooperation with treatment programmes while being unwilling to accept their word in connection with anything else.

able to do it. In practice, much violent behaviour is strongly influenced by the immediate situation that a person is in, and carefully learned patterns of self-control may well be discarded in the heat of the moment.

INTUITIVE BELIEFS AND FOLKLORE

It was noted earlier that some of those involved in delivering treatment programmes have unwarranted beliefs about how offenders carry out their offending, and that this can bias the way that these professionals 'formulate' problems. Treatment programmes themselves have been influenced by the same problem. This has affected both the selection of treatment goals and the methods used to tackle them. One example of this is the problem of denial. Offenders who deny committing their offences cannot by definition give an account of their thoughts and feelings before and during them. This has traditionally been regarded as a sign of risk, partly because the offender refuses to face up to what he has done, and partly because it means he cannot undertake a treatment programme and thereby (it is claimed) reduce his risk. This certainly sounded plausible, given official views about the effectiveness of treatment, but what is plausible is not necessarily true. Many psychologists and probation officers in many risk assessments over the years have stated that denial is a sign of serious risk, and this view became widespread, although it was not supported by any evidence. In fact, the classic studies of risk factors in sex offending (the most studied area) had already shown that this was not true.[10] Those

---

10   These were large-scale reviews combining the results of many individual research studies (Hanson and Bussière 1998; Hanson and Morton-Bourgon 2004). Systematic reviews are considered to provide the best evidence, simply because the results of individual small-scale studies vary so much. By combining them we get a more complete picture.

who denied their offences were no more likely to commit similar offences in future than those who admitted them. More recently, there have been some specific studies of denial in sex offenders.[11] Surprisingly, perhaps, the ones most likely to reoffend turned out to be those who had admitted everything they had been accused of. The researchers speculated that this was because these offenders understood how risky they were and wanted help in trying to change their behaviour. As one colleague pointed out, at least denial of an offence implies a recognition that it was wrong.

The fact that psychologists and other professionals may sometimes base their decisions on folklore or personal prejudice rather than evidence may be disturbing. It certainly should be. However, psychologists are human beings too, and it is always easier to detect other people's prejudices than one's own. A colleague who was working in prisons told me the following story:

> We were running a treatment programme for sex offenders when we ran into trouble with one of our staff. She was writing assessment reports on offenders giving them very high ratings of risk which were clearly not warranted. For example, one offender had said that he quite liked to have sex in a particular position which was by no means unusual. However, the staff member had very strict ideas about what

---

11 These were a series of studies carried out by Harkins and her colleagues at the University of Birmingham (Harkins, Beech and Goodwill 2010; Harkins *et al.* 2014). They looked at denial in detail, and noted that there were several different degrees of denial, including: 'the offence never happened', 'it happened but I didn't do it', 'I did it but it wasn't as bad as the victim claims'. The relationship between different kinds of denial and risk turned out to be much more complex than had previously been thought. This underlines the dangers of making assumptions about how things work which are not based on evidence. Apart from anything else, a (small, one hopes) proportion of those who claim innocence will actually be innocent!

was appropriate in the bedroom, and essentially regarded anything other than the missionary position with the lights out as a sexual deviation. Consequently, she was identifying sexual perversions right left and centre in people who were doing nothing out of the ordinary. She was highly religious, and this appeared to be related to her attitudes. She could not be persuaded to adopt a more reasonable point of view, and in the end she had to be removed from this kind of work.

There is no reason to think that lesser prejudices do not also affect professionals. At least one study shows that the emotions that assessors have towards offenders affect the way in which they complete the HCR-20 violence risk assessment tool, which is supposed to be a reasonably objective indication of risk.[12]

Another item of folklore concerns 'insight'. Indeed, this has long been an item on the HCR-20. According to this idea, insight into one's mental disorder, or violence risk, or need for treatment is necessary if one is to be able to manage one's antisocial impulses. Indeed, this was often cited in the past as one of the reasons why admissions of guilt were felt to be important: without admitting his offence(s), the offender could not be assisted in developing insight into his offending behaviour. There are problems with this notion. First, who decides what constitutes 'insight'? Normally, it comes down to the opinion of a professional, but as we have seen this may not be completely reliable. Essentially, for an assessor to say that someone has insight means that he agrees with the assessor's view of him. The sincerity of that agreement may be in doubt, and so may the accuracy of the assessor's view. The second problem is that expressing insight is verbal behaviour, and as we saw before this can be influenced by external factors not related to accuracy, perhaps a desire to gain favour with the

12   See Dernevik (2004).

professional in this case. A third and critical problem is that there is little evidence that the 'insight' item of the HCR-20, however assessed, is related to subsequent risk.[13] The basis for using treatment to improve it therefore seems obscure. Nonetheless, I have sat through countless parole hearings in which prison psychologists or probation officers have stressed the importance of a prisoner developing insight. Even when faced with the research demonstrating that there is no relationship between insight and risk, they tend to stick doggedly to their point of view.[14] I recall one parole hearing in particular where a trainee psychologist, faced with the evidence that insight and risk are unrelated, stated, 'All I can say is that he needs to develop insight into his offending.' Apparently, insight is officially demanded and therefore it must be pursued without question.

DYNAMIC RISK

The assessment of so-called 'static' risk has already been mentioned, static factors being those that are unchangeable, such as someone's criminal history or age. The whole basis of treatment in the forensic field is that there are such things as 'dynamic' risk factors. Unlike static factors, dynamic factors can be changed (at least in principle). Ostensibly, therefore, dynamic factors should make good targets for treatment programmes. However, we need to be cautious about this. The mere fact that a risk factor can change does not mean that changing it will

---

13   See Dietrich (1994) and Coid et al. (2007).

14   It may of course be that insight is critically important to reducing risk, but that we professionals are not very good at assessing it. Either way, the fact remains that our assessments of people's insight cannot reliably be related to risk. Therefore, it is totally unprofessional to recommend any treatment that is supposed to increase insight, because even if it is effective we have no means of telling. Indeed, we would have no means of telling if it made people's insight worse!

change risk. For example, it has been shown (unsurprisingly) that offenders tend to hold attitudes that are supportive of offending and other antisocial behaviour,[15] but it does not automatically follow that if we can change the attitudes there will be a reduction in risk. The example of the man who found religion made that point clearly. People are exceptionally good at moulding their attitudes to match their behaviour, and denying uncomfortable facts which they do not wish to acknowledge.[16]

There is in fact a logical problem in identifying dynamic risk factors. Identifying risk factors depends entirely upon establishing correlations between those factors and subsequent reconviction or lack of it.[17] Correlation is a mathematical technique, but for those who go faint at the very thought of maths, there is no need to understand the details in order to understand the principle. Essentially, correlation calculates the amount of agreement between two measures. Correlations range from −1 (one measure always shows the exact opposite of the other) to +1 (both measures always agree exactly). A correlation of zero indicates that there is neither agreement nor disagreement: there is no relationship between the two measures at all. In order to calculate a correlation between two measures, of course, they must be stable: if one measure was varying randomly all the time it would be impossible to show that it consistently agreed with the other. It wouldn't even be consistent with itself. One of the difficulties in weather forecasting, for example, is that nothing stays in the same state for very long. This makes it very difficult to predict the weather in any detail even a day or two ahead. Predictions constantly have to be updated in order to stand any chance of being useful. This is almost certainly why statistical predictors of reconviction work better than anything else.

---

15 See, amongst many others, Walters and Lowenkamp (2016).

16 For a very readable account, see *The (Honest) Truth about Dishonesty* by Dan Ariely (2012).

17 There are other mathematical techniques, but let's keep it simple!

They are dealing with static factors which do not change, rather than the constantly changing situation with which weather forecasters (and psychologists) work.

As an illustration, let us suppose that drug use and drug dealing are risk factors for a particular individual's offending. If he has been through a drug programme, and we know how effective it is, we may be able to calculate the probability that his risk of reoffending has been reduced by a given amount. Actually, we can very rarely calculate even that much with any certainty. However, dynamic risk factors may also be involved, such as peer pressure from his old drug-using friends, and financial hardship; there may also be 'protective' factors, which would reduce the likelihood of reoffending. These might include family support, support from a girlfriend or wife, somewhere to live and secure employment. We have absolutely no way of predicting any of these factors at the point where he leaves prison. They could all change in either direction: his old friends may have died or moved away, his partner could leave him, or he might unexpectedly get a good job, or a supportive new partner. Precisely because these factors are so changeable there is no way to predict them. If his parents are killed in a car crash, prompting him to fall into a depression and resume drug use to help him cope, we might *with the benefit of hindsight* think that we should have arranged some other social support network for him, but there would be no way to take this into account in advance.

Partly in response to this criticism, those seeking to develop treatment programmes have developed the concept of 'stable' versus 'acute' dynamic risk factors. Both of these are alleged to be changeable, but acute factors change over a very short timescale and are therefore not amenable to treatment programmes. They may nonetheless be amenable to short-term interventions as part of the risk management process when people are under probation supervision in the community, and one Canadian study identified a number.[18] However, stable dynamic factors are supposed to change only over a longer timescale, and in principle effective treatment programmes should help introduce change more quickly. Unfortunately, there is a question as to whether some of these factors truly are dynamic. For example, the Canadian study considered that for child sex offenders access to children (e.g. living or working in a situation close to them) was a dynamic risk factor. Once access to children exists, this may be true. However, in many cases the access will not be accidental; if such a person has *engineered* a situation so that he has access to children this is surely more likely to reflect a static risk factor, namely, having a sexual attraction to children. The Canadian study used an assessment tool that required a great deal of scoring by assessors. As so often in the field of assessment, reliability may be an issue – as a British government study using the same tool found, there were problems with differences between assessors (in this case, not psychologists, but police and probation officers).[19] This is not altogether surprising: several studies have found that assessments of alleged dynamic risk factors do not improve prediction over and above the results given by assessment of static risk factors alone.[20]

What all of this demonstrates, once again, is that psychologists are not yet in a position to identify treatment needs adequately, nor to measure the extent to which they are present (and therefore whether they, and the risk they are supposed to represent, have been reduced) in any individual. This raises the question of what treatment is actually doing, if it is not treating people.

---

18   See Hanson *et al.* (2007).

19   See McNaughton Nicholls *et al.* (2010).

20   See, for example, Philipse *et al.* (2006) and Morgan *et al.* (2013).

WHAT DOES TREATMENT ACTUALLY DO?

Let us leave aside for a moment the question of whether treatment works or not. This is considered in the next chapter, although it will be evident by now that I do not have much faith in the current fashion for cognitive-behavioural programmes. But whether it works to reduce criminal behaviour or not, what else does it do?

One thing the treatment programmes obviously do is enable politicians to say that they are treating prisoners humanely and protecting possible future victims. At the time of writing, concern for victims is a major political theme. It has become common to demand 'justice' for victims, even before anything has been proved against anyone, and to demand compensation alongside the justice. This has reached the point where many psychologists, lawyers and journalists are concerned about the growth of a victimhood industry, which may even encourage false claims of abuse.[21] Politically, however, concern for victims has to be paramount in the present climate. When a UK Parole Board judge was overheard in 2014 remarking that victim statements made no difference to parole board decisions, there was a media frenzy marked by outrage and indignation.[22] In fact, he was not only telling it like it was, but also as it was supposed to be, according to the Parole Board's constitution.[23] At the risk of stating the obvious, victims are not experts in criminology or in risk assessment, only in being victims. To say this is not to denigrate them, but to point out that the Parole Board is supposed to be considering likely risk in the future, not misdeeds of the past. There is little that victims can contribute to this, particularly since their opinion is likely to be swayed by emotion to a great extent. Studies in Alabama showed that

---

21   See, for example, Dineen (2004), Hewson (2014) and Parris (2015).

22   For one of the less emotional accounts, see the BBC (2014).

23   Downloadable document (The Parole Board for England and Wales 2015).

parole was less likely to be granted if victims were present or represented at the parole hearing, and more likely if the offender was present or represented. This may not be very surprising, but there was no evidence that the input of either side helped to bring about a less risky decision, the stated purpose of the process.[24]

Some studies have found that parole applicants were more likely to be successful if they had completed the recommended offending behaviour programmes.[25] It is not clear whether this was thought to indicate reduced risk, or simply compliance and manageability on the part of the prisoner. On the other hand, one study found that sex offenders were *less* likely to be paroled if they had completed a sex offender treatment programme.[26] This seems counterintuitive, but the authors speculated that this was because further treatment needs had been identified during the programme. The problem, as we have seen, is that the identification of treatment needs is speculative at best. If identification of further treatment needs is a common outcome of 'treatment programmes', there is a real risk that they could become self-perpetuating, each one identifying supposed needs to justify the next. This would reduce treatment needs assessment to a form of marketing for the offending behaviour industry. In the UK at least, there is a hierarchy of programmes. Individuals thought to pose a low risk undergo one programme,

24　Several studies were conducted, covering different aspects of the parole system (Morgan and Smith 2005a; Smith, Watkins and Morgan 1997).

25　For example, Bonham, Janeksela and Bardo (1986) in Kansas, and Hood and Shute (2000) in the UK. An earlier study, carried out before the introduction of offending behaviour programmes, found that participation in education increased the likelihood of parole being granted (Heinz *et al.* 1976).

26　See Welsh and Ogloff (2000). This was a more or less incidental finding, as the researchers' principal aim was to investigate possible discrimination against aboriginal Canadians. However, they also found that prisoners assessed as having important emotional or personal needs were less likely to get parole, which seems consistent with their interpretation of the finding about sex offenders.

while individuals thought to pose a high risk may have to undergo several programmes of increasing intensity. There seems to be no rhyme nor reason to this. Although there is a school of thought that holds that high-risk individuals should be targeted in preference to others, there is no real evidence that this approach is more effective than any other. The only strictly controlled study to look at this in detail concluded that there was no benefit to targeting high-risk individuals particularly.[27]

In fact, although the entire rationale of treatment programmes is that they should reduce the risk that criminals pose to the general population, and the official line is that they do, there is precious little sign that decision-makers believe this. They may believe it, but if so they do not behave in accordance with that belief (offenders are not the only people to behave in a way that does not mirror their stated beliefs). It will be remembered that in the UK life sentence prisoners are given a minimum term, after which they become eligible to apply for parole. Getting parole is in fact their only way out of prison, and very few obtain it at the earliest possible opportunity; they usually have to make several applications at two-year intervals. If the authorities really believed that offending behaviour programmes were effective, these prisoners should now be getting released sooner than they used to be. This is the logic if treatment programmes are genuinely thought to reduce risk, because risk reduction would make them eligible for parole sooner. However, on average, life sentence prisoners are now serving two years *longer* before being paroled than they used to before treatment programmes were introduced.[28] So much for treatment reducing risk. It is true that society in general is risk averse where criminals are concerned, but that has always been the case. No doubt several factors may be involved, but there is

---

27   See Hanson *et al.* (2009).

28   This is according to figures from the Ministry of Justice itself (Ministry of Justice, 2013).

no reason to think that prisoners are more risky than they used to be. Nor are they any cheaper: at current cost levels an extra two years means an extra £70,000 or more per prisoner.

If, as I have suggested, treatment programmes target attitudes and beliefs instead of the schemas which are supposed to underlie them, is there a risk of adverse effects? At the anecdotal level, there is evidence of this. A number of sex offenders have spoken to me about the adverse effects of prolonged discussions of sex offending. As one put it to me, 'I've never had so many deviant thoughts as I have in the last few weeks since I started this treatment programme.' This is probably not surprising when the subject matter fills a fair amount of their day. However, it is not just the subject matter that is important, but the manner in which it is handled. Part of the rationale behind sex offender treatment programmes is that 'deviant' attitudes should be challenged. Indeed, some colleagues who run the programmes have explained that they need to have a mix of different kinds of offender in order to make this happen. If the members of a programme were all child abusers, for example, they would probably not be so effective at challenging each other's views. On the other hand, a rapist who excuses his own behaviour will feel and express horror at the actions of child abusers, and they will similarly criticise his. One can see the logic, but only if this 'challenging' actually achieves what it is meant to. At least one experienced colleague, who formerly ran sex offender treatment programmes, doubts that. As she pointed out to me, there is a risk that people whose views are constantly attacked will simply generate new rationalisations for why they are right.[29] There is in fact good evidence that some attempts to change thinking patterns are counter-productive, and may result in an increase in the very preoccupation that one is trying to eliminate.[30]

29 This was a personal communication from Dr Clare Wilson, of the University of Portsmouth.

30 See Wegner (1994).

So far as I know, no research has thoroughly investigated the effects of these techniques in treatment programmes. It could be that they are more positive than I have suggested, or it could be that they are neutral, or even seriously counter-productive. Unless we research them properly we are not going to know. However, there is a lesson from history which is ominous.

THOUGHT REFORM: THE LESSON OF HISTORY

It is a truism that those who do not learn from history's mistakes are condemned to repeat them. In one form or another it has been attributed to the politician Edmund Burke, the philosopher George Santayana and many others.[31] The history of trying to change people's behaviour patterns by changing their attitudes and beliefs should have taught us that the whole idea is indeed a mistake. Modern offending behaviour programmes were introduced in the 1990s, but there is a much older example of the technique. This is 'thought reform': a collection of techniques used in the early days of communist China to 're-educate' Westerners who were living there in order to create political propaganda. Typically, the Westerners would be subjected to these techniques, popularly known as 'brainwashing', and then filmed as they confessed to various crimes, such as spying. After this they were generally deported, which was extremely convenient. It meant that any backsliding from their newfound political enthusiasm would not be apparent in China. If it occurred in the West it didn't matter, because the public in China had no access to Western media. The political purpose had already been served by demonstrating the untrustworthiness of foreigners, especially those from the West. The idea that people could be 'brainwashed' into believing (and therefore doing)

---

31   See https://en.wikiquote.org/wiki/George_Santayana.

anything their captors wanted them to was seized upon as a powerful theme in fiction, and contributed to more than one novel.[32]

But what did 'brainwashing' consist of? The subject was extensively studied by the psychiatrist Robert Lifton, who interviewed many victims of the process at length, following their return to the West.[33] He found that they had initially been placed in prison cells with several Chinese people, similarly accused of crimes against the state. They were required to reform their thought processes just as the Western victim was, but with an added twist: their own progress depended upon their success in changing his point of view. Thought reform was achieved by having prisoners challenge each other's beliefs and attitudes (sound familiar?). This was done by a verbal process, in which one prisoner would be the object of criticisms voiced by the others. He would be criticised for being an agent of Western powers (often but not always the United States), for undertaking activities intended to undermine Chinese culture and independence, and often for supposedly undertaking espionage. The allegations were not always related to spying; some of them were about fostering Western influence more generally – a sort of 'cultural imperialism'. However they were phrased, the activities were all regarded as anti-Chinese. Some victims were also required to read and formally study communist tracts, and even write essays about them. They would be questioned at intervals by a judge,

32 Most famously, and luridly, *The Manchurian Candidate* (Condon, 2004), in which an agent is brainwashed into assassinating prominent figures in the United States. The book was originally published in 1959, at the height of the Cold War. The US government was portrayed as the villain in *Vector* (Sutton, 1971), in which victims of a biological weapons accident are made to believe that it was a natural event as part of a cover-up. The effectiveness of real-life 'brainwashing' was rather less spectacular.

33 See *Thought Reform and the Psychology of Totalism* (Lifton 1989). The book was originally published in 1961, but later republished. It remains the definitive work on this topic.

who would remind them of how benevolent the government was being, because they could have been executed. The judge would determine whether their 'reform' had progressed far enough. When it had, often after two or three years, they would then be filmed making a public statement in which they admitted all the supposed wrongs they had committed. The Chinese would use these films for propaganda purposes, while the poor victim, often in a state of considerable emotional confusion, would be deported. It is worth noting that victims' confessions and expressions of enthusiasm for communism were often rejected in the early stages, on the basis that they were not genuine. The Chinese wanted the new ideas to be internalised, not just superficial compliance.

The emphasis was mainly on verbal methods, but these could include threats, and occasionally violence was used. The threat of execution has already been mentioned, but there was a running threat that conditions might be worsened if the victim did not cooperate. Violence was rare, but it did occur on occasions. Lifton describes a case in which a victim was chained in a kneeling position day and night, and was actually beaten up physically. Interestingly, he was then brought before a government official who formally apologised for his treatment. The official stated that violence and physical coercion were not intended to be used, and that this had been done without official sanction. The purpose of the victim's imprisonment was essentially re-education rather than punishment. However, the victim was not released any sooner on that account. It was never clear whether the apology was real, or simply a justification for the use of violence, but since the Chinese officials were not generally apologetic it may well have been sincere. They appeared genuinely to have thought of themselves as benevolent, despite the suffering that they were inflicting upon their victims. There is a clear warning here that belief in one's own benevolence does not necessarily guarantee the effectiveness or humanity of one's actions.

What of the state of mind of the returning victims? Lifton found that this varied considerably. Some victims recounted that they had become quite delusional when the process reached an advanced stage. Some reported auditory hallucinations, such as thinking that they could hear former colleagues talking outside their cell window. There is little doubt that it was a seriously harrowing experience for many, and the symptoms which some of them developed would nowadays be regarded as indicating post-traumatic stress disorder. When it came to their beliefs and attitudes, however, there was little long-term impact. Some of the victims had developed a greater understanding of the Chinese point of view, but none had developed any long-term admiration for communism. Indeed, although Lifton did not use quantitative research methods, he believed that in a number of cases the victims had become more anti-communist than they had been before. He estimated that only about one in seven had undergone any genuine change of mind during the thought reform process, and that this had only persisted while they were still in communist China. That is, any change of beliefs that did occur could only be sustained in a social environment where the individual was surrounded by like-minded people who were sympathetic to those beliefs. When this environment was swapped for the familiar environment of the West, the attitudes and beliefs were also swapped for those more appropriate in a non-communist society. There was no question of the victims having become clandestine communist agents. Lifton believed that the majority had not undergone any change of belief system; they had in fact undergone a feigned conversion in order to please their captors and obtain their release. As time had gone on they had simply got better at it. He concluded that thought reform was ineffective when it came to any permanent change in behaviour, attitude or belief.

I am sure that my colleagues would object to any implication that they are undertaking 'brainwashing' with prisoners, but the fact is that there is a great similarity between thought reform and the 'cognitive restructuring' that they consider themselves to be undertaking. Both processes depend upon the belief systems of prisoners being challenged by others. Both depend upon an extended verbal process, often involving discussions, study and written work. Both insist upon a genuine internalised change of beliefs, not external compliance. Both have claimed success in changing people's behaviour as a result of changing their attitudes and beliefs. Both have been studied, with results suggesting that these claims have been exaggerated. The main differences with offending behaviour programmes are that offenders are allowed to refuse to participate, and that violence and threats of execution are not permitted. However, threats do occur, both explicitly and implicitly. With life sentence prisoners there is the ever-present threat that without participation in 'treatment' they will never be able to progress to release. Participation in treatment programmes is necessary in order to 'demonstrate a reduction in risk', without which parole is unlikely. In other words, like the thought reform victims, they must show that their attitudes and beliefs are now more acceptable and the changes genuine. As will be seen in the next chapter, there is reason to doubt that these changes are likely to be reflected in subsequent behaviour, just as in the case of the religious convert mentioned above.

INTERVENTION: IMPLICATIONS

How is it that ineffective and untested methods have become so widespread? Is it simply that their proponents are good salespeople? To some extent, it is. There is no doubt that in the early 1990s persuasive individual psychologists in the criminal justice systems of the Western world managed to persuade those who hold the purse strings to fund their programmes.

They did so on the basis that these programmes could reduce recidivism among offenders, something which politicians were very eager to believe. This claim went far beyond any evidence that was available at the time. It is even further beyond it now, but once programmes like this are established they acquire a life of their own. Administrative organisations grow up around them, and administrators as well as professional specialists resist any interference with their empires. So, in the field of offending behaviour programmes, a plethora of vested interests has arisen. This is despite the fact that the programmes were originally regarded as experimental and there were good intentions to evaluate them strictly. These good intentions have not been realised.

Is it professionally ethical to recommend treatments for prisoners in order to 'reduce their risk' when we have no evidence that it will do so, and it might even increase risk? 'No' is the only possible answer. Unfortunately, it is an answer that is very hard to get out of professionals in this field. When I was a member of the BPS's Investigatory Committee I did raise this problem with other committee members. There were two responses. The first was an admission that many of the things psychologists do don't have any evidence for their effectiveness. That is an interesting statement about how much psychological practice is not evidence-based, but it overlooks the fact that the things most psychologists do can't affect whether somebody is allowed their liberty or not. In criminal justice settings the consequences of bad practice can be extremely serious. The second answer was that it was very hard for psychologists not to do something when their employers required it. This is a hopeless answer. It is, of course, a variation of the excuse for misconduct that 'I was only obeying orders', a defence that was ruled inadmissible at the Nuremberg war crime trials in the 1940s. But there is another issue: if we agree that psychologists have to do whatever their employers require we are in effect allowing employers to decide what is acceptable and ethical professional conduct for psychologists. This cannot be right. The problem is demonstrated in an extreme form by a story from a prison colleague who asked not to be identified. According to this colleague, a senior prison psychologist expressed the following opinion, 'Your job is to do whatever the prison governor wants you to do. If the governor tells you to go and walk his dog, then that is your job for the day.' I feel confident that few would agree, inside or outside the profession.

Psychologists are legally regulated in most countries, to ensure that they do not exploit or otherwise treat clients unethically, e.g. financially or sexually. Is there also a case for enforcing stricter scientific standards so that unproven methods are not oversold? In theory, this is already part of the code of conduct for psychologists, at least in the UK. I once lodged a complaint against a prison psychologist over just this issue. The complaint related to the selective misquoting of research findings in order to justify a particular decision. The regulatory authority, the HCPC, decided that it could not take up the complaint. Somewhat tongue in cheek, I wrote to ask whether the HCPC actually considered it part of its business to ensure that practising psychologists were professionally competent (as opposed to just dealing with gross misconduct such as fraud or sexual exploitation). They replied that indeed they were concerned with professional competence, but I think the irony was lost on them.

Let us be clear: as a profession psychology claims to be based on good scientific research evidence. Where it is clearly not, then that is not simply a matter of the professional reputation of those concerned, or even of the whole profession. Bad decisions based on bad practice have bad effects on real people in the real world. If we claim effectiveness for treatment programmes when there isn't any, we will be more likely to consider that the risk posed by an offender has been reduced when it has not. This may translate into his being paroled when he should not be. Indeed, this is exactly what happened in one of the most notorious UK parole failures of recent years.[34] On the other hand, if we allow spurious evidence to enter into risk assessment the opposite error may occur, and people who pose no significant risk may be detained for years or even decades of extremely expensive incarceration when it is unnecessary. If we do not insist on a strong evidentiary basis for our practice, we cannot avoid either of these errors.

Does the professional isolation of those working in prisons lead to a lack of accountability? My personal experience only extends to the UK, but colleagues in the United States assure me that there is a similar problem there. That experience suggests that colleagues in the criminal justice system in the UK are indeed very isolated. Most of their training is conducted in-house by other prison psychologists, and they are administered by other prison psychologists who are responsible for their professional standards. This is a classic example of a service marking its own homework.

The problems do not stop there. Organisations that operate in this way are politely referred to as 'inward looking' or having a 'silo mentality'. For both individuals and organisations, lack of contact with external views and factual contributions is unhealthy; frankly, it is a recipe for paranoia. The reason for this is that people's worldview is constantly reinforced by those around them because they hold the same view. If it is never challenged by evidence from outside, that worldview becomes entrenched and increasingly divorced from reality. Anyone coming from outside with a different view is therefore seen as a threat, and anyone with a different view inside the organisation is likely to be seen as disloyal. Not for nothing is paranoia sometimes referred to as the occupational disease of dictators! The isolation is therefore a highly undesirable feature of work in such organisations.

---

34 See the report into the Anthony Rice case by HM Inspectorate of Probation (2006).

– 7 –

EVALUATION

What Works and How Would We Know?

It's all very well going on about problems in assessment, formulation and treatment, but 'the proof of the pudding is in the eating'. Since offending behaviour programmes have now been running for over 20 years there must be some data available to tell us how well they are doing. In fact, a great many studies of programme effectiveness have been carried out, and it is perfectly reasonable to ask what they have shown. This chapter faces this issue squarely.

EVALUATING TREATMENT PROGRAMMES

At first sight, the evaluation of treatment programmes may seem simple: don't we just run a programme with a group of people (the treatment group) and compare the results with another group (the control group) who didn't undertake the programme? Then, if we find the treatment group was convicted of fewer further offences than the control group, the treatment works. Doesn't it? Unfortunately, things are not so simple.[1] In the early days, many of the treatment evaluations that were attempted were done on exactly these lines. However, any

---

1   And it's not news. Many of these points were made by Rice and Harris (2003), two of the most highly respected researchers in this field, but they were largely ignored.

comparison in outcomes between the two groups depends upon the fact that they differ *only* in one respect: that one underwent the treatment and the other did not. It soon became apparent that they often differed in other respects as well, and these other differences might account for the apparent treatment effect. For one thing, many of the early studies offered offenders the treatment programme and if they refused they were placed in the control group. By definition, treatment refusers could not be in the treatment group. If refusers were high in risk, this would mean that the control group would do badly by comparison with the treatment group. Few studies even considered this until recent years, but it has become apparent that refusers may indeed be higher in risk.[2] This invalidates most of the treatment evaluations that were carried out in the early days. Furthermore, the problem is still there even if we do not reassign refusers to the control group. The reason for this is that it will contain some high risk 'refusers' who weren't actually offered the programme (but would have refused if they had been), whereas the treatment group will still contain none.[3] There will still be a spurious 'treatment' effect.

Similar considerations apply to those who commence treatment but then drop out. It has long been known that these individuals are higher in risk, and in the early days it was even suggested that this was because the treatment had a confusing effect initially because of the way it attacked participants' existing beliefs and attitudes. It was claimed that the benefits of treatment required the person to stay the course, and risk would actually be raised if they dropped out prematurely. This is the sort of reasoning used in the example about power lines. There was not the slightest evidence for the process being claimed; it was purely and simply an idea that somebody dreamed up

---

2   Ibid.

3   Ibid.

to explain why a little treatment appeared to be a dangerous thing. It is now generally accepted that those who drop out of treatment are those who posed a high risk in the first place, and cannot cope with the assault on their belief systems. Whether effective or not, these treatment programmes can be very challenging, and require people to examine themselves, their motives and their beliefs in considerable detail, and to withstand criticism from others (this treatment is invariably conducted in groups). As one prisoner put it, 'Treatment programmes are basically organised nagging, and mind-numbingly boring.' It is not surprising if someone with those attitudes doesn't stay the course (and he didn't).

If the simple two-group design is inadequate to evaluate treatment, can we do better? We can, and some researchers have used the matched-pairs design. The idea behind this is that each participant in the treatment programme is paired with someone in the control group. Each pair will be matched on factors known to be relevant to reconviction, such as age, type of offence, number of previous offences, and so on. In principle, this ought to ensure that the two groups are the same in all important respects. If someone drops out of the treatment group, his match is removed from the control group as well, thus maintaining the similarity between the two groups. However, results have been mixed. One difficulty is that it is rarely possible to find exact matches, so approximate matches must be used. For example, we may have a 45-year-old in the treatment group, but be unable to find one for the control group who is a good match in the other respects necessary. We may end up with a 40-year-old instead, or perhaps there is one who is the right age but doesn't quite match with respect to offending history. Inevitably, the matching is a compromise, and compromise is the source of much error. What's more, we have to be certain that we have matched the two groups for everything that is relevant to future reconviction risk. In practice, we can never be quite sure of this. For example, it is often maintained that people need to be 'ready' to change, and the inadequacies of clinical interviews for assessing this sort of subjective characteristic have already been discussed above.

There is little doubt that the best way to evaluate treatments (and not just psychological treatments) is by a randomised controlled trial.[4] Some psychologists have gone so far as to insist that we have a moral duty to conduct such trials before we pronounce treatment to be successful.[5] With this design no attempt is made to match participants. Two groups are drawn at random from the same population, and one undergoes the treatment while the other does not. If the two groups have truly been drawn at random then they must be equivalent and the only difference is whether they have undertaken the treatment. However, randomised controlled trials are very rarely carried out, despite being the best method. The reason for this is almost certainly that they are expensive and take much more organisation than the other methods. For randomisation to work effectively the two groups must be large, and this requires expenditure of staff time and offender time. Generally speaking, it is difficult to conduct a randomised controlled trial on a reasonable scale without getting special funding for it. Furthermore, there seems to be a bias against randomised controlled trials in the field of forensic psychology; some practitioners have gone so far as to suggest that they are not possible.[6] Historically, they have been difficult to carry out, but this does not make lesser methods any better. If we cannot conduct a randomised controlled trial, it would be more honest to say that we do not know what the treatment does, if anything. Instead, a number of practitioners

---

4   It is just as essential with pharmaceutical treatments, and these days no new drug would be approved unless it had passed a randomised controlled trial (Goldacre 2008, 2012).

5   See Weisburd (2003).

6   See Clarke and Cornish (1972).

and researchers have adopted the principle that poor studies are better than none, and poor evidence better than nothing, which rapidly seems to morph into a belief that a lot of poor evidence is equivalent to good evidence. This is clearly not true, but the belief is exemplified by the answer that a highly qualified and experienced prison colleague gave to the question of whether the simple two-group design could be accepted as evidence of effectiveness. The reply was, 'Not if it was just one study, but if there are a number of them you could start to accept that as evidence of effectiveness.' In other words, failing to prove something once is no use, but failing to prove it lots of times means we have proved it. The logic is elusive.[7] One sceptical colleague was moved to remark that people involved in delivering programmes appeared to be adept at denying any evidence that failed to support them. The same colleague suggested that if randomised controlled trials showed programmes to be effective, the people delivering them would be shouting the results from the rooftops.

ARE TREATMENT PROGRAMMES BEING EVALUATED PROPERLY?

There may be arguments about what constitutes effective evaluation of a programme, but obviously some sort of evaluation

---

7   But widespread. Similar comments were made in review studies by Lösel and Schmucker (2005), who justified the inclusion of 'suboptimal' (p.118) studies, and Hanson et al. (2002), who noted the difficulties of randomisation in order to justify including 'research studies using methods other than random assignment' (p.186). In fact, they had found only one randomised study, still in progress at the time, which had found no treatment effect up to then. When the final report was published three years later it still hadn't (Marques et al. 2005). This was hailed in advance as the study that was going to demonstrate once and for all the utility of cognitive-behavioural programmes with sex offenders. Instead, it suggested that 'futility' would be nearer the mark. Programmes continued with undiminished enthusiasm.

must be carried out. If this were not the case, then we would not know what effect programmes were having; they might even be making people worse, and we would not know. So, obviously there is a comprehensive policy for evaluating programmes to see what works and what does not. Isn't there? After all, if there is no proof that a programme works there would be no lawful basis for denying parole to people on the grounds that they hadn't undertaken it. Actually, the system doesn't quite work like that, at least in the UK. What happens at parole hearings is that the parole panel can say they think a particular risk (e.g. attitudes to violence, or attitudes to women if the victims were female) has not been 'addressed'. In the UK, Parole Boards are actually not allowed to say *how* that risk should be addressed, i.e. which programme should be undertaken. However, Ministry of Justice psychologists can assure the panel that a certain risk can only be addressed by undertaking a certain programme, and the panel is not likely to challenge them. Indeed, a colleague of mine who was questioning the value of a particular programme was told by the judge who was chairing the parole panel: 'I don't care whether it works or not, I want him to do it.' Such obvious bias shows clearly how alleged treatment programmes have not become a means of achieving earlier release for those who undertake them, but a means of denying release for those who have not. Effectiveness has nothing to do with it. Coming from a judge, who ought to be aware of the legal implications of keeping people in custody on spurious grounds, it is a worrying statement.

The somewhat surprising truth is that most offending behaviour programmes have never been evaluated at all, let alone evaluated strictly. In the UK, there are a number of programmes which are currently being run, that have never been evaluated, and for which there is no plan to evaluate them, according to colleagues in the Ministry of Justice. Yet psychologists unblushingly advise parole panels that prisoners must undergo these programmes if their risk is to be reduced. Such a stance is professionally unjustifiable when there is no scientific evidence for it and there is no plan to obtain any. Prison-based colleagues often justify their stance by saying that the programmes which they are recommending have been 'accredited' and are proven to reduce risk. The Ministry of Justice is indeed advised by the Correctional Services Accreditation Panel (CSAP), a group of experts in offending behaviour programmes; it is probably fair to say that none of these experts is known for their critical stance towards such programmes. So it is not true to say, as many prison colleagues habitually do, that a programme's accreditation means it has been proven to reduce risk. What it actually means is that a group of experts in this field, who are generally in favour of offending behaviour programmes, have examined the rationale for the programme and declared that it looks okay to them. That's it. There is no proof, no evidence and in many cases no plan to obtain any. The approval is simply based on the fact that the programme conforms to the principles that the Accreditation Panel recognises.

A set of principles that is currently popular among psychologists working in the correctional field is known as the 'Risk, Need and Responsivity' principles, or 'RNR'.[8] According to these principles, treatment programmes should be directed at those who pose the highest risk of future offending, they should target criminogenic needs, and they should be delivered in a way that is appropriate to the learning style of the offender. Given the difficulties that we have in assessing risk accurately, and in identifying criminogenic needs, there is reason to doubt that RNR principles are likely to be easy to apply, regardless of how useful they are in theory. Responsivity appears to have been catered for (at least in the UK) by developing 'adapted' versions of programmes for those of low IQ. Attempts have

---

8   The classic expression of this philosophy is *The Psychology of Criminal Conduct* (Andrews and Bonta 2016), now in its sixth edition.

also been made to assess 'readiness for change', using the so-called 'transtheoretical model of change'.[9] This at any rate must win a prize for one of the most grandiose titles in psychology: it isn't clear what 'transtheoretical' could possibly mean.[10] It was originally developed in the field of health psychology, and was concerned with such things as giving up smoking and other problematic health-related behaviour. Its relevance to the very different sorts of behaviour involved in offending is not entirely clear, but it has been widely adopted anyway. The model envisages five stages: pre-contemplation (not yet thinking about change), contemplation (thinking about changing soon), preparation (taking small steps towards change, such as telling family that you're going to), action (actually doing it) and maintenance (doing things, like seeking support from others, which help to maintain the change once it has been made). A sixth stage, relapse, is sometimes added.

Without wishing to go into too much detail, the transtheoretical model of change has been subject to a great deal of research, and there appears to be no strong support for it. As so often happens, some studies appear supportive and others not. Criticisms include the fact that it assumes people make decisions on a conscious and rational basis, which is demonstrably untrue.[11] It has also been criticised on practical grounds, because the theory requires that different interventions should be more effective in some stages of change than others, and this appears not to be true.[12] If a model of behaviour change

9   The original publication of this model was in 1982 (Prochaska and DiClemente 1982), but much has been written since, mostly concerning undesirable or risky health-related behaviour.

10   Searches in the *Oxford English Dictionary* and on Google failed to find any definition of the term 'transtheoretical' apart from its use in the transtheoretical model itself.

11   As before, see Kahneman (2011) and Ariely (2012).

12   According to a systematic review, published by the highly respected online database The Cochrane Collaboration (Cahill, Lancaster and Green 2010).

in health psychology fails on its home territory, there seems very little reason to suppose that it will fare any better in a different field. Nonetheless, at least in the UK, forensic psychologists are still basing part of their work on this model.

Getting back to the RNR principles, these too have been investigated in various ways over the years and support has been mixed. However, an attempt to provide a definitive evaluation of the RNR model and its application to sex offenders was made in Canada in 2009.[13] The researchers collected details of 130 evaluations of sex offender treatment programmes, and rated them for the quality of the methods used. Of the 130, no fewer than 105 (81%) were rejected as being of too poor a quality to be included, which in itself says something about the preponderance of poor studies in this field. A further three studies were rejected for technical reasons, leaving only 22. The researchers rated these for their compliance with RNR principles and divided them into three groups according to how good their compliance was. They ended up with three classifications: weak, good and strong. Not surprisingly, the researchers found that apparent treatment effects were more powerful in the weak studies than in the good studies (that is, the stricter the evaluation, the less apparent treatment effect was found). However, there was no relationship between treatment effect and risk level, one of the three RNR principles. That is, programmes targeted at high-risk individuals produced no more treatment effect than those targeted at others. But what of the strong studies? Surely the most stringent tests of RNR programmes would provide the most convincing evidence? There was a problem here: the researchers did not rate *any* of the studies they found as strong. It is therefore possible that strong studies would have found no treatment effect at all. As they themselves put it, 'Reviewers restricting themselves to the better quality, published studies…could reasonably conclude

---

13   See Hanson *et al.* (2009).

that there is *no evidence that treatment is effective* in reducing sexual offence recidivism.'[14] Quite so.

Having mentioned publication, I should also mention the 'bound for publication' bias, proposed by two eminent statisticians, Copas and Jackson.[15] This derives its name from the fact that there is a tendency not to publish unsuccessful studies. Imagine you are a psychologist involved in treatment programmes, proud of your work and convinced of its effectiveness. Then you do a strict evaluation of one of your treatment programmes, and it turns out that there is no treatment effect after all. For someone convinced of the benefits of their work this is likely to be very disturbing. Furthermore, there are really only two possibilities. One is that your cherished treatment programme is useless. The other is that the treatment should work but that you just haven't done it very well. Do you publish, and thereby advertise your incompetence to all of your colleagues? Is it not easier to convince yourself that you have made a mistake in the evaluation somewhere and simply bury the project quietly? If so, this will result in a bias whereby studies that appear successful are published, and others are not. Copas and Jackson showed that it is possible to estimate the strength of this effect mathematically, and that it does occur in evaluations of medical treatments. There is no reason to think that psychological treatments would be immune from it. Unsuccessful evaluations are likely to end up being filed away somewhere and forgotten about, hence the other name of this effect: the 'file drawer' effect. There have been attempts to show that this does not occur in psychology, but none are very convincing. For example, a well-known systematic review of sex offender treatment evaluations was carried out by Lösel and Schmucker,[16] who studied the results

---

14   Ibid. (p.23, emphasis added).

15   See Copas and Jackson (2004).

16   See Lösel and Schmucker (2005). This study was a 'meta-analysis' which goes further than a review. Rather than simply discussing the findings from different evaluations, a meta-analysis combines them mathematically,

of 80 evaluations involving almost 23,000 offenders. This was a large study by any standard. As well as published evaluation studies they attempted to include unpublished ones by requesting them from colleagues. They considered that there was no difference in success rates between published and unpublished studies, and concluded there was no 'bound for publication' bias.

However, this is a pretty superficial examination of the problem. Even releasing a study to Lösel and Schmucker would be publication of a kind: it would still reveal supposed incompetence to colleagues. But Lösel and Schmucker's paper contained hidden within it some more interesting information. It turned out that in evaluations conducted on small groups (under 50) the treatment group did over four times as well as the untreated group. Quite a success rate. However, in studies of larger groups there was little difference, and in the largest of all (over 500) the treatment groups actually did *worse* than the untreated groups (about 12% worse). But does size really matter? In this case it does, and for the following reason. Small-scale studies are often done without any special funding and under the control of the practitioner conducting the treatment. This is why it is easy for them not to publish unsuccessful results, as no one need ever know the study took place. Large-scale studies cannot be done on this improvised basis. They are expensive and they require special funding, usually obtained in the form of grants from the government or from research organisations. Because they are spending public money, these organisations *require* that results should be published, in order that the public can see what it is getting for its money. There is no way of hiding the outcome, successful or not, and there can be no 'bound for publication' bias. So, when small studies which probably included spurious treatment effects were removed, no treatment effects were found. Lösel and Schmucker's paper contained another

---

effectively combining them into one very large-scale evaluation study. In principle, this ought to be a very effective technique.

interesting nugget: there was only a significant 'treatment' effect where the people evaluating the programme were also involved in running it. In other words, treatment only appeared to work when the treaters were 'marking their own homework'. Where evaluations were conducted by independent researchers, no treatment effect was found.[17] I do not suggest for one moment that professionals were being deliberately deceitful, but the fact is that it is very easy to make slight changes in the data or the statistical analysis because you are convinced (not always for good reason) that they should be made, rather than because the best methodology requires it.[18]

Another interesting finding, not emphasised in the paper, was that no treatment effect was found for studies involving randomisation or matched controls (the strictest methods for evaluating treatments). Essentially, what Lösel and Schmucker found was that most evaluations had serious problems but they put them into their meta-analysis anyway. This is not the way to evaluate whether treatment works. Nonetheless, this study has been quoted time and again in the years since it was published as evidence, or even 'proof', that cognitive behavioural treatments for sex offenders are effective.[19] What is the true position?

---

17 Ibid., Table 3, p.130.

18 See Ariely (2012), especially Chapter 3: 'Blinded by Our Own Motivations'.

19 For some reason, researchers and treaters in this field have been more interested in sex offenders than anyone else. They generate more programmes for them and publish more evaluations. It is not clear why, since sexual behaviour is notoriously difficult to change. It may reflect the current moral panic about sex offenders, despite the decreases in this offending across the Western world. Both the American Psychological Association and the British Psychological Society have issued position statements declaring that changing a person's sexual orientation is not a legitimate target for therapy. To be fair, sex offender treatment programmes tend to concentrate on discouraging the expression of illicit sexual behaviour, rather than changing orientation, but some still retain an element of this.

DO TREATMENT PROGRAMMES
MAKE PEOPLE ANY BETTER?

There is an old engineering adage that says an ounce of practice is worth a ton of theory. So, whatever the theory may say, and whatever the problems may be with evaluating treatments, what in practice is the evidence from good quality evaluations? As we have seen, actually finding good quality evaluations is the first problem. However, the Cochrane Collaboration, a highly respected online database of high-quality evaluation studies, has published a review of sex offender treatments.[20] They were only able to find 10 randomised controlled studies (generally accepted as the most definitive kind), and which they thought were of high enough quality to be worth considering. A couple of these did find positive results, but the studies were absurdly small, with only 20–30 participants. As we have seen, spurious positive results can easily be generated by such small studies, especially given the 'bound for publication' bias. There were two larger-scale studies, one using modern cognitive-behavioural methods, and the other using a more traditional 'psychodynamic' therapy. The cognitive-behavioural treatment evaluation involved 484 participants, but no treatment effect was found. The psychodynamic therapy evaluation involved 231 participants, and again no treatment effect was found. The authors concluded that there was an urgent need for more randomised controlled trials, as these were the only kind capable of determining the question of sex offender treatment effectiveness once and for all.

In 2015, subsequent to the publication of the Cochrane Collaboration study, a new review was published by Lösel and Schmucker, who repeated their 2005 review with the addition of new studies.[21] They also excluded some studies which they had used before, but which they could no longer regard as satisfactory.

---

20 See Dennis *et al.* (2012).

21 See Schmucker and Lösel (2015).

Altogether this new review considered 29 studies involving over 10,000 offenders. Again, this is a sizeable study. However, having excluded unsatisfactory studies which they had previously used, they now found no treatment effect for prison-based programmes, and only a very small effect for those conducted in the community (a number are carried out by probation services, or by psychiatric hospitals). As with the 2005 study, some of the most interesting findings were those least emphasised by the authors. Once again, studies appeared to have a treatment effect *only* if they were of relatively poor quality, with randomised and matched-control designs finding no effect at all. Again, as with the 2005 study, a treatment effect was found *only* in studies with fewer than 50 participants, and *only* in those studies where the treatment professionals were 'marking their own homework'. As with the Cochrane Collaboration study, Lösel and Schmucker recommended more high-quality randomised controlled trials. Strangely, given the negative nature of their own findings, they described the results as 'promising'. A more dispassionate assessment is that they were anything but.

What is clear, looking at those many studies which have been carried out in the last 20 years, is that no clear good-quality evidence has been found for the effectiveness of cognitive-behavioural sex offender treatment. It is also clear that many small-scale studies have shown a spurious treatment effect which has provided encouragement for treatment professionals inclined to believe in its effectiveness. It is equally clear that the stricter the methodology, the less of an effect is found. With the best-designed studies, no effect is found at all. Frankly, if this were almost anything else, we would be abandoning this kind of treatment as hopelessly inadequate. The reasons why we have not done so will be examined below in the section on the offending behaviour industry.

Although sex offending seems to have attracted most attention from programme evaluators, it is obviously not the only form of offending. Indeed, it accounts for a small minority of offenders and offences. Nonsexual violence is another form of offending which is rightly regarded as serious. In many respects it can be more serious than sexual offending, because it can lead to permanent physical incapacity or even death, and like sexual offending can lead to enduring emotional symptoms. It is also more common. Not surprisingly, cognitive-behavioural 'treatments' for violent offending have become widespread. These involve similar techniques to programmes used for sex offenders. Deeply entrenched attitudes are challenged, and participants are encouraged to seek alternative, non-violent methods of solving problems and disputes. They may also be encouraged to develop victim empathy through the use of such things as video statements by victims. As mentioned earlier, a distinction is often drawn between 'instrumental' violence and violence that has an emotional basis. Instrumental violence is carried out for some kind of gain, such as in armed robbery, where there is no personal anger towards the victim. The term 'instrumental' does not refer to an instrument or weapon, but simply to the fact that the violence is not motivated by anger but by some sort of indirect gain. Emotional violence is regarded as stemming from an inability to control angry impulses, but also from a tendency to perceive aggression in, and threat from, other people; it may also show an inability to choose non-violent rather than violent solutions to hostile social situations. The distinction is not entirely academic, because discouraging emotional violence tends to centre on such techniques as relaxation, seeing the other person's point of view, and reducing the tendency to act on impulse. Discouraging instrumental violence is more concerned with encouraging empathy for the victim, recognising that antisocial activity is morally wrong by challenging beliefs and attitudes, and considering consequences. Behaviour in the real world does not always fall into neat categories, so some individuals may have a history of both kinds of violence. Finally, the specific category of domestic violence, sometimes called intimate partner violence, is widely recognised and programmes have been developed specifically to target this. For all of these kinds of violence cognitive-behavioural programmes have been developed and are currently in use in thousands of locations all over the Western world.

So do they work? A widely used programme for instrumentally violent offenders is the Cognitive Self-Change Programme (CSCP), originally devised by psychologists working in the Department of Corrections in the American state of Vermont.[22] This programme was not originally intended specifically for those with a history of violence. However, for reasons that are not entirely clear, it quickly became a programme for violent offenders, and after being piloted in one prison was adopted throughout the state.[23] The initial results appeared promising, although the methods used for the evaluation were extremely poor – essentially our old friend the simple two-group design, which proves nothing at all. The researchers recognised these faults, and concluded, 'Further research is needed before one can conclude that the CSC program's emphasis on cognitive distortions is the primary contributor to the positive outcomes reported in this study. Such research should employ randomised designs...'[24] This research has never been conducted. Furthermore, the Vermont research included only 55 offenders, which makes it very small indeed as a basis for determining policy. What's more, these 55 offenders were not all violent offenders: 40 per cent of them were serving time for non-violent offences, some of them for such things as drunk driving. This did not stop it crossing the Atlantic, somehow becoming a specialised programme for instrumentally violent

22 See Henning and Frueh (1996).

23 Ibid.

24 Ibid., p.539.

offenders on the way, and being adopted all over the UK.[25] In fact, the evidence for the effectiveness of the CSCP was, and remains, exceptionally poor.

In 2007, a report commissioned by the Ministry of Justice for England and Wales examined the effectiveness of violence treatment programmes.[26] Their overall conclusion was that the Ministry was on the right track with its treatment programmes, which is rather surprising, given what they actually found.[27] First, they found that most treatment evaluations were of very poor quality (again, does this sound familiar?). Nonetheless, they reviewed 11 studies which had been conducted in various parts of the English-speaking world. Two of these they rated as being of low quality, eight as medium quality and only one as high quality. One study was of an attempt to monitor violent offenders by means of electronic 'tags', and as such is not really a treatment evaluation at all. Either way, it didn't work. Of the remaining ten studies, five failed to find any significant treatment effect. One of the five that did was the Vermont study mentioned above, which the researchers rated as medium quality, but I have suggested that it was actually poor. Another involved only 22 participants, which is risible as sample sizes go. Two of the remaining studies used matched pairs designs, and although one was only just statistically significant the other was much more so. The final study was also a good size, with 305 people in the treatment group. Those who completed treatment did significantly better than untreated men. Unfortunately, a very large proportion

---

25 In the UK, the CSCP has been shortened and so has its title. It is now the SCP (Self-Change Programme), and has been shortened from two years to only six months. There appears to be no rationale for any of this other than budgetary cuts.

26 See Jolliffe and Farrington (2007).

27 This kind of report, in which no good evidence is found for current policy but the authors endorse the policy anyway, is distressingly common. It appears to be a manifestation of what has been called 'policy-based evidence-making'.

(106, or 35%) dropped out of treatment. When these were included in the treatment group (which is normally done, as treatment is evaluated on an 'intention to treat' basis) the treatment group did no better than the others. It therefore looks as if the apparent treatment effect was actually a selection effect, the high-risk individuals having removed themselves by dropping out, making the treated men look better than they should.[28] It is worth noting that the *only* study rated as high quality (a randomised controlled design) found no treatment effect. To sum up, out of 11 studies, six (including the only high-quality study) found no treatment effect, and the others all had design failings which rendered their evidence suspect. Bearing in mind that violence programmes had been running for 20 years by this time, one might be pardoned for thinking this is not much of a result. It is also difficult to see the logic in rejecting many studies because they were poor quality, but still including in one's review two studies that were rated as low quality. You would have to wonder how bad the rest were.

A study of a treatment programme for persistently violent offenders in Canada appeared in 2009.[29] This noted that there had been a shift in emphasis in recent years from simple anger management with violent offenders to cognitive-behavioural techniques intended to modify their perceptions of social situations. The study aimed to evaluate this more sophisticated approach. Unusually, it compared the treatment group not only with untreated offenders, but also with a second treatment group using a different approach. The researchers found no differences between any of the groups.

28　The same effect that was noticed in sex offender treatment studies by Rice and Harris (2003).

29　See Serin, Gobeil and Preston (2009). Serin and Preston had published an earlier account of violence programmes in Canada (Serin and Preston 2000). This was in the early years of such programmes and had found little evidence at that stage for any effectiveness.

There have been other studies. In general, they have been of poor quality, which is a frustratingly common finding in the whole field of offending behaviour programme evaluation. It is not obvious why the editors of academic journals continue to publish studies that do not actually demonstrate anything. The fact remains that they do, and that such studies are not worth publishing. If that seems like a harsh judgement, then someone will have to explain to me the value of publishing studies that do not prove anything, and whose poor design means that they could not prove anything even in principle. All this does is muddy the waters, and provide encouragement to those who are already too easily convinced.[30]

As well as sexual and violent offenders, more general offenders have also been targeted for treatment. Once again, the rationale for this is that offenders tend to have antisocial attitudes, and that we may be able to change their entrenched behaviour patterns by challenging these. Those who commit relatively minor property offences – thefts, burglaries and the like – can still cause much harm. Burglary in particular is often experienced by victims as very intrusive and threatening, and can leave people with long-term anxieties. As with other kinds of offending, there is certainly evidence that antisocial people harbour antisocial attitudes, but not that changing the expression of those attitudes changes the behaviour. Nonetheless, a particular kind of programme has been widely adopted, generally going by the name of 'thinking skills' or 'cognitive skills' training. The idea behind this is that many offenders are impulsive, do not think through the likely consequences of their actions, and do not consider the harm that they do to others and, in the long run, to themselves. By confronting these attitudes, and encouraging people to adopt different methods of problem solving, the hope is that they will make better choices in future.

---

30 This observation has been made before, perhaps most outspokenly by Hagen (1997) in her book *Whores of the Court*.

As appears to be universal in this field, there are very few high-quality evaluations of these cognitive skills programmes. However, a study of the results of two programmes running in England and Wales at the time was published in 2003.[31] The study was commissioned by the Home Office, which was responsible for English and Welsh prisons in those days (they were subsequently taken over by the newly formed Ministry of Justice). The researchers found no treatment effect, but noted that an earlier study, also commissioned by the Home Office, had found positive results amongst men who had undertaken the programmes at an earlier period.[32] Both studies had a similar methodology, and treated and untreated men were matched on some known risk factors. It is not obvious why their results were diametrically opposed to each other, and the 2003 researchers considered several reasons why they might have failed to find the treatment effect that the previous study apparently did. They commented, 'Explanations for the current results are discussed; in particular, why they should not be taken as evidence that these programmes are ineffective.'[33] This is a clear example of the sort of thinking that prevails in this field. The researchers found no treatment effect. *Of course* this is evidence that the programmes are ineffective. It may not be definitive proof, but it is certainly evidence. If it is not, what on earth would be? The fact that it disagreed with a more palatable result obtained by someone else is just tough. There was nothing to indicate that the more positive result was the more reliable one.

In 2009 another evaluation appeared, this time of the Enhanced Thinking Skills programme run in English prisons at that period.[34] This was one of the programmes mentioned

---

31 See Falshaw *et al.* (2003).

32 See Friendship *et al.* (2002).

33 See Falshaw *et al.* (2003), p.1.

34 See McDougall *et al.* (2009).

in the previous studies. Unusually, the study was a randomised controlled trial, the kind of research design most likely to discover the true value of any treatment. It found an alleged treatment effect. I say 'alleged' because the purpose of prison treatment programmes is to reduce offending, which is normally measured by reconvictions after release, and the study did not measure this. Instead, its measure of improvement was...a questionnaire score. The questionnaire used was the Eysenck Impulsivity Scale, which has been shown to be correlated with offending. I have nothing against the Eysenck Impulsivity Scale as an assessment of impulsive personality, but it is not a measure of actual offending. Furthermore, as an indicator of treatment change a questionnaire measure is pretty much useless. During the course of the programme the participants must have been able to get a good idea of what the programme facilitators were trying to do, and what sort of answers they were hoping to get on the questionnaire following the programme. It was in the prisoners' own interests to show improvement, because reports on the programme might affect their future progress through the prison system. There are means of checking whether people are giving honest answers to questionnaire measures, or whether they are trying to slant them in a particular direction, but the researchers did not use any. Interestingly, the scores obtained from untreated men also improved over the same period, although not as much. As pointed out above, prisoners do talk to each other, and it is quite possible that some of those in the untreated group were prompted by their friends in the treatment group. To be fair, the researchers were fully aware that questionnaire scores were not a measure of reoffending, and recommended that the men in the study should be followed up after release to see if the treated men reconvicted less. To the best of my knowledge this has never been done, or at least never been published, so there is no evidence of success where it really matters: after release into the real world.

Many programme evaluations have only been conducted with male prisoners, possibly because they do constitute the large majority (about 95% in the UK). However, some women do commit offences and some of those end up in prison. One study funded by the Home Office for England and Wales considered the use of cognitive skills programmes with female prisoners.[35] This was a study in which 180 women who had participated in a programme were matched on various risk-related factors with 540 women who had not participated. The impact was measured by reconviction one year after release, and again two years after. There was no difference between treated and untreated women at either point. Yet again, the researcher called for randomised controlled trials. However, she also pointed out that there was little evidence that the cognitive deficits being targeted by thinking skills courses were of much relevance to the causes of criminality in women. She went on to suggest that no single intervention was likely to make much difference on its own, but that a combination of treatments might be necessary. This was a more thoughtful analysis than the 'there was no effect but it's very promising' conclusion which is so prevalent.

In 2010, another study of UK male prisoners who had undertaken a cognitive skills programme was published.[36] This was also government funded. The study began by noting that evidence from the earlier studies quoted above had been inconclusive. However, it suggested one reason for this might have been the methods used. Earlier studies had matched treated and untreated participants on various static risk factors, but had not been able to match them on dynamic risk factors. Given the doubtful status of most dynamic risk factors, one might question whether this was such a serious problem, but the researcher in this case decided to match participants on both kinds of risk factor.

---

35 See Cann (2006).

36 See Sadlier (2010).

Even more surprising is that some of the dynamic factors, such as motivation to stop offending, have generally not been shown to be valid by the research literature. By their nature these are clinical assessments, and known to have no reliability. Be that as it may, the study did at least use reconviction after release as one measure of impact. Reconvictions were measured one year after release. There was a small difference (six percentage points) in favour of the treated group. Not surprisingly, the total number of offences committed was also lower. More surprising, perhaps, was that the 'serious reoffence rate' was unaffected. The Home Office has a classification of around 3000 offence types, of which 150 are considered to be severe. These include serious violence offences, armed robberies, and the like. It is not clear why a treatment effect would only be seen in those committing less serious offences. There was a further problem: it turned out that the two groups were not in fact the same, despite the fairly detailed matching procedure. The researcher had selected men for the treatment group whose current sentences were on average 34 per cent longer than those in the untreated group. This is not simply an academic observation, because those on longer sentences have committed more serious offences in general, and crucially because it is well established that they tend to reconvict less, and more slowly. In other words, men with longer sentences would be expected to have fewer offences in the year after release, so the apparent superiority of the treated group may simply be an effect of not choosing two comparable groups: in the jargon, a 'sampling error'. There is no obvious way to test this retrospectively, although it might be done if given access to the original data.

There is a great deal more research out there, but to review all of it would take several books the size of this one. The vast majority is of very poor quality, biased towards producing a spurious treatment effect where there is none, and even many of those have failed to find one. Those quoted above are actually about the best in the field. As the quality of the studies improves, the likelihood of finding a treatment effect decreases. At the highest level, with randomised controlled trials, a large sample of participants and sensible outcome measures like reconviction, I have yet to come across a single study that shows a treatment effect.

Unfortunately, it may be even worse than that.

DO TREATMENT PROGRAMMES MAKE PEOPLE *WORSE*?

Curiously, although many people are prepared to believe on the basis of inadequate evidence that cognitive-behavioural programmes can change people's behaviour for the better, few seem to have considered the possibility that they can change it for the worse – that is, that they could make offenders *more likely* to commit offences than they were before. In part, this may be because practitioners are so convinced of the value of what they are doing. They might concede the possibility (in principle at least) that their work was ineffective, perhaps because of some flaw in the programme or in the practices of those conducting it. But it is at least aimed at discouraging offending behaviour, so how could it make it worse?

But the possibility has always been there. If we go back to the idea of thought reform in communist China, Lifton found that only a minority of people appeared to have undergone genuine change in their beliefs, and that this only persisted while they remained in China, surrounded by communists. Many of the returnees displayed considerable mental confusion, but not only did they exhibit no continuing adherence to communism, some of them seemed to undergo a sort of 'rebound' effect, whereby they became more anti-communist than they were before. On a commonsense basis this is hardly surprising: after all, the communist regime had put them through a gruelling and prolonged process, had filmed the results for propaganda purposes and then cast them out. In retrospect, it must have seemed like an extreme form of manipulation, as indeed it was. The idea that those who had been most persuaded by this manipulation would then turn against their former oppressors when the manipulation was revealed is not at all unlikely. Those who had maintained their scepticism throughout the process would probably have had it confirmed, but not necessarily increased. After all, this is what they thought the communist system was like anyway. Since I have drawn parallels between thought reform and cognitive-behavioural programmes, is there a parallel in the rebound effect?

Before looking at the actual evidence, I would mention again the suggestion by a colleague that treatment programmes might prompt offenders to generate more effective rationalisations for their behaviour than they had before. She also raised another problem: many of these programmes rely in part on the notion of 'thought stopping' and related techniques. That is, people are trained in ways of interrupting their own train of thought and diverting it onto other lines. In theory, this should help those who are plagued by thoughts of illicit behaviour of one kind or another. In practice, this may be doubted. The idea that thoughts can be inhibited by choice was studied in some detail by the late Dr Daniel Wegner. What he found was that in practice attempts to stop a particular train of thought actually rebounded so that people were *more* plagued by them than ever, an effect which he termed 'ironic suppression'. He theorised that this might be one reason for the development of obsessional thinking and compulsive behaviour.[37] Being a good experimentalist, however, he did not stop at theorising; he carried out a great

---

37 See Wegner (1994). I find it worrying that, whenever I have raised Wegner's work (which is mainstream and by no means obscure) with prison-based colleagues, none has ever heard of it.

deal of research which confirmed the existence of this effect in a variety of settings. Are there parallel 'rebound' effects in cognitive-behavioural treatments for offenders? No one has ever specifically looked for them, but there is certainly evidence of counter-productive effects.

It may be remembered that evaluations of sex offender treatment programmes found that most of the apparent treatment effect came from small studies. Indeed, the wide-ranging review by Lösel and Schmucker in 2005 went further and found that, in ten studies with over 500 participants, treated men actually did *worse* than untreated controls. On average their performance was about 12 per cent worse. However, this result could not be regarded as statistically significant because there was so much variation between studies, some showing a treatment effect and some not. When they revisited the subject in 2015, the same researchers only felt able to include five such large studies. Curiously, these five now showed a small effect in favour of treatment but again this was not statistically significant because of the large variations found between studies. However, in the later review the treatment effect in small studies was only about half as strong as in the 2005 review.

These researchers were not the only ones to find a difference in the 'wrong' direction. A 2003 review in the Cochrane Collaboration database concluded there was no firm evidence for the effectiveness of sex offender treatment, and some evidence that it might be harmful.[38] The review was hampered by the lack of good quality studies that had been carried out at that time. In 2005 a major study (which has already been mentioned[39]) found no evidence of a treatment benefit, and the untreated men in the study did better, although again this tendency was not statistically significant. The overall picture from sex offender

38   See Kenworthy *et al.* (2003). The Cochrane Collaboration review by Dennis *et al.* (2012) was intended to be an update of this one.

39   See Marques *et al.* (2005)

treatment reviews is that they have frequently found a small, but not statistically significant, difference in favour of the *untreated* men. In the case of sex offenders this is only suggestive of an alarming possibility, but in some other cases the evidence is stronger.

In my years of dealing with life sentence prisoners, I have met many who appeared to show genuine remorse for their crimes and tried to atone for them in various ways. Often this took the form of charitable work, fundraising for people with disabilities or for children's charities. One such activity was intended to divert young people away from crime. The idea was that young people who were getting into trouble would be brought into a high security prison to meet and talk with life sentence prisoners. It was assumed that this would deter them from their criminal activities by getting them to think about the consequences. I asked one lifer who was involved in the scheme whether he thought it was effective. He said he didn't know, but he was sure it shocked them. In an interview with me, he had been reduced to tears when describing the dreadful consequences of his crime, and appeared genuinely racked with guilt. When I asked him, he said that he regularly wept in front of the young people in the programme when recounting his sorrow at the part he had played in a robbery which resulted in the deaths of two people, and the loss of 20 years of his own liberty (so far). He just couldn't help it. It was clear that the young people had not really thought about these possibilities before, and the prospect alarmed them. The prison had had a number of letters from kids who had been on the scheme, saying that they were giving up drugs and cutting themselves off from their criminal friends. He didn't know whether that worked in the long term, but hoped that it did.

Sadly, it doesn't. This type of scheme, which is one of a number of so-called 'Scared Straight' programmes, is one of the few to have been subject to randomised controlled trials.

Another Cochrane Collaboration review,[40] published in 2009, is one of several that have shown that 'Scared Straight' programmes not only do not help youngsters, they lead them to commit more and worse crimes than they did before. How can this be? The truth is that we don't know for certain why it happened, but there is no doubt that it did. However, I do have a hypothesis. First, we know that deterrence (which is essentially what this kind of thing is about) has little to do with criminal behaviour. Deterrence is part of the mix of things that keeps law-abiding people in their place, but one of the problems with antisocial individuals is that they have never been taught to respond to deterrents in the first place. That is, they have a chronic tendency to look at short-term rewards and disregard long-term consequences, which is why thinking skills programmes were developed. In other words, increasing fear of the consequences does little or nothing to decrease their antisocial behaviour. Second, we know that simply punishing behaviour (and that includes increasing fear of the consequences, as with this scheme) is not a reliable way of changing behaviour. What is needed is to strengthen some alternative behaviour pattern which may replace the old undesirable one. 'Scared Straight' does not do this. Third, criminals are human beings, and they exist in a social environment. We hear a great deal about peer pressure on juvenile delinquents, but have failed to realise how it may interact with such things as 'Scared Straight' programmes. Imagine one of those young people who has written to the prison assuring them that he will give up drugs and cut himself off from his criminal associates. Who is he going to mix with now? All his friends are doing drugs and involved in criminal activity, and will probably revile him for leaving their group or gang and going soft. How will he spend his time? Cut off from his friends he will be lonely, isolated and deprived of any support for the stance that he has taken. The likelihood is that he will drift back to the group and

---

40   See Petrosino, Turpin-Petrosino and Buehler (2009).

ask to be taken back. This time, though, it is likely that he will have to do something to prove his 'love' for the group (and some juvenile groups really do talk in these terms). The likelihood is that he will do something worse than he did before just to show that he is as tough as the rest of them. I admit that this account is speculative, but there must be some social process like this which accounts for the fact that 'Scared Straight' programmes are not simply ineffective but actually make people more criminal. The truth is that adolescents are generally not concerned with being successful adults; they want to be successful adolescents. This means that peer pressure is exceptionally important in that age group, and likely to outweigh the influence of parents and other adults. This uncomfortable truth was demonstrated in 1995 by Judith Rich Harris.[41]

Another programme that has been shown to be counter-productive was the Greenlight programme, conducted in America with 735 adult male offenders.[42] This was a cognitive-behavioural programme intended to tackle some of the problems that men might face on leaving prison and reintegrating into society. It was a comprehensive programme, covering practical skills, assistance with job-seeking, drug and other counselling, and a probation familiarisation process which included meeting their probation officer and being familiarised with what was required. It was also a comprehensive failure. Men who had been through the Greenlight programme not only failed parole and committed further offences more often than those who took part in a traditional pre-release programme, they actually did worse than those who had no pre-release preparation at all. There was an inquest into this programme, but it is not clear why it failed. There were plenty of possible reasons, including poor implementation of the programme and the fact that men resented being moved to a different prison in

41   See Harris (1995).

42   See Wilson (2007).

order to undertake it. They had no choice about whether they participated or not, which has implications for the degree of coercion – explicit or implicit – involved in other programmes.

In the end we do not know for certain why these programmes failed. However, because they were evaluated using the best techniques, we can at least be sure that they did. More than that, because they were evaluated using the best techniques we can be sure that they were actually counter-productive, despite being launched with the best of intentions. The lessons for other programmes are clear.

WHY ARE TREATMENT RESULTS SO POOR?

To my mind there is no doubt at all that cognitive-behavioural offending behaviour programmes have comprehensively failed. As we have seen, there was a historical precedent for this in the form of Chinese thought reform programmes, which also failed, despite being able to put pressures on their prisoners which would never be permitted in a liberal democracy. But why did they fail? Perhaps one clue is in the alternative term sometimes used for thought reform: 're-education'. As used in this context, education is a verbal process. In both thought reform programmes and cognitive-behavioural programmes participants challenge each other's points of view, have debates about issues, role-play social situations and write homework. This is overwhelmingly verbal. It teaches people how to talk about various kinds of behaviour, but it does not teach them to do it. That requires changes to take place at a much deeper level in the human psyche; it requires change at a level of which we are not even consciously aware.

If that sounds too much like the psychoanalytic point of view popularised by Freud a hundred years ago, please bear with me. Although the terminology has changed, and although the subject has been approached in a way far removed from that of Freud, a great deal of modern research supports the idea that we are not aware of many of the influences on our conscious thinking and behaviour. Nowhere is this more clearly seen than in the phenomenon of hypnosis, a subject that was considered by Daniel Wegner as part of a wider study of 'free will' and why we think we have it.[43] It is fair to say that hypnosis is still poorly understood, partly because scientific study has been discouraged by its association with popular entertainment. Nonetheless, under hypnosis people can be persuaded to do almost anything if it is put to them in the right way.

More interesting from the point of view of the present topic is that people can be given posthypnotic instructions to perform some action after coming out of the hypnotic trance, *and to forget the fact that they received those instructions*. After being 'woken up' from the trance, they will perform the action. Wegner quotes the example of a hypnotic subject being given a posthypnotic instruction to pick up a book which is lying on the floor and put it in the bookshelf. When asked why she did it, she gave a valid-sounding reason to do with not liking things to be untidy and the bookshelf being its proper place. This is typical. When asked why they obeyed a posthypnotic instruction, approximately 50 per cent of people will say they do not know. Approximately 50 per cent will make up a rationalisation that seems plausible in the circumstances, as in the example of the woman and the book. Approximately 0 per cent will say they did it because the hypnotist told them to. In other words, it is perfectly possible for us to perform an action, and to generate some reason for

---

43   See Wegner (2002). There are examples other than those involving hypnosis, but they tend to be less fun. Still, under carefully established experimental conditions, people can be induced to think that actions that they have performed have actually been performed by some other agency. They can also be persuaded that actions performed by something or someone else were actually their own.

having done so, without actually having any conscious clue why we did it.

The work of Kahneman and Ariely, already mentioned, is very much concerned with why we do things, rather than why we *claim* to have done them. There is a parallel here with what was said earlier about the work of Sir Frederick Bartlett on schemas. This clearly demonstrated that there were structures and processes underlying our conscious memories and beliefs of which we are not normally aware. In my view, what cognitive-behavioural programmes are doing is challenging *conscious* attitudes and beliefs, but getting nowhere near the schemas or other structures that may underlie them. There is no straightforward way of doing this, but certainly bombarding people with verbal information is not going to do it. Not even if they are required to produce a large quantity of verbal material in response.

Since Sir Frederick Bartlett reported on his work in the 1930s a great deal more has been done, using techniques that had simply not been invented then. These include methods of brain scanning that can show which parts of the brain are being activated during any particular behaviour. There is not room here to review all of this work, but some key points have been drawn together by Kevin Creeden, a therapist who works with young sex offenders and has studied this field intensively.[44] First, many of the offenders whom we see (sex offenders and otherwise) have been through an upbringing that most of us would regard as abusive, neglectful and very probably traumatic. This has long-term damaging effects on the development of their brains, resulting in difficulties with impulse control and relations with others later in life.[45] This is not an attempt to resurrect the 'cycles of abuse' theory, which suggested that child abusers are in some

---

44   See Creeden (2009, 2013).

45   See, for example, a review of the neuroscience of child development by Twardosz and Lutzker (2010).

way acting out the abuse that happened to them as children. In fact, there is a high incidence of abuse (physical, sexual, emotional and plain neglect) in the backgrounds of all offenders. Sexual abuse is not especially characteristic of the backgrounds of sex offenders, nor of other offenders, neglect and physical abuse being more typical.[46] The second point is that a history of such abuse has an effect on the developing brain. Specifically, it results in an enlarged amygdala, the structure that is most concerned with identifying and responding to threats in the environment. People with an enlarged amygdala are more likely to perceive situations as threatening, and more likely to respond impulsively to them by 'getting their defence in first'. The third point is that, when we perceive something, sensory input from the eyes, ears, etc. travels to the amygdala 40 times faster than it travels to the cerebral cortex, where more rational thinking and decision-making takes place. Impulses then travel from the amygdala to the cerebral cortex, effectively telling it what kind of situation has been perceived. The cerebral cortex then selects a course of action to deal with the perceived situation. It will be obvious that the choice of action will be greatly affected by the way in which the amygdala has classified the situation.

Interestingly, although Kahneman's work on human decision-making did not delve into neuroscience, it did demonstrate that we first of all have an emotional response to something, and only secondly decide how to respond to it.[47] A fourth point, extremely important in the context of cognitive-behavioural treatment, is that one effect of trauma is a reduction in the brain's ability to handle language. In other words, we are asking

---

46 See Stewart, Dennison and Waterson (2002). They studied the relationship between abuse in childhood and subsequent offending in an Australian sample of over 41,000 children.

47 Kahneman refers to 'system one' (fast, emotional, impulsive and irrational) and 'system two' (slow, rational and deliberative) but he makes clear that he is not referring to specific brain structures. These 'systems' are just a shorthand way of referring to different types of decision-making.

offenders to handle very large amounts of verbal information and process much verbal activity (discussion, debate, written work, etc.) but they are less well equipped than most people to do it. This would still be true even if the basic concept behind the treatment were sound.

What this has led us to is a series of conclusions:

- Treatment programmes are often poorly evaluated, possibly because some professionals have a vested interest in not evaluating them strictly.

- There is no good evidence that treatment programmes reduce risk in offenders.

- There is strong evidence that some treatment programmes actually make people *worse*.

- Treatment results are generally poor, partly because they are using ineffective methods and sometimes because they are targeting the wrong things.

There still remains the question of how this situation has arisen, and why the correctional systems of the Western world persist in running (and expecting taxpayers to fund) programmes whose effectiveness cannot be demonstrated after 20 years, and which in some cases risk making offenders worse. To answer this, I believe we have to address the idea of the 'offending behaviour industry'.

THE OFFENDING BEHAVIOUR INDUSTRY

When the late US President Dwight Eisenhower was stepping down from office in 1961 he made a speech warning against what he called the 'military-industrial complex'. Despite having been a career soldier, one of the military heroes of the Second World War and Republican President at the height of the Cold

War, he warned that there was a risk of a commercial alliance between members of the military and the purveyors of military equipment. He outlined a risk that this alliance would lobby Congress and press for increased military spending so that the military would get their hardware and the industrialists could sell it to them. Thus, the American government would be persuaded of the existence of illusory military threats (and the means of countering them) in order to justify public expenditure on the defence industry. The situation was not helped by the fact that many ex-members of the military joined defence companies as advisers or salespeople.[48]

Something similar has now happened with psychologists and the criminal justice system. In the 1990s, despite the fact that crime was actually decreasing, it was a topic that was frequently aired in apocalyptic terms by the tabloid newspapers. Crime was widely described in terms that suggested that it was out of control. Politicians were under considerable pressure to do something about it. Treatment programmes were introduced at the instigation of a few persuasive professionals who managed to get the politicians of the time to fund their pet projects. In my opinion, one of the reasons for the present unsatisfactory state of affairs is that treatment programmes were not introduced on the basis of a proper theoretical understanding of the behaviour at which they were directed. They were provided in response to politicians who demanded a solution for the problems that they were experiencing. We did not have a scientific model of how offending behaviour arises, based on our extensive knowledge of such things as genetics, child development, brain development, socialisation and learning. On the other hand, we

---

48   See *The Sovereign State: The Secret History of ITT* (Sampson, 1973) for a fascinating account of how International Telephone & Telegraph benefited from this policy in the Second World War. Amongst other things, they made American munitions used to bomb German factories that they also owned, and later claimed compensation for the damage!

had some politicians who badly wanted to be convinced, and some opportunists only too eager to convince them. The result has been massive public expenditure on programmes and risk assessment methods that are not effective but which make some people a great deal of money. Many of the individuals who began this trend have since moved on, having built academic and professional careers on these projects. A clear illustration of this unscientific approach can be seen in the personal qualities and behaviour that are targeted in cognitive-behavioural programmes. In essence, programme designers have simply thought up a number of things which they think should be targets for change. They have done this on the basis of clinical experience (in other words, a clinical assessment of risk factors, and we know how well that works).

As an example, consider victim empathy. One of the things that psychologists have noted in sex offenders is a lack of empathy for their victims, assessed clinically of course. This has coincided with increased lobbying from victims, and growing public concern about sex offenders, encouraged by inflammatory (and usually highly inaccurate) press campaigns. It has therefore become routine in sex offender programmes to try to develop empathy in offenders. This may be done by showing videos of abuse victims, who explain the emotional impact that their abuse had on them, and perhaps following up with discussion and written work in which the offender enumerates all the possible impacts on victims. Of course, this does assume that offenders are capable of empathy (one of the other areas impaired by trauma) and that we are not simply teaching them how to manipulate others. It has certainly been suggested that psychopaths can learn manipulative techniques from some of these programmes.[49] But even if this is not the case, we know that empathy training is useless as a means

---

49   For example, Hare (1999).

of reducing risk. Not only that, we have known it for many years, as it was demonstrated in the last century in the earliest comprehensive studies of risk factors in sex offenders.[50] Along with other treatment targets proven to be ineffective, it has remained in many treatment programmes to this day. One study concluded, 'Many of the variables commonly addressed in sex offender treatment programs (e.g., psychological distress, denial of sex crime, victim empathy, stated motivation for treatment) had little or no relationship with sexual or violent recidivism.'[51] In short, even if the treatment could work in principle it was targeting the wrong things and so it wouldn't work anyway. Those conducting the treatments were astoundingly slow to react to this knowledge, which was actually available before most of the programmes were devised. But careers have been built on this work – not only academic careers but in some cases commercial ones as well. Still, why worry about effectiveness when there's money to be made?

And there is indeed money to be made. Serious money. As an example, the National Offender Management Service for England and Wales (as well as many similar services in the United States and other countries) has been running an anger management programme called 'Controlling Anger and Learning to Manage it', or CALM. This programme is actually bought in as an off-the-shelf package from a North American company called Multi-Health Systems. At the time of writing their website advertises a 'CALM kit', consisting of '1 set of 6 Group Leader's Guides, 10 Group Member's Workbooks, 1 Master Package, and 1 CD' at a cost of $549. No doubt much of this material is reusable, although the group members' workbooks will obviously not be: not to worry, you can order a new set of 10 workbooks for

---

50   For example, Hanson and Bussière (1998); Hanson and Morton-Bourgon (2004).

51   See Hanson and Morton-Bourgon (2005), p.1154.

only $260. If you should need another Group Leader's Guide it will only set you back another $306.[52]

I once telephoned the UK publisher of this material to ask what the evidence was for its effectiveness. They were completely unable to tell me, but suggested I contact a practitioner who was running it somewhere. I did indeed contact a prison colleague who was freshly trained in the programme (at great expense) and starting to run it, but she too was completely unable to refer me to any published evidence about its effectiveness, although she felt there was some evidence 'somewhere in the Ministry of Justice'. She had certainly undergone the training for programme leaders, but clearly no one had really gone into the effectiveness of the programme. Effectiveness appeared not to have been the primary concern of the practitioner, the trainers or the publishers. It was like the TV comedy *Yes, Minister*, in which the wily civil servant Sir Humphrey describes the usual political response to a crisis as: 'Something must be done! This is something. We'll do this.' Nonetheless, this programme has been running in thousands of locations throughout the Western world. I have carried out Internet searches, but failed to find any evaluations of the CALM programme, let alone any randomised controlled trials.

In the chapter on assessment I mentioned the Hare PCL-R psychopathy assessment schedule, which is intended to be a measure of personality although it has often been used as a risk assessment tool. I also mentioned that one of the difficulties

---

52 See the company website: https://ecom.mhs.com/ (S(zfpeqs45l2bo3z2vknmvbo55))/inventory.aspx?gr=saf&prod=calm&id= pricing&RptGrpID=clm. When I visited it in 2016 the website also listed three documents referred to as the 'Research Library'. I downloaded all of these, but found that one was a reprint of a *Guardian* newspaper article containing merely anecdotal evidence about a few cases, one was a description of the programmes sold by the company (there were a lot of others, as well as risk assessment instruments) and the last was a brochure. None contained any scientific evaluation of effectiveness, nor any reference to any.

with the PCL-R is that it has come to be regarded almost as the very definition of psychopathy, which tends to inhibit further research into the concept. In particular, researchers have questioned whether measures of past criminal behaviour should feature so prominently, given that many psychopaths have no criminal record. However, when two prominent and respected researchers decided to go into print and question this openly, Hare did something that no academic ever does over a professional matter. He threatened legal action. He threatened to sue Skeem and Cooke, the authors, and also the academic journal in which they were proposing to publish the article. He claimed that his position had been misrepresented (a matter that would normally be resolved by a letter to the journal editor), but also claimed a threat to his commercial interests. It took three years to resolve the dispute without recourse to the law, and resulted in considerable opprobrium being poured upon Hare by professional colleagues for allegedly trying to stifle academic discussion for commercial reasons.[53] Hare denied that this was his motive, and has since stated that his earnings from PCL-R royalties amount to less than $35,000 a year. It is not clear whether this includes money earned from providing training in the use of the PCL-R, or licensing others to provide that training, but many would think it a useful sum. Either way, it is clear that Hare's financial interest in the commercial success of the PCL-R raised doubts in some of his colleagues about his academic credibility. Financial motives muddy the waters in evaluating psychological products just as much as they do in evaluating pharmaceutical products.[54]

Leaving crass commercial considerations aside, there is no doubt that the offending behaviour industry has a stake in the continuation of cognitive-behavioural programmes, effective

---

53   A brief summary was published in the Scientific American (Minkel, 2010).

54   And that is a lot (Goldacre 2012).

or not. This is simply because so many professionals have built their careers and professional reputations on the delivery of these programmes. In many cases, they have not learned how to do anything else of any substance, so restriction to programmes of proven effectiveness would leave most of them unemployed. It would also leave most of them professionally discredited; millions upon millions of taxpayers' dollars, pounds, euros and other currencies have been expended on offending behaviour programmes based purely on the opinions of these professionals. If this seems unduly critical, consider the opinion of the American psychologist mentioned earlier, Professor Margaret Hagen. Referring to an early review of sex offender treatments that found no treatment effect[55] she stated, 'There is just too much money involved, too many careers, livelihoods and reputations to just shut down the whole scam. Sex offender therapy *must* be shown to work.'[56]

One of the ways in which the offending behaviour industry protects itself against evidence-based criticism is what I think of as the 'flight of names'. When a particular programme is looking beleaguered in the face of the evidence, a standard ploy is to change the name and repackage the programme. Very often, there is little but the name that has changed. For example, since I became involved in parole cases about 15 years ago, I have seen cognitive skills programmes through several incarnations. Over the years essentially similar programmes have been labelled 'cognitive skills', 'reasoning and rehabilitation', and 'thinking skills programme'. Also, whilst in the final stages of writing this book I heard that the two main sex offender treatment programmes in England and Wales were being scrapped. The reason for that has not been made explicit, but the wording of official documents suggests that there were anxieties about

---

55 An evaluation that she felt should have stopped the whole movement in its tracks (Furby, Blackshaw and Weinrott 1989).

56 See Hagen (1997), p.156.

ineffectiveness. Since no scientifically respectable evaluations of these programmes have been carried out in the UK, the inference is that evidence from abroad is felt to have undermined them. As we have come to expect by now, these programmes are not simply being ended, but replaced. The new programmes will be called 'Horizon' for medium risk sex offenders, and 'Kaizen' for high-risk offenders. The Kaizen programme will consist of a core programme for various offenders, with 'bolt-on' editions for specific types (kaizen is a Japanese word meaning 'improve'). Unfortunately, it is clear that cognitive-behavioural techniques will remain the basis of treatment. The most important thing to have changed is the name.

The Horizon and Kaizen programmes have been piloted for about the last three years. We need to be clear what this means: the pilots appear to have been concerned with making sure that the programmes can run smoothly, not with effectiveness. There has not been a randomised controlled trial to determine if the programmes actually *work*. Official documents claim that evaluations of the programmes will be built in from the start, but it is hard to accept this when the opportunity to evaluate pilot programmes has not been taken. As with all previous programmes, these are being rolled out on a national basis without any proof of effectiveness being obtained first. I confidently expect that, in a few years' time, the new programmes will also be quietly shelved in favour of some new name.

As we have seen, it has become routine for programme evaluators to find poor or no treatment effect, to call for more research, particularly randomised controlled trials, and equally routine for no one to come forward to carry it out. There comes a point where we have to stop fooling ourselves and accept that, unpalatable as it may seem, the evidence is not there. If we leave it to the offending behaviour industry itself this will never happen. Treatment needs analysis has become a marketing exercise, a way of recruiting more programme participants rather than a way of assessing any genuine treatment need. Reviews of treatments by 'independent' evaluators still find no treatment effect but declare the results to be 'promising'. They have been 'promising' for over 20 years and that promise has never been fulfilled. The truth is that most of these evaluators are not independent. They need access to government records and to prisons in order to continue their research. Very often they need access to government money to fund it. They are not going to bite the hand that feeds their research, and if they do they may suffer the kind of attack visited upon my colleague over the SARN-TNA (see the section above on assessing treatment needs). They have their own careers to worry about. Perhaps the ultimate proof of this is the tendency in recent years for leading figures in the offending behaviour industry to question whether randomised controlled trials are possible or desirable in this field. In fact, such evaluations are the *only* way to demonstrate the effectiveness of treatments one way or the other. Questioning whether one's products should be evaluated on the basis of accepted and orthodox scientific method is the hallmark of the charlatan and the snake oil salesman. Most modern psychologists thought we had left that behind.

Hagen referred to offending behaviour programmes as a 'scam'. I don't believe that they are a scam, if by that we mean that people are deliberately and knowingly selling ineffective treatments just to make money. I believe the processes are much more subtle than that; they still involve dishonesty, but it is the sort of intellectual dishonesty by which clever people fool themselves. Until we apply our knowledge of psychological decision-making processes to psychologists themselves, these fundamentally dishonest processes will continue.

EVALUATION: IMPLICATIONS

It is generally accepted that individual studies, especially small ones, are not sufficient for deciding issues of policy. In order to evaluate what the evidence is one must look at all of it. The way to do this is to carry out a systematic review of all the evidence available. In this context the word 'systematic' means that an objective selection system has been used to decide which published studies should be included in the review and which should be excluded. This method of selection is made clear in the research report so that anyone else can see exactly how it was done. Put bluntly, it gives your colleagues the chance to check your homework. It is a hallmark of good systematic reviews that they only include studies of sufficient quality to test scientifically what is being investigated. Systematic reviews based firmly on these principles do not show that there is any benefit from cognitive-behavioural offending behaviour programmes. Indeed, when these strict criteria are applied, several studies have found that some of these programmes actually *increase* risk. I must stress, though, that the problem is not the science. The problem is that the science was not applied.

I do not think this is entirely to do with vested interests, at least in any financial or career sense. One of the problems in psychology is that very often we have good science but very poor technology. Science on its own increases our knowledge of the natural world (including ourselves) but not our ability to control it. Turning the scientific information into reliable technologies enables us to affect the world in a practical way, whether that is assessing the safety of bridges, curing diseases, or developing new machines. The development of reliable behavioural technologies has acquired the status of a holy grail in psychology. In my view, cognitive-behavioural techniques have acquired their dominance partly because some practitioners were so keen to develop a reliable technology that they were only too willing to ignore the mounting evidence that these programmes were ineffective. I believe there are five main reasons why people reject the evidence.

First, there is loss of face. These programmes have been approved and implemented by 'experts' who were convinced of their effectiveness. Having to face the truth now would mean having to face their own poor decision-making. I well remember discussing sex offender treatment with a prison colleague, and suggesting that there was no evidence of effectiveness. 'Thanks,' she replied. 'That's all the work that I have been doing for the last ten years thrown out of the window.' I sympathise with anyone who feels like that, but the responsibility for that lies with those who rushed these programmes in on the basis of ill-considered evidence in the first place. We cannot protect these practitioners' feelings if it means retaining programmes that may actually raise risk to the public. Not to mention the waste of taxpayers' money involved.

A second, and somewhat related, factor is that of career interests. Dropping ineffective programmes would not only mean loss of face for those who approved them, but loss of careers for those who carry them out. As I pointed out earlier, many of them are not trained to do anything else. It is hardly surprising that there is immense resistance to the evidence among practitioners.

Another related consideration is the third factor: empire building within organisations. Some practitioners, and some others, like administrators, have risen to senior positions as treatment managers, and regional and national supervisors of such programmes. Others have consultant positions advising correctional systems on which programmes to use. Potentially, there are salaries and status to be lost here.

The fourth factor that I see is the co-opted critic. I have suggested earlier that academics have been reluctant to criticise programmes for fear of offending correctional organisations.

Certainly in the UK, and I am sure in other countries too, losing the goodwill of the criminal justice system would cost researchers dear. Criminologists and forensic psychologists need access to prisoners in order to conduct their research. They will be reluctant to bite the hand that feeds them. And many academics and researchers, too, have built careers and reputations for expertise on work in this field.

Fifth, and finally, there are commercial interests. As I pointed out earlier, some of the programmes in widespread use are bought as packages from commercial providers. Not only do practitioners buy the materials, they often buy training as well. As with published risk assessment schedules, there is money to be made in this field and companies are eager to make it.

There is no shortage of vested interests in the offending behaviour industry.

− 8 −

COMMUNICATION

Who's Listening?

According to Thomas Paine, 'A body of men holding themselves accountable to nobody ought not to be trusted by anybody.'[1] It is a truism often noted that power without accountability leads inevitably to abuse. This is not, I suggest, because people in powerful positions are inherently evil, but because people whose power is never challenged inevitably drift towards a position in which they can justify to themselves anything they do. Of course, whether a body of people holds itself accountable verbally is not altogether the point. The point is that accountability should be genuine, whatever they may pay lip service to. In any profession whose members have power over others, it is therefore extremely undesirable that they should be cut off from outside observation and potential criticism.

Lack of transparency is the friend and protector of arbitrary power. Anyone who doubts this would do well to consider the Guantánamo detention centre set up by the Americans to detain suspected Taliban guerrillas involved in the war in Afghanistan. Assisted by psychologists, detainees were tortured using methods very similar to those used by the Japanese against American prisoners in the Second World War. After that war some of the Japanese interrogators were hanged by the victorious Allies for these disgraceful abuses of human rights. At Guantánamo, however, similar practices were justified as 'harsh interrogation'.

---

1   See Thomas Paine's *Rights of Man* (1791).

The American Psychological Association suffered a major scandal as a result, prominent members resigned and the APA commissioned a report on the involvement of some of its members in this mistreatment.[2] There can be little doubt that if the behaviour of these individuals had been more open to scrutiny, it would have been challenged sooner and perhaps would not have occurred at all. The American Psychological Association, like similar bodies in most other countries, has a code of conduct that embraces the highest standards of professional ethics. In practice this was not enough.

BEING ACCOUNTABLE FOR WHAT WE SAY

What has this to do with communication? First, communicating the results of your work necessarily entails telling people what you have been doing, aiding transparency. Second, it offers people the opportunity to correct you when you have made errors of fact. Third, it offers other professionals the opportunity to challenge what you have done on the grounds of either ethics or scientific knowledge. Fourth, it gives you a learning opportunity through which you can improve your practice.

Psychologists in criminal justice systems are subject to the same ethical guidelines as other psychologists. They are not, however, subject to the same scrutiny.[3] In health service

---

2   See the downloadable report (Hoffman 2015).

3   An American colleague pointed out that many prisoners have little to fill their time with except the construction of legal arguments against those who detain them. There is truth in this, but those who seek to hold psychologists to a high professional standard must understand what that standard is, and how best to challenge professional conduct when it falls short. This is less straightforward than being able to read laws which are available to all and the transcripts of court cases. When I was a member of the BPS's Investigatory Committee we often received complaints which were very poorly phrased and targeted by people who simply did not understand what they could and could not complain about. Furthermore, legal challenges might result in freedom, but misconduct complaints

settings, for example, the reports of psychologists may be read by psychiatrists, nurses, occupational therapists and other medical staff. In the UK, and probably other jurisdictions, prison psychologists' reports may be read by no one except the prisoner concerned, at least until the point where the report has to be produced as evidence for a hearing or a decision-making board of some kind. Since a great many reports are actually produced by trainees, and all trainees have supervisors who are professionally responsible for their work, scrutiny of the reports is in theory quite close. In practice, this does not seem to help, probably because the scrutiny is not external. Both supervisor and trainee are part of the criminal justice system, and they operate according to the same philosophy and within the same rules. As examples of the resulting problems, consider the following, all actual cases from my own experience:

- A prisoner who spoke virtually no English was supposed to be risk-assessed by a prison psychologist. Ethical guidelines make it clear that in such a case an interpreter should be used, not simply for the assessment itself, but also to feed back the results. The prison psychologist did neither, but produced the report based on the second-hand opinions of other people, who had also not used interpreters. Apparently, communication was too much trouble.

- An elderly life sentence prisoner had killed his wife. He had been quite elderly when he committed the offence, which occurred in very unusual circumstances in which no serious harm had been intended. This was apparently accepted by the court, which imposed a very short minimum period, but he had pleaded guilty to murder despite having grounds for a manslaughter plea. A trainee

---

will not. So, many prisoners challenge 'the system' legally, but few make misconduct complaints against psychologists.

prison psychologist was deputed to report on him. For whatever reason, she appeared to have an obsession with domestic violence and opposed his release on parole, making multiple insinuations that the man might have a history of domestic violence, including during his first marriage, which had lasted for many years. There was absolutely no evidence for this supposed violent history. His first wife and the grown-up children from their marriage actually submitted statements supporting his position that no domestic violence had taken place during it. The reaction of the prison psychologist was to suggest (without any evidence) that they had all been unfairly influenced in some way; she continued to insist that he should undertake a domestic violence programme. At the subsequent parole hearing the Parole Board psychologist cross-examined the trainee author, systematically unpicking the report, revealing the trainee's embarrassing lack of objectivity, and indeed lack of psychological knowledge. This also revealed the poor quality of supervision. Nothing happened as a result of any of these demonstrations of poor practice.

- Another trainee prison psychologist, giving evidence at a parole hearing, was asked why she had laid such great stress on the development of insight, when it was known from research that our estimates of insight were of no relevance to risk. Essentially, she could not answer this question, and ended up saying there was nothing else that she could say except that insight was terribly important. She had to say this because it was one of the stated purposes of the treatment programme that she was advocating, but it had no basis in fact.

- In another hearing, a fully qualified senior psychologist was cross examined by a prisoner's legal representative about the evidence for the effectiveness of the sex offender treatment programmes that she had been conducting for years. Eventually, she was forced to admit that there really wasn't any, and was reduced to tears. The very fact that this admission was so stressful says something about the way in which programme enthusiasts have identified their sense of professional self-worth with treatment programmes, despite their lack of an evidence base. But if they cannot admit it to themselves they certainly won't be able to admit it to anyone else.

- In another case a prisoner was elderly and physically disabled, and used a wheelchair. Despite several specialist medical opinions supporting the severity of these disabilities, the senior prison psychologist involved insisted that the man was perfectly fit and only malingering. The purpose of this malingering was not entirely apparent; the man was coming up to a parole hearing, but it is not at all clear that a disability would make parole more likely as it can make resettlement more difficult. The psychologist's qualifications for overruling the opinions of several medical specialists were non-existent. The prisoner pre-empted the issue by dying, which some of us thought was taking malingering a bit too far.

- I have mentioned that in the UK, trainees' reports must be supervised by qualified psychologists; they must also be countersigned by supervisors to certify their approval. In one case a trainee submitted four different versions of her report at different times. Only one of these was countersigned, and on closer examination it appeared that she had countersigned it herself. Under cross-examination at a parole hearing she admitted that this was the case.

To my mind, what these examples illustrate is the rigid orthodoxy prevalent in UK prison psychological circles, and an inability to exercise professional objectivity despite the lack of an evidence base. They also illustrate the slackness of supervision. These examples come from the UK, which may be unusual in several respects, particularly in the extensive use of partially qualified trainees to carry out work that has serious implications for prisoners. However, discussions with American colleagues suggest that the situation may not be very different there. They report that much of the work in prisons is carried out by people of a similar level of qualification to UK trainees (a master's degree in psychology), under the supervision of licensed psychologists qualified to doctoral level. Also, there seems to be a similarly strong commitment to the idea of treatment programmes, regardless of the evidence base. Inevitably, this means that reporting on prisoners at various decision points in their sentence becomes a search for what programme they can do next. The alternative is to allow prisoners to progress through the system, perhaps even to be paroled, without some notional remaining risk having been 'reduced'.[4] Certainly, the treatment programme culture is as deeply embedded in the American system as it is in the UK, and the supposed value of treatment programmes is widely quoted as a reason for the decisions taken about prisoners.[5]

PROFESSIONAL ISOLATION

Another problem which may be as prevalent in other countries as it is in the UK is that of *professional* isolation, as opposed to isolation from public scrutiny generally. In their day-to-day work, psychologists working in the criminal justice system tend to

---

4   There is, of course, another process at work here, namely, covering one's back.

5   As well as my own work in the UK (Forde 2014), see Blasko (2013), whose work was in the United States.

associate professionally only with other psychologists working in the same system. It is almost inevitable that they become inward looking, and convinced of the rightness of their own position, because they will never hear it seriously questioned. I have given a number of public presentations to those involved in forensic psychology, and on several occasions I have been approached afterwards by prison trainee psychologists seeking advice. The problem is always the same: they have dared to challenge the prison service orthodoxy, usually by questioning the effectiveness of programmes, and the response has been authoritarian and robust. Threats of dismissal are not unknown, and threats that trainees will have a difficult time qualifying unless they learn to toe the line are reported to be common. There is little comfort to offer trainees in this position. Essentially, they will not be free to question the system unless they place themselves outside it, and qualifying outside the system is very difficult. Questions from within may be a treated as disciplinary offences. Questions from without are treated as politically motivated attacks.[6]

As an example, consider a misconduct complaint that was made against me a few years ago. When such a complaint is made, it is referred to a three-person panel of the regulatory body, the HCPC, to consider whether there is a prima facie case to answer. If there is not, the complaint is dismissed at that point; otherwise it is referred to a hearing on whether the practitioner concerned is fit to practise. This particular complaint was made because of a statement in one of my reports about a life-sentence prisoner who had committed rape many years before. As well as the normal evidence about the decline in risk with age, etc., I stated that people convicted of rape do not pose a

---

6   One public statement about criticisms from outside the system referred to them as a problem that 'plagues' prison psychologists, and as challenging 'the government point of view' (O'Toole 2010). The point that the standard of psychology was being challenged and not government policy per se was completely (and perhaps conveniently) overlooked.

significant risk of further sexual offending, but they do pose a risk of further violent offending. This statement is contrary to prison service orthodoxy, according to which all rapists must attend a sex offender treatment programme to deal with their alleged preference for violent sex. However, the statement is completely correct: a rape conviction is predictive of violent, not sexual, offences.[7] Several major studies of risk factors have shown this. However, a group of no fewer than seven senior prison psychologists lodged the complaint, alleging that I was not sufficiently familiar with the professional literature. Initially, the HCPC refused to accept the complaint because it does not adjudicate on differences of professional opinion. However, the prison psychologists (all trained to doctoral level) insisted on pressing the complaint on the grounds that it was not simply a difference of opinion, but that my statement was factually incorrect, which threw doubt upon my familiarity with the professional research in this field, and therefore my ability to practise in it. Their case rested principally on one single published academic paper. This was not one of the classic studies of risk factors in sex offenders, but a paper that one of the complainants had co-written. It had been published in a respectable academic journal. The HCPC referred the matter to a panel. I need hardly point out that a guilty verdict would have had the potential to have me struck off.

The paper on which their case rested was statistically rather peculiar, and I was surprised that any editor had accepted it for publication as it stood. It had taken data from two research studies, the larger of which had found no relationship between rape and further sexual offending. The smaller (less than one third the size, based on about 300 offenders) had found that

---

7   See, amongst others, Hanson and Bussière (1998) and Hanson and Morton-Bourgon (2004, 2005). The last-named states that the amount of violence used in a sexual offence is 'potentially misleading' as a risk factor for sexual offenders.

there was, but small studies are notoriously prone to fluke results, as we saw earlier in the chapter on treatment evaluations. The authors of this paper had then pooled the results of these two studies, and found that a barely statistically significant relationship between rape and further sexual offending still existed. In rebutting their complaint, I pointed out that this was statistical sleight of hand. Overall there might have been a tiny (and it was indeed tiny) statistically significant relationship between rape and sexual reconviction. The fact remained that three-quarters of the evidence reported in this paper had *not* supported the supposed relationship between rape and further sexual offending. It was as if the complainants had mixed three cans of white paint and one of royal blue and declared the resultant pastel shade to be royal blue because it was not white. This was the least of it. The complainants showed no appreciation of the fact that the paper they were quoting was only a very small part of the published evidence on this point, and that all of the other published evidence (based on data from over 30,000 offenders) did not show the claimed relationship between rape and further sexual offending, but did show one with further violent offending,[8] as I had stated.[9] Embarrassingly,

---

8   I am indebted to Hugh Marriage, OBE, former Crime Reduction Director for the South-East Region of England, for pointing out that the risk of a further rape conviction is higher in men acquitted of rape than in those convicted of it. Although they don't address this point specifically, a number of Hugh's entertaining and informative speeches about crime policy may be found at: www.marriages.me.uk/hugh. Interestingly, the relationship between a rape conviction and violence extends to offences committed before the rape as well as after. When I collected a sample of life sentence prisoners, those convicted of rape averaged significantly more previous violent offences (3.58) than those convicted of murder (1.48), or manslaughter (0.50). See Forde (2014), Table 11, p.83.

9   This finding is as near universal as it ever gets, according to reviews that looked at risk factors (Hanson and Bussière 1998; Hanson and Morton-Bourgon 2004). Both reviews showed that even a preference for rape was not predictive of further sexual offences. Hanson and Morton-Bourgon (2005) listed the degree of force or violence used in a sex offence as one of

some of these papers had been written by some of the same authors as the paper they were quoting. I concluded, 'In effect, the complainants have accused me of misconduct because I follow the conclusion indicated by 99 per cent of the evidence, while they insist that the other 1 per cent should be accepted in preference to it.' The complaint was dismissed and the panel commented that I had defended my position by reasoned reference to published literature. I commented further:

> I suggest it is the *complainants* who have misrepresented the research evidence on this point. They can hardly do otherwise: to accept the truth would be to undermine the policy of their service, which they have been carrying out for some years. Furthermore, undermining the policy would open the door to compensation claims by thousands of offenders who have been retained in custody unnecessarily to undertake sex offender treatment programmes when they did not pose a significant risk of further sexual offending. The political nature of their complaint is therefore clear.

The point of describing this incident, however, is that no fewer than seven experienced prison psychologists had a severely limited understanding of the professional literature, while thinking that someone who disagreed with them must be the one at fault. It is hard to see this as defence of a genuine intellectual or professional position – hence my comment about the political nature of the complaint.[10]

---

several 'potentially misleading' alleged risk factors. It seems that most (not all) rapists go through a phase of their lives in which they pose a threat to women but this comes to an end.

10   Strangely, perhaps, they did not complain about my report's conclusion, which was that I felt the Ministry of Justice had proved its inability to handle this complex case, which had probably resulted in the prisoner serving about ten years longer than he should have done. I recommended that he should be released immediately. The Parole Board apparently agreed, and went with

This is not how professionals with any pretensions to scientific credibility are supposed to communicate with one another. If someone is presenting inaccurate evidence, then this should be challenged by reference to the whole of the evidence available, not just one or two cherry-picked studies. Furthermore, it is customary to contact colleagues direct when we think they are at fault, and invite them to either explain or change their position, rather than rushing into the disciplinary procedure. Such a reaction suggests a defensiveness based on insecurity – essentially, a fear that the challenger may be right – so that the raising of any question is seen as a threat rather than a contribution to professional debate. As a threat, it elicits an overreaction intended to maintain the status quo. Maintaining the status quo is not a valid scientific goal.

Lest anyone should think that I have a personal axe to grind, I would remind them of the treatment meted out to the researcher who challenged the SARN treatment needs analysis (referred to in Chapter 3). I would also cite the case of a well-qualified UK prison psychologist who dared to question treatment policy. This resulted in such an abusive response, which included personal attacks and being removed from the work which she was undertaking, that she eventually resigned. She sued for constructive dismissal, but the Ministry of Justice made clear that it was prepared to spend unlimited amounts of taxpayers' money in defending the case, and in the end she received legal advice to the effect that any compensation she might receive would not be worth the cost of obtaining it. She became a very effective independent psychologist, but several years after leaving the service was still suffering attacks on her personal and professional integrity in reports written by senior members of the service who saw her work. At least in the UK, the response to any unwelcome evidence has been to ignore it and shoot the messenger.

---

the recommendation (ah, maybe that's why they didn't complain about it). This was several years ago, and he has not been in trouble again since.

CO-OPTING THE CRITICS

Another difficulty related to communications in this field is that of obtaining access to data for research purposes. Some universities have made good arrangements with individual prisons in order to obtain access to data. In general, however, it is quite difficult to do this, and certainly in the UK the prison system has not been very effective at carrying out the research itself. Some examples have already been given, and there are exceptions, but in general prison research has not used the strictest methods based on acceptably large samples. It will be obvious by now that I think this is at least partly because of a fear that the best scientific methods will not produce the 'right' answers, especially with respect to treatment programmes. There is no way of knowing how many studies came up with the 'wrong' answers and were filed in the bottom drawer, thus contributing to the 'bound for publication bias'. Offenders who refuse to admit their offences are often said to be 'in denial', a Freudian concept that denotes an inability to recognise consciously something of which one is ashamed or afraid. One result of this denial can be that the individual attacks (sometimes very angrily) anything that threatens to reveal the truth. Denial is clearly not the sole province of offenders.

Having mentioned the fact that psychologists can be seriously lacking in professional knowledge in some fields, it is worth pointing out that there is a legal requirement to keep up to date. There is also a legal requirement to have professional indemnity insurance, so that any compensation claims made in connection with misconduct complaints can be met. This insurance could be invalidated if a psychologist was found not to be professionally up to date with developments in their own field. In the UK this is emphasised by a requirement that every psychologist should undergo at least 20 hours of 'continuing professional development' (CPD) per year. This may consist of formal training courses, but may include such things as participating in discussion groups, reading books or academic research papers and attending conferences. Records of CPD have to be kept, and when psychologists' registrations come up for renewal (every two years) a random selection of these records is examined. In the United States CPD is referred to as 'continuing education' (CE). Because American psychologists are licensed by individual states, each state has its own CE requirements, and these vary considerably. For example, at the time of writing, the state of Arizona requires 60 hours of CE every two years and Wisconsin requires 40, whereas New York state has no minimum requirement at all. Some states may require that a proportion of CE is spent on a specific topic, such as professional ethics or suicide prevention.[11] It is worth pointing out that psychologists employed by criminal justice organisations do not need professional indemnity insurance. If anyone sues, they sue the organisation and not the individual. Therefore, even with the legal obligation to do so, there is no practical incentive for psychologists working in such organisations to keep themselves up to date.

COMMUNICATION: IMPLICATIONS

It will be obvious that a few hours a year will not be enough to keep up to date with all new developments in any professional field. It may be less obvious that a legal requirement to spend a minimum amount of time doing so does not legally oblige any employer to provide paid time for it. Enquiries of colleagues both in the UK and in the US suggest that employers in neither country provide any such time at all. They may provide training courses, but these will generally be restricted to training in the

---

11   See www.continuingeducation.com/psychology/state-ce-requirements.

organisation's activities, such as running treatment programmes, or administering a particular risk assessment tool. It is not likely that this training will include keeping up to date with research findings in any wider sense. In other words, any psychologists wishing to keep fully informed of developments will have to do it in their own time. This is much easier for independent psychologists, who are self-employed. In my case, I used to allow 20 per cent of my time just for keeping up to date with research. Expressed in hours, this was probably about 20 times the legal requirement (but worth it as it enabled me to see off spurious misconduct complaints taken by less well-informed colleagues!). The situation could be improved if employing organisations were required to give psychologists at least the amount of study time that is legally required.

Again it will probably be obvious that communication between two groups of colleagues will be difficult if one has a view based on wide-ranging consideration of up-to-date knowledge and the other has a narrow training in the requirements of their employer. For example, one problem in discussing the effectiveness of treatments is that many of those carrying them out are not familiar with the evidence about them, or even the merits of different evaluation methods. A colleague who is an experienced psychosexual therapist was approached by representatives of the Ministry of Justice (an administrator and a psychologist) when changes in the laws on pornography were being considered by the government. As a self-employed professional who had worked in this field for many years, she was well informed and up to date. She was very surprised when the two Ministry representatives arrived to find that the psychologist was a trainee, despite being in charge of a national treatment programme. She was also surprised to find out in the course of their discussions that this person appeared to know almost nothing of the professional literature concerning sex offenders. If someone who is heading up a national programme knows little of the professional literature, what hope is there for the rest? It is worth mentioning also that some people remain trainees for extended periods of time. The record that I have come across so far is nine years. Trainees, of course, are cheaper to employ than fully qualified psychologists. There is a reason for this.

This state of affairs can only continue because one section of the profession isolates itself from other fields. Its lack of communication with others prevents people from finding out how ill informed it actually is, but also prevents it from becoming better informed. Whether the isolation is deliberate or accidental the results are the same: a lack of self-awareness, out-of-date knowledge and attitudes, and a defensive and even aggressive attitude towards those who try to change this. This cannot be in the best interests of either the profession or the public.

THE PAROLE PROCESS

Who Goes Home?

Why examine parole decisions in particular? There are three main reasons: first, I have about 15 years of practical experience in dealing with parole cases, so I know the field well; second, the process illustrates a great many of the concerns that I have raised; third, having made a special study of parole decisions in my doctoral work I have amassed a good deal of knowledge of the research in this area. Or, as one university professor put it, 'You will probably be the world expert in your field after finishing your doctoral research. No one else will have studied your particular area to as great a depth. That is, until the next doctoral thesis is published about 15 minutes later!' My doctoral thesis is available online, and contains amongst other things a brief history of the parole process, especially as it applies to the UK.[1] It also includes a review of the published academic research on what determines parole decisions, from the 1960s until 2014, as well as original research on a sample of life sentence prisoners in England and Wales.

PAROLE IN THE UK

The first schemes that allowed prisoners early release on condition of good behaviour in the community were tried in

---

1   See Forde (2014), especially Chapter 1.

overseas penal colonies in the 19th century. However, a formal parole system was introduced in the UK in the 1920s, and has undergone various developments since then. A major consideration has always been the safety of the public, so risk assessment has always been of paramount importance, even before there was any formalised way of carrying it out. Unfortunately, research carried out at the end of the 20th century showed quite clearly that the Parole Board for England and Wales was not carrying out systematic risk assessment. Furthermore, a consequence of this was that parole failures could only be kept down to an acceptable rate if parole was refused to most people. The researchers suggested that people should be released automatically at a certain point in their sentence, and kept under supervision for a period in the community after that.[2] This suggestion was accepted and put into law. For determinate-sentence prisoners (those on a fixed term), release henceforth took place at the halfway point of their sentence and they remained under supervision until the two-thirds point. This meant that the Parole Board no longer had to consider such cases. But there was a problem with life sentence and other indeterminate-sentence prisoners: they did not have a fixed sentence, so no halfway point could be calculated. Therefore, the parole system was kept in place for these prisoners, although there was no evidence that the Parole Board could assess risk any more accurately in these cases than it had been able to in determinate-sentence prisoners.[3]

Since the abolition of the death penalty in the UK (in 1965 in Great Britain, and 1973 in Northern Ireland) a life sentence has been mandatory in the case of a murder conviction, but may also be imposed for other offences, such as rape, manslaughter and armed robbery. The rules have changed a little from time to time,

---

2 See Hood and Shute (1999, 2000).

3 For subsequent evidence that it can't, see Padfield and Liebling (2000) on life sentence cases and Bradford and Cowell (2012) on so-called 'Imprisonment for Public Protection' cases (IPPs).

but the current system is that where a life sentence is imposed the judge also stipulates a minimum term (sometimes known for largely historical reasons as the 'tariff'). The offender concerned cannot be considered for parole until that minimum term has expired. After that, release is not certain, but depends upon a judgement by the Parole Board that the prisoner no longer poses a significant risk to the public. There is no basis for the popular perception (evident when I have given talks on the subject) that murderers are generally released after ten years or even less. In practice, the decision is taken by a three-member panel of the Parole Board, normally chaired by a judge or senior lawyer and including a psychologist or psychiatrist. It is possible to receive a whole-life tariff (that is, life without the possibility of parole at all) but it is extremely unusual. The minimum term is supposed to represent a punitive or retributive element in the sentence. After that, a prisoner ought to be released unless he is judged to pose a continuing risk to the public. Parole panels in the UK can make one of three decisions: they can turn down the parole application, they can recommend transfer to an open prison (a prison without walls) or they can direct release. Transfer to open prison conditions is only a recommendation to the Minister of Justice, and is not binding. A direction for release *is* legally binding and the Minister must comply. Systems in other developed countries differ in various ways, but they broadly follow a similar pattern, with most life sentence prisoners being eligible for parole at some point. Most countries have an equivalent of the Parole Board, and in the United States each state has its own parole authority, while another deals with federal prisoners.

However, although most parole systems are broadly similar, the details of the process can vary enormously from one to another. What they all have in common is that they place a high priority on avoiding risk to the public. In most jurisdictions, unlike the UK, the parole process is not restricted to lifers and other indeterminate sentence prisoners.

PAROLE AROUND THE WORLD

I mentioned above that I had carried out a systematic review of published academic literature on parole.[4] Specifically, it was a review of academic literature which examined the factors that correlated with parole decisions. This showed that it was commonplace for parole boards to claim that they considered cases on one criterion (often, risk to the public) but in practice their decisions related to other factors, such as the type of offence (regardless of risk) and perhaps behaviour in prison (most of which is unrelated to risk to the public after release). However, as the work of Kahneman and Ariely shows, people's stated reasons for taking decisions are often quite different from the real ones. Again, it is important to stress that people are usually not lying when this happens. They are simply unaware of their true motivation. They have a view about how they ought to conduct their work, and that view influences how they perceive it. It is more a question of self-serving rose-tinted spectacles than any deliberate intention to mislead. Everyone wants to think that their work is of value and adheres to sound principles. Most people find themselves able to adopt the beliefs and attitudes that help to maintain this delusion.

So what did the review show about the reality of parole decisions the world over? Frankly, it was pretty chaotic. Also, it was not much studied. Between 1966 and 2014, when the review was completed, only 29 papers had been published on what determines parole decisions. This number is tiny for such a long time period. There were plenty of papers discussing parole, particularly what policy ought to be, but very few that actually took a scientific look at what influenced parole outcomes. Because of the way the computerised library searches for papers had been conducted I was confident that no significant paper had been inadvertently passed over.

---

4   See Forde (2014), Chapter 2.

One reassuring finding was that, although a number of researchers had examined the issue, there was little evidence of bias against any ethnic groups. This had been examined in the United States and in Canada. Another finding was that it was usually possible to predict the results of parole board deliberations using only a few variables. In other words, although parole boards typically portrayed their task as one of immense complexity, considering and balancing many different sources of information, the decision ultimately rested on just a few (sometimes only one or two). Unfortunately, these few factors were different in almost every jurisdiction, making it impossible to generalise. One could not, for example, say that in general prisoners who behaved well in prison were more likely to obtain parole. Likewise, one could not say that violent or sexual offenders were necessarily less likely to do so. Any of these things might be true in some jurisdictions but not in others.

Another finding was that parole boards did not always follow their own terms of reference in taking decisions. For example, in a number of jurisdictions they were instructed to ignore the length of sentence imposed, as this was properly the consideration of the sentencing judge. Nonetheless, it was clear that in some cases parole boards were less inclined to parole serious offenders because they felt that they had not yet received enough punishment! Essentially, this meant that some parole boards were acting unlawfully. In one jurisdiction the victims of offences could make a statement to the parole board, sometimes in person. Equally, the offender could make statements and appear in person. It was shown that the decision tended to be swayed more towards the victim or the offender depending on who had appeared. Neither of these sources of information is related to subsequent risk to the public.[5]

---

5   In 2014 there was a minor furore when an English parole board judge was overheard saying that victim impact statements didn't affect parole board decisions (Dearden 2014). Later statements clarified this, saying that they

An important finding was that, despite the emphasis on risk to the public, little systematic risk assessment was actually carried out by any of the parole boards in any jurisdiction. This was not always because of a lack of availability: statistical predictors were quite often available. However, parole boards resisted the use of statistical predictors; they wanted to be able to exercise their own discretion. In other words, they wanted to be able to judge each case individually. The problem with this, of course, is that risk is statistical by its very nature. An individual risk assessment is a contradiction in terms.[6] Given what we know about human decision-making, we would expect that leaving decisions to a parole board's discretion would inevitably result in decisions being made on the basis of subjective ideas about risk. We have seen some evidence of this already, in the findings that boards took decisions with reference to factors of which they were not even aware. There was more evidence earlier when considering assessment methods, and more will be referred to in the next chapter. Given the impact of things like victim and offender statements, we might also expect that the personal presentation of someone at a parole board hearing would make a difference to the decision. Even though it is totally unrelated to risk, it is not unrelated to the subjectivity of

---

contributed important information to consideration of the case, but it would be very unusual that the victim would have information about the offender's risk. Hard though it may seem, the fact is that victims are experts on being victims, but not necessarily anything else of relevance to making a parole decision.

6   This point of view has been challenged, but an individualised risk assessment means making judgements about individual factors in a case which we know to be relevant to risk. The only way we can know this is by knowing about the prevalence of these factors in high and low risk cases. Otherwise, we are back to subjective judgements. Nonetheless, I have endlessly discussed questions in parole hearings along the lines of, 'Might this factor not result in … [pick consequence of choice]?' The truthful answer would probably be, 'I don't know, and neither do you, and nor does anyone else. This is complete speculation.' However, one is not encouraged to talk to Parole Board judges like this.

decision-making. Given Kahneman's work, essentially showing that we have an emotional reaction to something and then create a rationalisation which justifies it, we might expect that if we warm to someone we would be more likely to grant them what they want. Unfortunately, these expectations were fully realised.

Very few of the research projects covered in this review were truly experimental in nature. Indeed, such a thing would be very difficult to organise, given that there are legal constraints. We cannot, for example, conduct a randomised controlled trial to investigate parole decisions. However, there were a couple of exceptions. One of these was a simulation study, which does permit experimental manipulation. Studies like this are often criticised because they frequently use students, but this one used experienced parole officers to make the judgements.[7] They were asked to examine copies of actual case papers and recommend whether or not the prisoner described should get parole. The recommendations were swayed heavily by any aggravating factors in the original offence. Sexual and violent offenders were mostly not recommended for parole. Interestingly, the parole officers rated some supposed (but not actual) indicators of risk as being very important in their decision, but only when they wanted to justify refusing parole. Once again, it seemed that the decision was taken first, and reasons for it decided later.

This was perhaps even more clearly demonstrated in another North American study. This used the PCL-R measure of psychopathy to see whether 'psychopaths' were more or less likely to be paroled.[8] The main finding was that prisoners who scored highly on the PCL-R psychopathy measure were two and a half times *more* likely to be paroled. Psychopaths are notoriously good at manipulating people and giving a plausible

---

7   See Turpin-Petrosino (1999). This study was conducted in the state of New Jersey.

8   See Porter, ten Brinke and Wilson (2009). This study was conducted on Canadian sex offenders.

impression of themselves, which is one reason why they make such effective criminals. The suggestion from this research is that they are equally good at manipulating parole boards and those who provide risk assessment reports to them. Once again, the influence of the offender's personal presentation was out of all proportion to its actual importance: personal presentation is, of course, not related to risk. Indeed, the psychopaths who were so successful at obtaining release were much more likely to be reconvicted afterwards. Considering the problems related earlier with the PCL-R, it is interesting that, although this study found PCL-R 'psychopaths' to be successfully manipulative, this was not related to their score on item 5 of the PCL-R: 'conning and manipulative'. Instead, it was related to those items that reflected previous criminal history. In other words, the psychopaths were successful manipulators because of their previous experience of the criminal justice system, not because of the personality characteristic that the PCL-R tries to measure.

Two other studies are perhaps worth mentioning here. The first was another part of my doctoral research, which included a study of those factors relating to parole decisions in a sample of a hundred British life sentence prisoners.[9] This examined the relationship between parole decisions and risk assessments which I had carried out on the parole applicants. The Parole Board had this information in front of them when they made their decision, but those making recommendations to them (such as probation officers) generally did not. The risk assessments varied from one case to another, but most included the PCL-R psychopathy assessment and the HCR-20 violence risk assessment or the SVR-20 sexual violence risk assessment. In some cases both risk assessments were carried out. Parole decisions proved to be related to the HCR-20 assessment, but not in a straightforward way. It may be recalled that the HCR-20 contains three sections

---

9   See Forde (2014), Chapter 3.

relating to Historical, Clinical and Risk Management factors and that there are 20 items, hence the name. It may also be recalled that the Historical scale was the least subjective and also the best predictor of violence. It is not clear how well Historical items would predict in lifers, whose offences had taken place many years before. However, the Clinical and Risk Management scales are not any better on that account. They remain quite subjective and presumably not very predictive of violence. What I found was that the recommendations of expert witnesses (probation officers and prison psychologists) were largely predictable from the Clinical and Risk Management scales, the ones *least* related to actual violent reconvictions. This was despite the fact that these professionals had not seen the HCR-20 scores before making their own recommendations. The decision of the Parole Board was in turn highly predictable from the recommendations of the expert witnesses. It appeared that the Clinical and Risk Management scales and the professionals' recommendations were both independently reflecting something about how the parole applicants presented themselves in interview. It is likely that this had little to do with risk, even though it ended up being a major influence on the Parole Board decision.

It may be objected that a sample of a hundred prisoners is not large enough to base policy on, and I would agree. However, shortly after my thesis was published, a Californian study found essentially the same results in a much larger sample of over 5000 parole applicants. The authors of that study interpreted their results as meaning that the HCR-20 was being used correctly. That is, they thought the Californian parole board (the Board of Parole Hearings) was using the measures most related to *current* risk, as opposed to historical items reflecting risk in the past. The Board had the assessments in front of them when they made the decision. It is possible that the researchers were biased in favour of the HCR-20: one was one of its co-authors, and another had conducted extensive postgraduate research with him and his colleagues. The study was not able to follow up their cases and see whether the risk assessments were highly predictive of behaviour in the community, although earlier research suggests not. However, given that the Clinical and Risk Management scales of the HCR-20 reflect the current *presentation* of the prisoner, and given that presentation has been shown to affect parole decisions (both in the study of psychopaths and in the study of who attends the parole hearing and gives evidence) I had a different interpretation. It appeared likely to me that the parole decision was being influenced by the recommendations of professionals, as other research has shown, and in turn the professionals were being influenced by the presentation of the prisoner in interview.

If this view is correct there are implications for how we arrive at parole decisions, and even whether we should have a parole process at all, as opposed to some more automatic (and very much cheaper) procedure. In the first place, it is clear that parole decisions in general are not taken on the basis of risk to the public, even though that is the basis that is claimed. In the second place, there are obvious political pressures to keep the number of spectacular parole failures down, especially serious reoffences. If the parole decision is not genuinely governed by risk, then the only way to keep the more dramatic failures down is to parole very few people, which is exactly what was happening with determinate sentence men in the UK when the parole system applied to them. In my experience of carrying out risk assessments for 15 years this is also what happens with life sentence men. It has been dispiriting to sit through hundreds of parole hearings and to present evidence that a person poses a low risk to the public by every measure that we know, and yet still see the parole applicant turned down. He may have served 20 years or more (the record in my experience was 41) and he may be getting on in years (the record for *this* in my experience was 80), at which point violence risk is almost non-existent. However, if there is any factor in a case which somebody does not understand or does not trust, however slight, the chances are it will be used as a reason to refuse parole. Most of these factors have no relationship whatever with risk. I have even seen cases of parole being refused because a parole panel was worried by a factor in the applicant's history which was known to be *protective*!

This is simply not a rational way of taking decisions about people. Furthermore, as with fixed-sentence men before the policy was changed, it is virtually certain that many low-risk individuals are serving longer than they need to. In the case of life sentence prisoners this can be years or even decades longer, and generally the period between parole hearings is two years. This costs the taxpayer thousands of pounds per case. There is a further consequence: if there is essentially no relationship between a prisoner's real level of risk and his chances of being paroled, then some high-risk individuals are also being released. The number will be very small, because the total number being released is small, and genuinely high-risk individuals are rare in the lifer population. However, if genuine risk assessment could be incorporated into the release decision it would be possible to release more lifers with no increase in danger to the public. This is of critical importance at a time when the prison population is high and still rising, and much of this problem is due to the number of indeterminate sentence men serving very long periods.[10]

THE PAROLE PROCESS: IMPLICATIONS

Why, you might well ask, do professionals give 'expert' opinion about risk on the basis of factors that we know are not related to risk? There is one basic reason why this happens: professionals are not thoroughly evidence based in their thinking. But there

---

10   According to the Ministry of Justice (2013).

is more to it than this. Psychologists within the criminal justice system are committed to identifying risks and prescribing offending behaviour programmes which are supposed to address these. They usually have very limited room for manoeuvre. Furthermore, at least in the UK criminal justice system, there is considerable organisational pressure to drum up 'custom' for these programmes, with budgets being geared towards participation targets. Add to this the fact that professionals in the system are not allotted any time at all to keep up to date with the research, and are under great institutional pressure to ignore anything that challenges existing policy and practice, and it is not surprising that those psychologists are committed to running programmes, effective or not. In order to justify running the programmes, one must identify risks which those programmes are intended to reduce. It is thus commonplace to see that offenders who exhibit no known risk factors at all will have risks attributed to them on the flimsiest of grounds.

There is an additional factor in the case of people who are applying for parole. This is simply that the Parole Board is very powerfully motivated to avoid releasing people who might later reoffend seriously. This is understandable, and indeed it is what they are supposed to be trying to do. Nonetheless, it results in them putting great pressure on expert witnesses to give certainty or something close to it. I have said it earlier in this book, and I say it again here: we can predict statistically with approximately 70 per cent accuracy whether someone will reconvict with a serious violent or sexual offence. That's it. That is as good as it gets on the basis of our present knowledge. No amount of anxiety on the part of parole authorities, no amount of heckling from the tabloid press, and no amount of wariness on the part of politicians can change that. Furthermore, it is known (repeat, *known*) that augmenting statistical prediction with supposedly expert knowledge, in the form of clinical judgement or clinical override, makes prediction worse.

It follows from this that any search for additional risk factors to give us greater 'certainty' actually makes our risk assessment worse. In other words, the political and institutional pressures upon risk assessors make them perform even less well than they otherwise would. These pressures nonetheless cause risk assessment professionals to augment objective measures with others that have no value. What seems to happen is that 'experts' feel that they have to support their opinions with complex rationalisations. Parole boards do not want to hear that 'this is as good as it gets', so many professionals won't tell them that. I have witnessed this regularly for 15 years. I have also been arguing against it, but I fear to little effect.

It is very clear from the research by Kahneman and others that people are often unaware of the true reasons why they take decisions. It is equally clear that they tend to make decisions on the basis of an initial and emotionally biased impression, and then justify them afterwards by more rational arguments. Again, from the work of Ariely and others it is clear that people are often very resistant to acknowledging the true reasons for their decisions, even to themselves. In short, if decision-makers (including parole boards) refuse to use objective risk estimates and insist upon their 'discretion', what they are actually insisting upon is that they must be allowed to make flawed decisions without hindrance. They will not, of course, see it like that.

To be fair, parole boards are not supposed to be automatons slavishly following an objective risk assessment. They are generally required to balance risk to the public against the possible benefits of parole. These might include the successful reintegration of the offender into society, which theoretically gives greater long-term protection. But the difficulty here is that this is also a judgement which they cannot make. No one can make it. The further ahead in time we try to predict anything, the less accurate prediction can be. This is inevitable, because we cannot foretell the future, and we therefore do not know what circumstances will prevail in the offender's life in ten years' time, or five, or probably even two. Whatever the circumstances are, they may affect the level of risk posed. Or they may not. Parole boards therefore have no basis for taking this kind of decision, and the evidence is that they do not. The research which showed that psychopaths were good at talking their way into parole bears this out. Parole boards were impressed by their talk, but objectively these people were a high risk and prone to reoffending.

To take a specific example which is in the public domain, consider the case of Anthony Rice. Rice was a man who had committed a number of sexual offences between the ages of 15 and 48. For his most recent offence, an attempted rape, he had received a discretionary life sentence with a minimum term of ten years, although he had in fact served 15. A life sentence would not normally be given for attempted rape, but discretionary life sentences may be given where the judge thinks there is evidence of continuing risk, often due to mental health problems. He was released in 2004 and went on to commit very serious assaults against two women, one of whom died. From the circumstances, including his own account of the events, it is clear that he deliberately intended to kill the final victim because of the extreme anger against women which he was experiencing at the time. The Probation Inspectorate enquired into these events and made a number of criticisms. Some are not relevant here, but two definitely are: the parole panel's reliance on 'overoptimistic' assessments of Rice's improvement during treatment programmes, and its inadequate risk assessment.

Rice had undergone the standard Sex Offender Treatment Programme, and a seven-year stay in the therapeutic community regime at Grendon Prison (much longer than most prisoners). I have argued in earlier chapters that these interventions are not effective and that we cannot reliably measure any change that may have taken place during them. It seems that the parole panel believed that they could be effective and had been in his case.

They were wrong. The Inspectorate criticised the parole panel's risk assessment on the basis that it was inadequately informed. Specifically, they stated that the details of his earlier sexual offences had not been made available. The panel knew that he had committed previous offences, but not that some of the victims were children. To my mind this criticism makes very little sense. For one thing, men who commit offences against children are not necessarily especially high in risk, and for another both of the offences he committed on parole were against adult women, so any risk to children seems a bit academic. His offences against children had been committed when he was still very young himself, two of them against fellow teenagers, and there was no indication that he harboured any sexual attraction towards children by the time he was in his 40s. This is a red herring. What is not a red herring, however, is that the information available was not correctly incorporated in a *statistical* prediction of Rice's risk of a repeat offence. Had it been, his risk would have been rated as 'Very High'. Although at age 48 he would have been past the peak age for committing sexual offences, he would not have been so far past it that his risk would have been discounted on the basis of age alone. In other words, if the parole panel had ignored reports about Rice's progress in treatment, and correctly assessed his risk using just the statistical information available, they would probably not have released him.

It is easy to be wise after the event, but practitioners like myself were advocating reliance on statistical predictors and questioning the alleged evidence in favour of treatment programmes well before these events. The case of Anthony Rice illustrates how right we were to do so, and how objective information, imperfect as it is, is nonetheless much more reliable than 'clinical' judgement. All too often retaining discretion over such decisions simply guarantees that they will be made less well than they would otherwise be.

The research evidence clearly implies that decisions are taken on a chance basis and not on the basis of risk to the public. Despite this, serious failures are very rare, at least among UK lifers. As pointed out earlier, the UK parole system now only involves those on indeterminate sentences, with those on determinate sentences being released automatically. In other words, the risk is extremely low anyway, whatever the periodic outbreaks of moral outrage exhibited by the tabloid press. Given that objective criteria do exist for determining risk, it is certainly possible that parole applicants could be placed in risk bands. It is likely that most of those objectively assessed as being low in risk could be released with minimal supervision.

As outlined earlier, UK lifers are given a minimum term which they must serve before becoming eligible for parole. It is clear that in the majority of cases they could be safely released after finishing this minimum term. We can be sure of that because most of the arguments against doing so are spurious, and because the end result is not related to risk. This does not mean that all lifers should automatically be released as soon as they have completed their minimum term. However, it does suggest that the test for release could be reversed: instead of asking whether someone has proved his lack of dangerousness (an impossible task anyway), we could ask whether there is any case for saying that he still remains too dangerous to release. In the absence of any such case, based on objective evidence of risk, he could then progress to open prison with a view to being tested in less secure conditions. The main difference between this scheme and what happens now is that many lifers would be released earlier. It should be remembered that the minimum term, or 'tariff', is meant to be the punishment element of a life sentence in the UK. Thereafter, a prisoner is supposed to progress towards release, unless he is thought to be too dangerous. The problem currently is that our basis for deciding whether a prisoner is too dangerous is deeply flawed.

However, in most systems in the Western world, once a person has been paroled he is then handed over to the care of a probation service or similar organisation. The logic behind this is not immediately obvious. It is true that parole authorities are treated as being very similar to courts, and once the decision is taken they often have no more contact with the parolee, but this does not have to be the case. Arguably, parole authorities would appreciate the difficulties of supervision much more if they were responsible for that as well as the release decision. This would involve considerable reorganisation of the institutions concerned, but it would make parole authorities more directly responsible for the outcome of their decisions, and give them much more feedback about the results of those decisions. Currently, in most jurisdictions, parolees can be returned to prison for a variety of reasons (not usually because of reoffending, but for minor violations of parole conditions) but the parole authority never knows. It is only when a major crisis occurs, such as a very serious offence by a parolee, that there is usually an enquiry and the parole authority may be held to some account.

Another feature of the present system in most jurisdictions, and not just the UK, is that when a released offender fails parole he is returned directly to closed prison. The effect of this is very often to incarcerate him for a very long period, perhaps months or years, before he can apply for parole again. This is very wasteful of resources, and mostly unnecessary. If someone breaches the conditions of his parole it should normally be punishment (and warning) enough for him to be returned to prison for a short period. Unless he has committed a further offence, it might not even be necessary to return him to a closed prison. An open prison, or even a semi-secure hostel, might well be warning enough. In the UK currently about one third of lifers are recalled to prison when on parole, usually for breaches of parole conditions and not for further offending. For example, they may have missed appointments with their supervising officer, or they may have been associating with other known criminals, or were perhaps found to have been drinking heavily when they were supposed to avoid this, or anything else that their supervising officer perceives as increasing their level of risk (and we know how reliable that kind of judgement is). There is no immediate appeal against being recalled on the unsupported word of a probation officer. Recalled individuals are supposed to get a 'recall hearing' in front of the Parole Board within six months, although I have known cases where it has taken three or four times as long. Yet the decision may well be that the recall was unnecessary and the man can be released again immediately. A range of recall possibilities would save huge amounts of money without putting the public at any greater risk than it is now. So would a policy of granting recall hearings very quickly.

These are only some of the possibilities, but none of them represents change for the sake of change. They are suggestions for more efficient use of public finances, as well as more efficient handling of parolees' cases.

– 10 –

HEURISTICS AND BIASES

How Can We Be So Stupid?

By now it will be obvious that I believe psychologists make some of the mistakes they do because they are human beings, and all human beings are subject to making judgements on the basis of flawed processes. All human beings, regardless of intelligence, emotional stability or professional training. This does not mean that I think all human beings are equally prone to error, or that they all make the same kinds of error to the same degree. The details may depend upon their upbringing, personality and many other factors. Nonetheless, there is now considerable evidence that our brains are hardwired in a particular way which causes us to make systematic errors in thinking.

THE DANGERS OF A BAD DECISION

The reason for this is often framed in terms of evolutionary theory. The argument goes something like this. When our remote ancestors were surviving on the tropical grasslands of ancient Africa, they needed to react fast in order to stay alive. The tropical savanna is the home of many dangerous animals. Not only are there lions and leopards which may attack and eat humans, there are poisonous snakes, other snakes that kill by constriction and many poisonous insects. Not only that, there are many other animals, especially those with young, which may object to your presence and attack you anyway, possibly fatally for you. Being able to throw stones and spears may offer some protection, but probably not enough. Evasive action may be essential to survival. Either way, early humans needed to make very fast judgements which increased their chances of surviving. The ones that could not make these fast judgements didn't survive. We are by definition the descendants of those that did.

Of course, having made a quick judgement about a situation, our remote ancestors would still have to take action. In some cases, the action might have to be equally fast, such as leaping for a tree or crouching behind a large rock. However, in many cases a more leisurely and rational plan would be necessary. This would not always be developed by an individual, but sometimes by a group such as a hunting party. Nonetheless, the nature of the situation would be assessed in the initial quick-thinking phase of the process, and this would tend to define what sort of action was taken afterwards, even if it was slower and more rational. But (I hear you cry) psychologists are not hunters on the savanna. This is true, but the evolutionary explanation is simply a hypothesis about how the functioning of our brains came to be the way it is. Even if it is wrong, that does not change the way our brains work.

HEURISTICS AND BIASES

Mention has already been made of the work of Daniel Kahneman,and I intend to look at it in more detail in this section.[1] Essentially, what Kahneman has shown is that our initial assessment of the situation is quick but sometimes wrong. However, whether it is right or wrong, the behaviour that is then set in train is based on this initial assessment. Furthermore, the

---

1   See Tversky and Kahneman (1974) and Kahneman (2011).

initial assessment is subject to a great variety of biases of which we are generally unaware, and which are not easily subject to correction. Not only are we unaware of these biases, but the work of Ariely has shown that we are adept at keeping ourselves from becoming aware of them: once made, the assessment is very resistant to being changed.[2] The flaws in decision-making which have been discovered are generally known collectively as 'heuristics and biases'. Heuristics are essentially rules of thumb, or simple and fast automatic judgements which help us to get a task going. These are often contrasted with 'algorithms', which will inexorably lead to the correct answer, but may take a very long time doing it (as an evolutionary psychologist might put it, the lion would have eaten you by then). Biases are simply effects that slant our judgement one way or another. As we shall see, there are ample opportunities for both heuristics and biases to enter into the decision-making processes of psychologists, probation officers and parole panels. And, indeed, everyone else.

AVAILABILITY

One common heuristic, the 'availability heuristic', has been shown to affect people's judgement of risks and benefits across a wide range of topics. What it means is that some items of information are more readily available to us than others, and therefore influence our judgement. For example, people who are favourable to technological development tend to overestimate its benefits and underestimate its costs. Because they are used to thinking about the benefits, these are the first things that come to mind when they are being asked for an opinion. For psychologists, a parallel might be that when they are considering someone's possible risk of violence in the event

---

2   See Ariely (2012).

that he is released, they may overestimate the importance of minor disputes in which he has recently been involved. Since a large part of the dossier of papers concerning a prisoner consists of statements about risk, it is almost inevitable that parole panels will tend to concentrate on this issue. However, some factors (usually called 'protective factors') are known to mitigate risk. It is highly likely that, if the same prisoner were to be considered for parole on the basis of statements about his protective factors, he would be much more likely to be released.

A somewhat related heuristic is what Kahneman calls 'What You See Is All There Is', or 'WYSIATI'. Essentially, this means that we construct a narrative based on the information that we have, and can be absurdly confident in the validity of this narrative even if it is based on very little information. Having formed the view on the basis of this information, we may then be quite resistant to changing it when new information becomes available. Rather, we try to explain the new information away. Returning to the parole scenario, my own research made clear that parole boards are often influenced disproportionately by a few items of information. Furthermore, although their decisions are influenced by these items of information, they are often unaware of the fact, and when it is pointed out to them are very resistant to the idea. They generally persist in thinking that they can come to an individualised decision that is fairly based on all the information they have.

ANCHORING

Another source of error is what Kahneman calls 'anchoring'. This means the tendency for one's judgement to be influenced by a decision suggested beforehand. This bias has been demonstrated in a variety of situations. For example, real estate agents who were required to value properties were shown to be influenced by values suggested by the potential vendors beforehand.[3] The agents were utterly unaware of this bias, and firmly maintained that their valuations were completely objective. They understood property values, and the vendors did not, and they would not be influenced by such amateur ideas. Nevertheless, they were. In another experiment, it was shown that the mere mention of a possible prison sentence of a certain length could influence the sentence that legal experts thought was appropriate in a particular case.[4] The anchoring bias was so strong that it continued to be displayed even when the legal experts had generated the suggested prison sentences themselves by rolling dice, so they knew it was a random figure! My own survey of the literature on parole decisions showed that these were influenced by the recommendation of the prisoner's home probation officer, even though the parole panels making these decisions also complained that the home probation officer did not know the prisoner very well. This bias was not confined to the UK, but occurred wherever it had been investigated.[5] It does suggest that, despite the poor risk assessments on which these recommendations were based, parole panels were influenced by them nonetheless. It could be objected that parole panels might not *know* the risk assessment was poor, but the psychologist or psychiatrist member (and there would certainly be one in the UK) should certainly have known. In any case, if legal experts can be influenced by a figure known to be derived from throwing dice, it must be obvious that they can be influenced by recommendations that appear to be more systematic.

Another opportunity for anchoring to occur is in the assessment of treatment needs. We have seen already that the accuracy of treatment needs analysis is very poor. We have also

---

3   See Northcraft and Neale (1987).

4   See Englich, Mussweiler and Strack (2006).

5   See Forde (2014), especially Chapters 2 and 3.

seen that offenders who do not meet the criteria for participating in an offending behaviour programme are often selected for it anyway on the grounds of 'clinical override', a wholly invalid procedure. But, just as with other kinds of assessment, needs assessment is virtually certain to be susceptible to anchoring. If a clinical opinion has suggested participation in a programme, regardless of what the more objective assessment of risk may be, it is likely to sway the judgement of the treatment managers who have to select participants. As noted earlier, this is not because they are incompetent, but simply because they are human.

If the idea that anchoring could have such a powerful effect seems implausible, consider the work of Dr Itiel Dror and his colleagues.[6] Dror is a cognitive scientist who has studied the decisions made by forensic scientists. By "forensic scientists" I mean those who deal with physical evidence, such as fingerprints and blood, taken from crime scenes. Their evidence may be crucial in deciding whether someone is found guilty of a serious crime or not, and it is obviously very important that it should be accurate. Fortunately, these physical sciences involve indisputable physical evidence: things like counting features in two fingerprints to decide whether they come from the same person, so there is not much room for error, is there? Unfortunately, Dror's work shows that there is.[7] First, he has shown that the interrater reliability of such experts is surprisingly low (that is, they often disagree with each other). Second, he has shown that even an expert who is given the same evidence on two separate occasions may not come to the same conclusion both times. Third, he has shown that one reason for this unreliability can be bias induced by irrelevant information. For example, knowing whether the

---

6   See Dror (2016). One of his more surprising findings is that these 'hard sciences' had not established any standards for what constituted adequate performance, despite having been in use for around a century. It seems that no one realized the reliability problem might exist.

7   See Dror and Rosenthal (2008).

suspect has confessed to the crime, or whether he has an alibi, should make no difference to the experts' judgement about whether the evidence is incriminating or not. However, it does; in the first case experts are more likely to judge the evidence incriminating, and in the second to judge that it is not. If even experts in the 'hard sciences' can make errors like this because of irrelevant information, what chance have psychologists got? Dror is now tackling this question too, reviewing some of the evidence I am presenting in this chapter,[8] and coming to similar conclusions about forensic psychological assessment.

REPRESENTATIVENESS AND BASE RATES

The 'representativeness heuristic' is the tendency to overestimate the likelihood of something because it looks like something else with which we are more familiar, but which is actually rare. In other words, if A looks like a typical example of B, we may estimate it to be as likely as B, even if B is improbable. Kahneman uses the example of a fictitious student called Tom, supposedly selected at random from those enrolled at a particular university. When people were asked to choose from a list a field of study that Tom was likely to be following, but given no information about him, they correctly concluded that he was likely to be following one of the most popular courses in which most of the students were enrolled. However, another group of people were given the same task but also read a description of Tom, which described him as intelligent but not very creative and something of a social isolate. The people faced with this task tended to choose a field of study such as computer science, because the description of Tom fitted their stereotype of such 'nerdy' people. However, they also had been given statistical information about

---

8   See Dror and Murrie (in press).

how many students enrolled in each of these different courses. They should have been able to see that computer science (which enrolled very few students) was still statistically unlikely. However, their feeling that Tom resembled their stereotypical idea of a computer geek outweighed the other information.

In another example, the researchers gave people a description of a man ('Mr P') who was supposedly charged with a serious offence of fraud.[9] Following their reading of the description, participants were asked to place a number of statements in order of likelihood. One of the statements was that Mr P had murdered an employee, and a second statement was that he had murdered an employee to prevent him from talking to the police. Participants rated the second statement as more likely than the first. However, this is not correct. Clearly, if Mr P had committed a murder it could have been for a number of reasons (perhaps the employee was having an affair with Mrs P, or had stolen money from the business). No one single reason can be more probable than all of the possible reasons combined. But, given the information that Mr P was suspected of a crime, people were misled by their stereotypical views of the reasons why a suspected criminal might commit a murder.

In dealing with offenders, I have often come across examples of this sort of fallacious reasoning among psychologists, probation officers and others. Often, these have been in cases where the motive for a crime is not entirely clear. A common example is that men who have murdered women are often accused of having done so for a sexual motive. This accusation may be levelled even though there has been no charge or conviction of rape, and no evidence of any sexual assault, and no confession of such a motive from the offender although he admits the murder.[10] As with Mr P, there may be many reasons

---

9   See Neal and Grisso (2014).

10   The situation is complicated by the fact that, even if the murderer has a known sexual motive, the perpetrator is often simply convicted of murder, rather than rape and murder. Presumably, it is felt that the indeterminate

why murder is committed and no single reason can be more likely than all of the reasons put together. What appears to be at the root of this fallacy is the fact that the victim is female and the perpetrator male. For some psychologists this appears to be enough. Gender politics, I would suggest, have no place in what purports to be an objective assessment.

There is a similar problem with cases of rape, where the offender may admit the offence but deny that he has any particular interest in forced or violent sex. Again, rape can be committed for a variety of reasons,[11] but any one reason cannot be more likely than all of the possible reasons combined. Nonetheless, for many psychologists the fact of rape having been committed leads to insistence that the perpetrator has a 'deviant' interest in violent sex and must undergo 'treatment' for this or he will pose a danger to all women for many years to come. In fact, as noted earlier, a rape conviction is predictive of future *violence* rather than future sexual offending, and *acquittal* on a rape charge is more predictive of future rapes than a rape *conviction*. In other words, for most men who have committed rape the offence relates to a particular period in their life when they posed a danger to women. Those having an obsession with sexual violence per se, who may continue to be a threat, are a minority who cannot outnumber all men who have committed rape.

One of the reasons why the representativeness heuristic leads people astray is that they tend to ignore base rates (sometimes called 'prior probabilities'). The base rate may be thought of as the rate at which something occurs naturally, before we intervene

---

nature of the sentence allows every angle to be covered when considering possible release. Alternatively, in some cases it may be felt that rape cannot be proved beyond a reasonable doubt, whereas murder can. We are thus in the strange situation where the courts have decided there is insufficient evidence to prove rape, but the 'experts' insist that there is.

11   There is quite an extensive research literature on this. For a summary, see Office of Justice Programs (2014).

in a situation or select a particular group. For example, when evaluating treatments we are really comparing the performance of treated individuals with the base rate, which is shown by those who have not had the treatment. In the example given above of the student whose field of study we were trying to guess, the base rates are the proportions of the student population opting for various courses. Kahneman gives another example, which he has used in experiments on thinking. He described an individual ('Steve') as being meek and shy, something of a loner, not much interested in people but helpful if needed, and with a passion for tidiness. Then he asked participants whether they thought Steve was more likely to be a librarian or a farmer. Almost invariably, they decided that he was more likely to be a librarian. But there are very many more farmers than librarians (over 20 times as many in the United States, where this experiment was conducted), and as Kahneman puts it, 'it is almost certain that more "neat and tidy" souls will be found on tractors than at library information desks'.[12] However, the information given about Steve's personality matches the popular stereotype of librarians, and the fact that librarians are much rarer is forgotten.

Professionals are not immune from this bias. In particular, in the field of parole with which I have been much involved in recent years, there is a tendency to over-identify people as posing a serious risk of violence. Now, it may be argued that the Parole Board has a duty to err on the side of caution, and this is true. However, the rate of grave offending amongst released life sentence prisoners is extremely low. Indeed, if we were to predict that all life sentence prisoners applying for parole would not reconvict with a serious violence offence, we would be right nearly all the time. Certainly, the accuracy of such a prediction would far exceed that of most other human risk assessments. The problem is that many of these offenders have a turbulent

---

12   Kahneman (2011), p.7.

history of serious problems and offences, which causes anxiety; the difficulty is that most such people do not go on to commit one murder, let alone two.[13] Similarly, sex offenders have been shown to have a hard time obtaining parole in many jurisdictions,[14] despite the fact that their risk of reconviction is very low compared with that of other prisoners. The problem is that they *look* dangerous to the parole authorities because of the offences they have committed, and sometimes because of personal characteristics that are nothing to do with risk.

'Personal characteristics that are nothing to do with risk?' Surely not. Even if, as we have seen, risk assessments are much less than perfect, surely professionals would not make judgements about such a serious matter based on irrelevant personal characteristics? Would they not base their decisions about people on risk assessments that were known to have some validity? Not according to a study carried out in Canada, where offenders judged to pose a serious risk to the public may be denied parole or any other form of early release when they would normally be able to at least apply for it.[15] The researchers, Nugent and Zamble, assessed two groups of offenders, some who were detained without parole and some who were released. They used four different risk assessments, including the PCL-R psychopathy assessment mentioned earlier. They found that detained and non-detained prisoners were indeed different according to the four risk assessments. However, the difference was not in the direction one might expect; it was the *detained* men who scored lower on the risk assessment tools. Neither did the detained men (by definition, those thought to pose a higher

---

13   In a total of over 25 years of dealing with prisoners, including hundreds with a murder conviction, I have never met a serial killer (defined as one with three or more known victims). Indeed, I have only met two with as many as two victims.

14   See Forde (2014), Chapter 2.

15   See Nugent and Zamble (2001).

risk than others) commit more offences after their eventual release; indeed, they actually committed fewer, had committed fewer in the past, and had a better employment record prior to their current offence (a protective factor). In short, there was absolutely nothing to suggest that the detained men were higher in risk than those who were allowed to apply for parole. There were other differences, however. They were older, more likely to have been convicted of a sex offence, more likely to have shown poor progress in institutional treatment programmes, and more likely to have denied or minimised their offending. It may be recalled that being older and denying one's offence are actually *protective* factors. These findings are consistent with those reported for structured professional judgements in the earlier section on risk assessment. In those cases also risk assessments owed much to personal reactions to the person being assessed, and little to objective indicators of risk.

The PCL-R psychopathy assessment was also considered in an earlier section, and its use in risk assessment questioned. Nugent and Zamble assessed their offenders using the PCL-R, and found something very interesting. The PCL-R produces two scales, called Factor 1 and Factor 2. Factor 1 is supposed to be based on the core personality characteristics of the psychopath: such things as manipulativeness, callousness, impulsiveness and so on. Factor 2 is based more on the offender's record of behaviour: such things as leading a parasitic lifestyle and having an extensive and varied criminal record. The two Factor scores are added together to produce the total PCL-R score, along with a couple of 'orphan' items which do not relate to either Factor. The same research that showed that many risk assessment items did not predict violence also showed that Factor 1 of the PCL-R did not predict it either. It was Factor 2 that was predictive, and this is also the factor that was judged to be more objectively scored and which demonstrates higher reliability (it depends significantly on counting items in someone's criminal record and assessors are unlikely to disagree on these counts). Factor 1 simply records aspects of an offender that are rated as unpleasant. However, Nugent and Zamble found that detained men had higher Factor 1 scores. In other words, detained men were judged high in risk and served months or years more in prison than others because they were personally less pleasant and *not* because they were more dangerous. In my own research on parole I found something very similar, and again it was having a high score on Factor 1 that was associated with being refused parole, rather than any genuine indicator of risk.[16] Small wonder that Nugent and Zamble concluded:

> It is easy to understand how detained offenders have been unsuccessful in endearing themselves to staff and associates within the correctional system. It is important to recognise that decisions based on personal reactions may not provide better protection to the public.[17]

If anything this is an understatement, but perhaps the main point is that the professionals involved in taking these decisions were prone to a bias that affects all of us. They took harsh decisions, not because of genuine evidence that the people in front of them were dangerous, but because they *seemed* like most people's stereotype of a dangerous person. This stereotype is wrong. It is even more wrong when, as we saw earlier, it allows more psychopathic but charming individuals to talk their way into release in preference to those who are less attractive but less dangerous.

---

16   See Forde (2014), Chapter 3.

17   See Nugent and Zamble (2001), p.29.

FRAMING AND RARE EVENTS

One of the findings of psychological research into financial decision-making is that losses and gains are not treated equally. According to the classic Bernoullian formulation of risk, which held sway in economics for hundreds of years, there should be no difference. Risks that are mathematically equal should be equally attractive or unattractive. In fact, it is now well established that losses have a greater emotional impact than gains, even if the two are financially equivalent.[18] People are less willing to bet a sum of money when told there is a 10 per cent chance of losing than they are when told there is a 90 per cent chance of winning, even though the two risks are identical. This does not only apply to laboratory betting experiments, and not only to financial decisions. When groups of highly qualified surgeons were asked whether they would prescribe a risky treatment for a seriously ill patient, they were more willing to do so when told that 90 per cent of patients survived the treatment than they were when told that 10 per cent did not.[19] The difference was substantial: 84 per cent were willing to prescribe in the first group and only 50 per cent in the second. Clearly, not everyone was affected by this bias, but a substantial number certainly were. Yet the two statements about survival are logically identical. The difference is that it is more scary to talk about 10 per cent of patients dying than it is to talk about 90 per cent of patients surviving. Again, the work summarised by Kahneman has shown that the emotional vividness of a possible outcome influences decision-makers more than the actual probability that it will occur.

In a forensic context, a similar experiment was carried out with forensic psychologists and psychiatrists who were given reports on a supposed psychiatric patient with a history

---

18   See Kahneman (2011), Part IV.

19   See McNeil *et al.* (1982).

of violence.[20] These included an expert evaluation of risk. In a similar way to the surgeons, they were presented with two statements about the violence risk that the patient might pose. One group was told that, within a given time period, patients like the one in question had a 10 per cent probability of committing an act of violence. Another group was told that out of every hundred patients similar to this man, 10 were likely to commit an act of violence in the same time period. Again, these two statements are exactly equivalent, if you are thinking logically. However, 41 per cent of the professionals who saw the second statement recommended against discharge, and only 21 per cent of those who saw the first. In other words, the way in which the statement was formatted seriously affected the decision adopted by these experienced forensic professionals.

This formatting or 'framing' of statements has been shown to have a major impact on decision-making in a variety of fields. Clearly, in the context of forensic decisions the last example is particularly relevant to the subject matter of this book. UK parole panels are regularly given statements about risk which have been derived from statistical risk assessment instruments, particularly the Risk Matrix 2000. The sex offender version places scores into four categories indicating the risk of reconviction for a similar offence. The four categories are: Low, Medium, High and Very High. The 'Low Risk' category represents a 3 per cent risk of reconviction within five years. Probably most people would agree that a 97 per cent chance of *not* reconviction did indeed represent low risk. However, the 'High Risk' category represents a 26 per cent risk of reconviction within five years. To put it another way, 74 per cent of people in this category will *not* reconvict, virtually three-quarters. Is it really reasonable to say that one in four represents a high risk? And is it reasonable to use an emotive label in considering something about which

---

20   See Slovic, Monaghan and MacGregor (2000).

emotions run deep to begin with, when we now know that framing the risk statement in this way can affect important decisions taken about the offender? Incidentally, the 'Very High' category represents a 50 per cent chance of reconviction within five years. Most gamblers would call that 'evens': men in this group are as likely to stay conviction free as not.

If framing can have such an important influence on how we react to information, it may be that we should reconsider how we present it. For example, what might the effect be of relabelling the Risk Matrix 2000 categories as Evens, Low Risk, Very Low Risk and Extremely Low Risk? If that seems too radical, what about relabelling them as A, B, C and D? The fact is that we do not know what effect this might have without conducting experiments to discover that. However, in the past the issue has been totally neglected on the implicit assumption that it makes no difference. It does.

CONVINCING NARRATIVE

Human beings are great story makers. In essence, this is the fundamental problem with human judgement. We are constantly scanning our environment for information, and creating for ourselves a convincing narrative of how it all fits together. As mentioned before the whole process is rather like one of those 'join the dots' puzzles, in which we draw lines from one dot to the next and gradually a line drawing emerges to make sense of the apparent random group of dots. There are two errors identified by Kahneman which affect this convincing narrative: the illusion of validity and the illusion of understanding.

The illusion of validity refers to our belief that many processes are systematic and controllable when in fact they are not. One example of this is investment in the stock market. A wealth of research has demonstrated that this process is not systematic and it is not based on genuine knowledge and understanding of how investment works. Indeed, investment does not work in any normal sense of the word. It is a game of chance. Nonetheless, economists and investors who understand all of this perfectly well still maintain a belief that they can do better than chance when it comes to making a profit from their investments.[21] This belief is an illusion, if not actually a delusion. The same illusion seems to govern our decisions about offenders. For example, it is widely believed by professionals employed in the offending behaviour industry that they can assess certain failings or deficits in individuals and prescribe a treatment programme that will tend to reduce those deficits. The objective evidence for this is currently zero. Nonetheless, while people cling to this illusion the industry continues to flourish, just like the investment management industry. Equally, we cling to an illusion that we can improve upon a statistical predictor of risk by augmenting or overriding it with professional judgement, again just like the investment management industry. There is no evidence for this either. Indeed, there is clear evidence that these adjustments make prediction worse. The problem seems to be that risk assessment is not very good and so we constantly strive to make it better. Even though we are fooling ourselves, we tolerate such fallacious concepts as 'clinical override' because it gives us the intuitive feeling that we are doing better than the statistics. This leads on to another illusion, the illusion of understanding.

The illusion of understanding is particularly important in clinical or quasi-clinical situations. Clearly, if we understand the processes going on in a person we should be able to predict their outcomes. Therefore, if we have a clear understanding of why someone committed his offence, we should be able to tell whether he is likely to repeat it. This kind of thinking is exceptionally important in sentencing, and in parole decisions. Now, as we have seen, statistical risk assessments may not be terribly good,

---

21   See Kahneman (2011), Chapter 20.

but in practice they are better than any of the alternatives. In other words, if a parole panel wants to have the best chance of paroling people successfully, it should use a statistical predictor. However, this is something they rarely if ever do, and their performance appears to be roughly what one would expect if they took decisions by tossing a coin. Interestingly, when I put this to members of the Parole Board for England and Wales, their only suggestion for improvement was that parole panels needed yet more information about the offender if they were to take better decisions. But parole panels already receive *hundreds of pages* of information about parole applicants, and there is no reason to think that hundreds more will help. Anyway, most of it is irrelevant to the task in hand. The problem is not that parole authorities fail to create convincing narratives for themselves about offenders and their behaviour. The problem is that these narratives do not help. The illusion of understanding is thinking that they will.

CONFIRMATION BIAS AND HALO EFFECTS

Mention has already been made of confirmation bias. I return to it here because it is probably obvious now why it occurs: it helps to make our narrative, or illusion of understanding, more complete. But seeking confirmation of our ideas is no way to test them. After all, many deep-seated beliefs which were held firmly by many people over the years have turned out to be false. Some of these seem laughable to us now, like the belief that the world is flat, or the belief that heavenly bodies are mounted on spheres of invisible crystal which revolve around the Earth. It is easy to laugh at these things, which probably appeared very sensible in their day, but seemingly more rational scientific beliefs have been strongly held, although they also turned out to be erroneous. For example, it used to be thought that diseases were caused by air which was in some way polluted.

Indeed, 'malaria' actually means 'bad air', a reference to the fact that malaria was more common in marshy regions. This fact tended to confirm the idea that swamps and marshes somehow gave off contaminated vapours which caused the disease, a bias which tended to confirm the 'bad air' hypothesis. Nowadays, we know this is because it is transmitted by the malarial mosquito, which is also more commonly found in marshy regions.

In conducting assessments of individuals it is very tempting to fall into the error of confirmation bias, and there are usually plenty of opportunities. For example, suppose that we are examining someone who has been described as a psychopath. One of the characteristics of psychopaths is that they are famously lacking in empathy for others. Indeed, their emotions in general are described as blunted or numbed. They often exhibit very little emotional warmth, even when expressing sympathy for someone. It is as if they know the right words, but not the right way to say them. Items describing these characteristics are included on the PCL-R psychopathy assessment, and I have seen many assessments in which these characteristics are listed as evidence of psychopathy. However, they are not the only characteristics to result in reduced emotional expression. Unlike most forensic psychologists, I have experience of dealing with people suffering from the aftermath of traumatic experiences. One of the classic symptoms of post-traumatic stress disorder is 'emotional numbing', which often appears very similar to the lack of emotional expression seen in psychopaths. The assessor who is too tightly focused on the criminal aspects of an individual may assume that this is evidence of psychopathy, when in fact there is clear evidence of trauma in the person's past. I have seen many examples of this.

A somewhat related flaw in assessment is the 'halo effect'. This has been well known in psychology for many decades. What it means is that an opinion formed of someone at an early stage in assessment influences one's interpretation of information received later. In particular, forming an especially positive view of someone may cause an assessor to interpret later information rather more favourably than it ought to be interpreted. Of course, if an especially negative view has been formed the opposite will occur! It would be nice to think that professionals were immune from this effect, but this is not the case. We have known for decades that clinical judgement was unreliable and difficult to improve. Furthermore, there is little evidence that experience or training make clinical judgement any better. Neither does more information improve judgement (in spite of the views of parole board members), although it has been found to increase clinicians' confidence in their own judgement.[22] None of this is new (some of it dates back as far as the 1960s), but it has been largely ignored, probably because there is no obvious alternative to clinical judgement. As I hope to show later, alternatives are available, at least for forensic psychologists.

Both confirmation bias and halo effects may help to account for something called 'outcome bias'. This is the tendency to remember our predictions as being more accurate than they were. For example, it is common for people to say that they 'knew' in advance that an economic recession was going to occur, or that a child was going to be troublesome in later life, or that a certain marriage was going to fail. An example from my own prison experience may illustrate this. I wrote a report on a long-term prisoner, suggesting that he would be safe to be moved from a high security setting to an open prison. He was keen to follow a course of study which he would only be able to do if he could attend college on a daily basis. One of the prison governors took issue with me, saying that the prisoner would abscond once he got the chance. I replied that I thought absconding was extremely unlikely as I knew the man was keen to follow the college course. I predicted that if he got into trouble

---

22   This work has been summarised in one of the classic works on violence risk assessment (Quinsey *et al.* 2006).

at all it would be over women: he seemed to have a weakness for them, and they for him.

Unfortunately, some time after transfer to open conditions the prisoner was found to be having an affair with the wife of a prison officer. That was the end of his college attendance, and he was returned to closed prison. The governor claimed with some amusement that he had been right and I had been wrong. However, I had to point out that he had not predicted what had happened; he had predicted that the prisoner would run away, and this he had not done. I have no doubt that the story was retold in a way that reflected badly on the predictive powers of psychologists as compared with those of prison governors, but if so it was really a question of selective memory.

STATISTICAL EFFECTS: BIASED BY EXTREMES

Before leaving the subject of heuristics and biases and how they mislead us, I would like to mention some purely statistical effects which often cause us to misjudge events. One of these is the law of small numbers. Essentially, what this means is that we are prone to inferring generalisations from numbers that are too small to support them. People can make up quite complex theories on the basis of such unreliable information. Kahneman gives an example of kidney cancer statistics in the United States.[23] When told that the lowest rates of kidney cancer have been found in rural counties of the United States, people tend to suggest an explanation in terms of clean living, clean air and natural fresh foods without industrial additives. However, when told that the highest rates of kidney cancer have been found in rural counties, they tend to explain this in terms of issues like poverty, poor medical cover, and too much drinking

---

23   See Kahneman (2011), Chapter 10.

and smoking. Obviously the rural lifestyle cannot explain both rates. In fact, both statistics are true: both the highest *and* the lowest rates are found in rural counties, but this has nothing to do with lifestyle. It is to do with the fact that they are sparsely populated. Extreme or 'fluke' statistical findings are commonly found in small samples of data. However, as Kahneman's example shows, this does not stop people from generating wholly invalid narratives about the statistics. In forensic settings, such over-interpretation of too little information is rife. This is an additional reason for some people's enthusiasm for offending behaviour programmes. In many cases the samples have been small, but they have been published because people liked the results. This is the origin of the 'bound for publication' bias. It occurs in a slightly different form when we examine the events of a single person's life and try to draw dramatic conclusions from them. The truth is that we have no idea how the person might have behaved if the events had been different, and without that we have no idea how significant they are. In short, we may *think* we know why people behaved as they did, but we will never be able to test out our hypotheses about them.

Another statistical effect is known as 'regression towards the mean'. It is a cumbersome term, but it basically means that extreme events are usually followed by less extreme ones. Most events are close to the mean (average), and when unusual circumstances occur which give rise to an extreme event they are not normally maintained for long, and neither is the extreme event which they have caused. Regression towards the mean occurs across a wide variety of events, and is found in meteorology, genetics, psychology and almost every other field of science. It also occurs in the lives of individuals. Very few people lead totally humdrum lives in which nothing out of the ordinary ever happens. Much more commonly, we go through a relatively narrow range of events, better and worse, with extreme ones cropping up in response to unpredictable circumstances.

Some of these might be: losing one's job because of an economic recession, losing one's spouse or partner through illness or accident, or winning the lottery. None of these could be predicted, but they are likely to be isolated extreme events.

Fortunately, it is unusual that a person will experience a whole series of job losses, and sadly a run of lottery wins is pretty unlikely. If a run of extremely good or bad events does occur, we tend to attribute this (correctly) to chance. If just one or two extreme events occur we often try to explain them 'rationally', but it is usually just chance all the same. In forensic settings there is a tendency to attribute too much meaning to everything a person has ever done. Parole panels appear to be seriously worried by cases in which a person with an otherwise unblemished (or at least only slightly blemished) record has committed a serious act of violence. The truth is that this has usually occurred in response to extreme events, and the principle of regression towards the mean indicates that it is not likely to be repeated. Nonetheless, because parole panels find isolated events very difficult to explain to their satisfaction (they can't create a narrative around them) prisoners in this position often find it difficult to obtain parole. The fact is that an act that is out of character is *by definition* an extreme event and not likely to be repeated. Such individuals pose a low risk, but parole panels seem to prefer those with very wild pasts who can show a gradual and steady improvement throughout their sentences.

We seem to have a great deal of difficulty in coping with simple statistical effects like this. We have trouble accepting that much of what happens in the world is just random fluctuation.[24] Or, as Kahneman puts it, 'Our comforting conviction that the world makes sense rests on a secure foundation: our almost unlimited ability to ignore our ignorance.'[25]

---

24 For a great discussion of this whole subject, see Mlodinow (2009). No maths qualifications required.

25 See Kahneman (2011), p.201.

ARE WE HARDWIRED FOR POOR JUDGEMENT?

It's all very well talking about instant decisions being made on one basis and then rational arguments being made to justify them on another basis afterwards. But all behaviour depends upon brain functioning. Is there any evidence that the brain functions in the way that I have described? For example, is there evidence that information from the senses goes to parts of the brain concerned with emotional functioning before it arrives in the 'higher' centres concerned with reasoning? In the 1950s it was widely believed that this was the case, but very little was known about the functioning of different parts of the brain at that time. Most of the professional opinion about this was derived from psychoanalytic thinking, according to which a great deal of mental life took place at a level of which we were not conscious. But this idea was based on a particular view of the mind, rather than the brain.

UNCONSCIOUS PROCESSES

A clear example of an unconscious process was said to be 'perceptual defence'. Experiments were conducted using various words which were presented in a tachistoscope. This is a machine in which cards with words or designs on them can be presented to people for specified lengths of time, ranging from a few thousandths of a second upwards. It was soon found that some words were not reported by participants until they had been presented for much longer periods of time than others. In particular, it was found that some so-called 'taboo' words, such as obscenities or sexual words, were apparently not perceived by the participants until the time period was quite long: in the jargon, there was a higher threshold for these words. A theory was developed according to which the use of these taboo words had been heavily discouraged in childhood, and consequently aroused feelings of guilt when they were presented to participants.[1] In order to avoid this, the threshold was raised so that the observer didn't have to acknowledge these naughty words.

Unfortunately, this was too simple an interpretation. A group of researchers including Leo Postman, one of those who had conducted some of the early experiments, later published a retraction.[2] They pointed out that the participants in these experiments (usually psychology students) were required to actually speak the words once they had observed them. Professor Bruner, a senior academic in the department, and his young female assistant were conducting the experiment. Postman suggested, not unreasonably, that the (predominantly male) students would be very unwilling to voice the socially unacceptable words they had seen until they were absolutely certain that they were not making a mistake. Neutral words would not pose this problem, and could happily be uttered as soon as they were identified. A mistake with them would not matter, but mistaking an everyday word for an obscenity might make the student look rather peculiar. This suggested that what

---

1   See McGinnies (1949).

2   See Postman, Bronson and Gropper (1953).

the experiments really demonstrated was an unwillingness to appear dirty-minded.[3]

The design of most of the experiments meant that shyness about speaking taboo words was at least a partial explanation. But back in the late 1960s a fellow student of mine, Mike Heap, developed another method of testing the idea of perceptual defence. He showed people five-letter neutral words in a tachistoscope, and these were the only words that people actually had to speak. However, in between the five letters were the four letters of another word presented in a smaller size and in a different colour, so that the two words had clearly different characteristics. Some of the four-letter words were neutral, and some of them were four-letter words in the colloquial sense of not being fit for polite company. What Heap found was that when the four-letter word was neutral the observer's perceptual threshold was not raised, but when it was a taboo word the threshold went up, just as the perceptual defence hypothesis predicted. However, before rushing off to announce that Freud was right all along, we need to consider another possibility. It might simply be that, if a taboo word aroused emotions, these emotions might simply disrupt perception. It might not be a defence at all. Again, what evidence is there that the brain can in some sense recognise a word and react to it emotionally, before it is consciously recognised?

A (VERY) BRIEF ACCOUNT OF THE HARDWARE

As it turns out, studies of brain functioning since the 1960s have come a long way.[4] One of the things we now know is

---

3   There were other factors, including how familiar participants were with the words in question, how common they were generally and how well prepared they were to expect taboo words.

4   See Beech (2016).

that, when information is transmitted from sense organs (such as the eyes) to the brain, the information does not simply go to one place. It goes to several. For example, neural impulses coming from the eyes go to the occipital cortex at the rear of the brain. They also go to the cerebral cortex on the outer surface of the brain, where most rational and conscious thinking takes place. More importantly, another set of impulses branches off to the amygdala, which was mentioned earlier. The amygdala is situated at the base of the brain, and one of the things it does is to control many functions associated with fear, and the direction of attention towards incoming information. The amygdala decides whether something is a threat, and therefore whether some sort of defensive reaction should be prepared. It does this extremely quickly, and we are not aware of it. Impulses from the eyes travel to the amygdala roughly 40 times faster than they do to the cerebral cortex. Indeed, incoming impulses go to the amygdala, are processed, and the result transmitted onward to the cerebral cortex before any impulse has reached the cerebral cortex by the direct route. To put it another way, much of the emotional processing of the incoming information has been done before the observer is even aware that there is anything to be processed. The result of that processing will determine much of what the observer decides to do about it when it does reach awareness. Coincidentally, this may provide an explanation for much criminal behaviour, especially since we know that many chronically violent individuals tend to over-identify situations as being threatening when they are not. Much of their violence may be seen by the offenders themselves as defensive.

These neurobiological studies do not only have a value in explaining criminal behaviour, but also flaws in judgement. What these studies show quite clearly is that when we are making judgements about incoming information we have already formulated an emotional reaction to it before we become consciously aware of it. This is what researchers like

Kahneman mean when they refer to the brain being 'hardwired' to use faulty heuristic methods for making judgements. It is also why they think that it is impossible to train people out of these habits. Strictly speaking, they are not habits at all, which implies that other habits could be learned to replace them; they are simply the way the brain works. It follows from this that 'experts' are no different from any other human beings in the way that they make judgements. Much of the research which I have quoted supports this view. This does not mean that they know nothing about their subject. It simply means that their technical knowledge is better than that of other people, but that they may do no better than anyone else when asked for an 'off-the-cuff' opinion. When judging people's ability, for example, there is a world of difference between testing their ability using a wide variety of reliable and well-validated tests, and simply making a judgement based on how they look or behave in a short interview.

It may be remembered that psychopaths were found to be much more effective than other prisoners at talking their way into parole.[5] This makes sense if parole boards are making a judgement that is heavily influenced by their initial impression of someone. Psychopaths are notoriously good at presenting themselves favourably, and using this to manipulate others; we should therefore expect that they would impress parole boards with their apparent sincerity. But once this initial impression has been formed in the amygdala, it will colour the thinking of parole board members as it moves to their cerebral cortices.[6] Research showing that parole boards are more likely to decide in favour of prisoners if they actually attend the hearing also supports this

---

5   See Porter *et al.* (2009).

6   Any neurobiologist reading this will probably cringe at the oversimplification. But please bear with me: this is not a neurobiology textbook. It is the general principle that is important, rather than explaining the process in technical detail.

view.[7] Again, I have cited research showing that people's ratings of offenders on risk assessment schedules were influenced by their prior emotional reaction to them.[8] Other research has shown that similar assessments are influenced by whether the assessor is working for the prosecution or the defence in a trial.[9] The implication is that their initial impression is influenced by their awareness that they are being hired by one side or the other. Research has also found that there is greater variation between assessors on those items of risk assessment schedules that are less dependent on objective information.[10] It has even been found that parole assessments are influenced more by those items of risk assessment schedules that relate to the parole applicants' current presentation, although these are less useful as predictors.[11] I would suggest that these findings are all compatible with the neurobiological findings I have outlined, and consequently that psychologists' judgements are strongly influenced by initial emotional impressions which we then use our higher reasoning centres to rationalise. These findings are *not* compatible with the view that we make these judgements scientifically and rationally. Nor is there any indication that experience or qualifications do anything to improve this judgement process. The implications for the practice of psychology are profound and far-reaching.

DENIAL IN PROFESSIONALS

Why do practitioners appear to avoid using the most rigorous methods to evaluate treatments and risk assessment methods?

---

7   See Morgan and Smith (2005b).

8   See Dernevik (2004).

9   See Murrie *et al.* (2009) and Murrie *et al.* (2013).

10   See Rufino *et al.* (2011).

11   See Forde (2014), Chapter 3, and Guy *et al.* (2015).

Are they really afraid to know the truth? There cannot be a definitive answer to this question. All one can say with certainty is that there are a great many practitioners who seem overeager to accept very poor evidence in favour of the programmes that they run. This is evidence which their professional training should tell them is inadequate, and whose inadequacy would be quite apparent to them if it were presented in favour of some rival school of thought. Likewise, the same people seem overeager to dismiss the very high-quality research methods that have been proven time and again to deliver the truth about treatment effectiveness. I refuse to speculate on the size of these people's amygdalae, but it is very clear that for many of them good quality evidence is threatening. When people are faced with a threat, they defend themselves. This is only human, and perhaps forgivable.

It is not, I suggest, so easily forgivable in psychologists whose decisions grossly affect the lives of other people, as they often do in the criminal justice system. This would be true even if cognitive-behavioural programmes were only neutral: in that case the worst that could be said is that they were a waste of money. However, when it is possible that some of these programmes may actually *increase* risk in those who undergo them we are talking about something much worse than wasted money. I mentioned earlier Professor Hagen's description of treatment programmes as a 'scam', but disagreed with her on the basis that this implies conscious deceit. *Unconscious* deception is another matter, particularly self-deception, but the effects can be just as damaging. This phenomenon, known as 'denial' in the psychoanalytic tradition, is often applied to offenders by criminal justice professionals, but anyone can be in denial if they are strongly motivated enough not to accept the truth.[12] The fact is that we know how to evaluate treatment strictly,

---

12   See Ariely (2012).

but those in favour of cognitive-behavioural programmes shy away from using strict standards. More than that, some of them even question whether the strict standards are the right way to approach the subject at all. There are tell-tale signs that indicate when people are in a state of denial. In this context, a preference for weak standards whose results are preferable is a bit of a giveaway.

Denial is not the sole province of offenders. It can happen to everyone, even psychologists.

– 12 –

THE FUTURE OF FORENSIC (AND MAYBE OTHER) PSYCHOLOGY

Back in 2005 I attended a presentation for psychologists who were supervising a trainee, as I was doing at the time. The presentation was given by the then Chief Supervisor for the training route being run by the British Psychological Society, Professor Brian Thomas-Peter. If that name sounds familiar, it may be because he was mentioned earlier as co-author of an article which concluded that the PCL-R psychopathy assessment was not fit for clinical use.[1] This might suggest that he was not afraid of speaking his mind, and so it proved. Amongst other things, his presentation outlined the changes in criminal justice policy in the Western world over the previous few years. These had resulted in increased sentence lengths, harsher penalties, and a totally unjustified optimism about treatment interventions and risk assessment. This has mainly been at the prompting of politicians rather than because of any improvement in the science. Professor Thomas-Peter described a 'nightmare scenario' which he feared we might be approaching. This would result in a whole generation of UK forensic psychologists:

- who no longer think for themselves, but who allow others to think for them

---

1   See Thomas-Peter and Jones (2006).

- whose training does not achieve the competence to derive a sophisticated, unique psychological solution to a complex psychological problem

- who provide 'treatment by numbers', following an 'accredited' process from which they dare not deviate and which they cannot question

- who write 'fill in the blank' reports, having used 'join the dots' assessments that they do not fully understand and which typically do not influence the nature of intervention.[2]

In my opinion this 'nightmare scenario' has now come to pass. Professor Thomas-Peter's description gives a pretty accurate picture of current practice in forensic psychology in the UK and, as far as I can ascertain, throughout the Western world.

In this book I have tried to give an explanation of how we got here. There remains the question of how we move on towards genuinely effective practice. In trying to answer that I want to return to the model of psychological practice that was outlined in Chapter 2, which listed the processes of assessment, formulation, intervention, evaluation and research, and communication. I will also suggest ways in which this model could be strengthened, and how regulation of the profession could be improved, and will add some comments on mental health problems in the criminal justice system.

---

2   The bullet points are adapted with permission from slides used in the original public presentation. Although this was not published, Professor Thomas-Peter has discussed similar concerns elsewhere in published form (Thomas-Peter 2006, 2015).

ASSESSMENT

One point which has been returned to in different ways throughout this book is that psychologists are human beings. Human beings' personal judgement is subject to a great many flaws and biases which psychologists themselves have researched extensively. It follows that the personal judgement of psychologists is also subject to a great many flaws and biases. Many psychologists will argue that they do not use personal judgement in their professional work. They will refer to 'professional' judgement, and especially to 'clinical' judgement, implying that this is somehow different and superior. This argument is not new; Paul Meehl described arguments in similar terms well over half a century ago.[3] As he pointed out, if clinical judgement is based on a clinician's experience of a lot of cases, then it is really only a statistical judgement in disguise: the judgement is being made on the basis of what these previous cases have shown. However, given what we know about the fallibility of human memory, it is not likely even in principle to be better than an explicitly statistical judgement. He went on to demonstrate that it was not only unlikely but in fact had been found to be untrue even at that time. Since then, his view has been substantiated by scientific research many times over.

This research inevitably undermines the validity of clinical assessment. It may be recalled that a valid assessment is one that measures what it is supposed to measure. In fact, clinical judgement is rarely a measurement at all, in the sense that it doesn't produce a number on any scale. It is mostly expressed in phrases like 'I feel that…', 'It seems that…', or 'In my opinion…'. That's fine if we are talking about the weather, but not if we are talking about whether or not someone is going to commit a violent crime, or whether a particular treatment programme will reduce the risk of this. It may also be recalled that an

---

3   See Meehl (1954), especially Chapter 7, 'Remarks on Clinical Intuition'.

assessment is *reliable* if it consistently measures the *same* thing. Unfortunately, scientific research has demonstrated that expert opinion is very unreliable, a finding that has been replicated across a variety of fields including psychology.[4] To make that absolutely clear: experts in a variety of fields are prone to drawing different conclusions when they are presented with the same information on different occasions. Not every time, but in a significant proportion of cases.

Before leaving this topic, I should address an objection that is often made. Psychologists, we are often told, are highly trained and experienced. This gives them an ability to make judgements about people's risk or treatment needs which the rest of us don't have. (Actually, that's the rest of *you*, as I'm a psychologist too.) The trouble with this objection is that it is simply not true, for two main reasons. First, many of the people making these judgements are not in fact highly trained and experienced. As described earlier in this book, many forensic psychologists carrying out assessments and running treatment programmes have trainee status, and many of them never carry on to qualify. They leave to do other things. Because they have a high level of ability, there are many other things that they can choose to do; this is not in any way a criticism of these trainees as *people*. They are not stupid, and they are not acting in bad faith. However, to claim high-level professional skills for them on the basis of extensive training and experience which they have not yet gained is clearly nonsensical.

Second, there is little evidence that highly trained and qualified psychologists make any better predictions. Indeed, there is considerable evidence that they do not. This has been extensively researched, and it turns out that professionals of all levels of training and experience predict about as well as lay people.[5] Furthermore, it appears that people – even those who are

---

4   See Kahneman (2011), especially Chapter 21, 'Intuitions vs. Formulas'.

5   See Quinsey *et al.* (2006), Chapter 4, 'Clinical Judgement'.

highly expert in their field – are prone to claiming knowledge of topics that do not even exist. In experiments, when professionals were given a list of topics (some of which were fictitious), many claimed that they knew all about them.[6] Significantly, they were more likely to do this the more confidence they expressed in their professional knowledge. Those who were less sure of themselves were less likely to 'overclaim', as this phenomenon is called. This ought to worry forensic psychologists, as we know that witnesses, including expert witnesses, who are highly confident in court are also judged to be more believable.[7] Whilst these experiments did not involve psychologists, but experts in several other areas, there is no reason to suppose that psychologists are any more immune to this effect than they have proved to be to the other errors in judgement that have previously been described.

None of this means that psychologists, or other experts, are unable to carry out or evaluate research. Nor does it mean that they are unable to practise technical skills which they have learned. However, it does mean that as they drift away from these technical skills into areas in which personal judgement plays a larger part, their accuracy falls off rapidly. Therefore, I would suggest that in the criminal justice field we need to make the following improvements:

- *We should stop basing risk assessment partly or wholly on 'clinical' (subjective) methods which are of proven ineffectiveness.* The truth is that psychologists know comparatively little about risk. Insurance companies, on the other hand, know a great deal about it, and would probably be perfectly capable of developing actuarial risk assessments whose accuracy would far outstrip anything

---

6   See Atir, Rosenzweig and Dunning (2015).

7   See Benforado (2015), especially Chapter 6, 'The Corruption of Memory – The Eyewitness', and Chapter 7, 'How to Tell a Lie – The Expert'.

produced by psychologists. If ever there was a case for 'contracting out' services, this is probably it.

- *Assessment methods should be based on techniques whose reliability and predictive accuracy have been demonstrated through high-quality scientific research.* If no such method exists for a particular task (whether it involves treatment or parole decisions), psychologists should ask for it to be developed, rather than using something that they know to predict only at the chance level.

- *Decisions about treatments/interventions should likewise be taken on the basis of proven methods.* That is, it should be possible to show that the measured characteristics of the offender or client in question relate in a predictable way to the outcomes of the proposed treatment/intervention. If this is not the case, we simply cannot say whether the intervention has been effective or not. If the assessment shows that a person is not suited to the intervention, it should not be possible for a treatment manager to override this decision. 'Clinical override' is *always* wrong.

- *We should stop using risk assessment instruments with groups for which they were not designed.* As we have seen, assessment techniques developed on one group of people may not be applicable to a different one. This may mean a different gender, a different ethnic group, a different age group, or a different offence or sentence type, amongst a range of possibilities.

- *Psychologists should never be afraid to say 'I don't know'. If that is the truthful answer, all other answers are misleading.*

FORMULATION

In most fields of human activity we are aware that human beings vary considerably, and for this reason may not all respond to something in the same way. For example, we assume that children differ considerably and will not all benefit from the same educational programmes. Criminal justice systems claim to recognise this principle, but largely do not. In most jurisdictions it is now assumed that the identification of a 'criminological need' leads inexorably to the programme that is intended to address that need. A concession is sometimes made for intelligence, and special programmes may be developed for those with low IQs (80 or under in the UK), but people differ in many other ways than IQ. The idea that one form of 'therapy' is going to suit everyone is not accepted in any other field, so why should it be accepted in the criminal justice system?

As an example, consider the case of a life sentence prisoner I worked with some years ago. He had been the victim of sexual abuse when in a children's home, and again when in prison later on. Indeed, he received his life sentence for killing the abuser. The abuse that he suffered in the children's home had left him very confused about his sexuality, and in his late teens he had committed two indecent assaults against younger boys. Thereafter, he had committed no further sexual assaults and had settled happily into a typical heterosexual life and married successfully. However, when he was convicted of the murder it was decided that he should undergo the SOTP (sex offender treatment programme). This was despite the fact that there had been no sexual offending in his record for more than 20 years, and that even the prison psychologists who dealt with him were satisfied that he posed no risk of further sexual offending. He was not keen to take part, but he wanted to show that he was prepared to comply with the demands the authorities made of him, and undertook the programme. Unfortunately, since it is policy that different types of offender should be mixed on these programmes, he found himself in a group of men some of whom had a record of sexually abusing children. During the proceedings he was required to give extensive details of his own experience of being abused, and was convinced that some of the child sex offenders were pressing him for details because they were becoming sexually aroused by them.

He found this deeply upsetting, and began to re-experience symptoms of trauma which had been dormant since the abuse he had suffered originally. That was not the end of it. By the time I became involved in his case he was being pressed to undergo a further and more advanced sex offender treatment programme, 'to help him address his previous experience of being abused'. The fact that he had been judged to pose no risk of sexual offending, and the fact that the SOTP programme group is most emphatically *not* therapy for abuse victims were apparently irrelevant. After his previous re-traumatising experience he was desperate not to have to undertake this, declaring tearfully that he would rather do an extra five years in prison. In my own report I argued strongly that the treatment recommendation was inappropriate, and the Parole Board must have agreed with this opinion as they sent him to open prison.[8] It remains a mystery why anyone, let alone a psychologist, could imagine that a treatment was appropriate for someone who did not exhibit the risk that it was supposed to reduce. This is even before one considers the trauma element in his case. The treatment recommendation had clearly been made on a more or less automatic basis: he has X kind of offence in his record, so he must do X kind of programme, however unsuitable it may be. Clearly, there is no sense in this (unless the staff concerned were desperate to get more people on their programmes).

---

8   This resulted in another misconduct complaint against me, which also failed.

Obviously not all cases will have individual factors as extreme as this. However, people differ in many ways; sociability, social anxiety, verbal ability, guilt, and many other things may affect their suitability for programmes that are conducted in groups. Occasionally, where resources permit, UK prisoners may receive something that is mysteriously referred to as 'one-to-one work'. In this context, it is not at all clear what 'work' actually means. From reports that I have seen it varies, although it is generally intended to have a 'cognitive-behavioural' character. There is no scientific evidence that any of this achieves anything, because (according to my Ministry of Justice colleagues) such 'work' has never been subjected to any kind of evaluation, and there are no plans to evaluate it. Since much of it seems directed towards developing 'insight', and our assessments of this quality do not relate to subsequent risk, it would be surprising if it made any difference. One thing that may be said for it is that it at least tries to treat people as individual human beings, rather than as clusters of 'criminogenic needs'.

It seems to me that forensic psychological formulation could be improved in the following ways:

- *We should stop making detailed formulations of how people came to commit their crimes.* Useful formulation depends upon reliable and valid assessment, and much forensic assessment currently has poor reliability and validity. This applies both to risk assessment and to the assessment of alleged treatment needs.

- *We should stop treating alleged criminogenic needs as if they existed in isolation from everything else.* Human beings are complex and have many different characteristics which interact with each other. Altering one will probably have consequences elsewhere. It is not possible to separate criminogenic needs from all other needs, and there is no real evidence that developing formulations about criminogenic needs has ever contributed significantly to reducing criminal risk. A human being is not like a car being put in the workshop to have one component fixed in order to make it roadworthy.

- *Formulation should always be provisional.* It is something that may need to be revised in the light of experience, including the individual's response to interventions. Formulations are sometimes wrong, but the present system leaves very little room to correct them if they are. This is even more likely if the system is resistant to external scrutiny, quality research and the expression of contrary views by professionals from within or without.

INTERVENTION

As I have demonstrated in earlier chapters, many of the existing interventions currently practised in the criminal justice systems of the UK and the rest of the Western world have little or no scientific support. The reasons for their continuation have been explained at some length: the influence of over-enthusiastic practitioners, political pressure to come up with answers, empire-building, career-building, etc. But perhaps above all, there has been a massive unwillingness to accept what the research clearly shows: that a very big mistake has been made. To be clear, I am not suggesting that these interventions should never have been tried. My own view is that they were never very promising, but it is easy to be wise after the event. The point is that no intervention of any kind should have been rolled out on a national basis until it had been clearly supported by scientific evidence in a properly conducted and fully evaluated trial scheme. Instead, the schemes have been rolled out across the prison and probation systems of the Western world on the basis of the flimsiest of evidence.[9] Only later have strict scientific evaluations been carried out, and instead of accepting the unpalatable conclusions, those with a vested interest have challenged not only the findings but even the methods by which they were obtained. This is despite the fact that these research methods have long been accepted as the only scientifically valid way to evaluate treatments, and have been standard in the medical field for decades.

Consider those plausible-sounding interventions which have been proven to be ineffective or even counter-productive – in particular the 'Scared Straight' programmes which have now been conclusively shown to be counter-productive. In this context, 'counter-productive' means people who had been through the scheme committed more crimes than would otherwise have been the case. Necessarily, this involves creating more victims. One may be grateful that the effects of the programmes have been identified by researchers. However, it is disquieting to note that even today similar programmes are still being advertised in the United States as helpful and effective. Once again, intuition about the effectiveness of interventions means more to people than the scientific evidence, of which they are often apparently unaware. In the absence of evidence, it is understandable that practitioners may be strongly influenced by their own experience, which wrongly appears to demonstrate effectiveness, as well as the fact that there is money to be made. Oh, and they may be influenced by profit, as these US programmes are not being offered free of charge.

---

9   Many of these programmes have their origins in a group of publications known collectively as the 'What Works' literature. However, as Professor Brian Thomas-Peter has pointed out, 'Somewhere during the 1990s the question mark was lost from the expression "what works?"' See Thomas-Peter (2006), p.33. The original expression was rather more tentative than the confident assertion of effectiveness which is now widely used.

To overcome these problems:

- *We should never develop interventions on the basis of intuition, personal opinion or our own subjective experience.* Proposed interventions should be based firmly on theory that is supported by scientific evidence. Psychology purports to be a science, and this is how science works.

- *Interventions should only be adopted after a trial programme in which they have been evaluated according to strict scientific criteria and found to be effective.* There should be no more rolling out of programmes on a national basis, with under-resourced scientific evaluation trying hopelessly to play catch-up.

- *Interventions should be conducted and evaluated on the basis that they may be more effective with some populations than others.* 'One size fits all' interventions should be avoided.

- *There should be studies of the interventions used in those few countries that reportedly have recidivism rates dramatically lower than those in the UK and the US.*[10] Both Norway and the Netherlands claim to have far lower recidivism rates, and imprison a much smaller percentage of their populations. There has been almost no effort to find out why this is.

INTERVENTIONS WORTH TRYING

One of the most pernicious aspects of the stranglehold that the cognitive-behavioural school of thought has on the field of offender treatment is the fact that it has blocked out consideration of anything else. There is virtually no form of

---

10   See Sterbenz (2014).

offending behaviour programme that is not based on (or at least claims to be based on) cognitive-behavioural principles. This is despite the fact that cognitive-behavioural therapy, from which these programmes are allegedly derived, was not intended for the alteration of complex habitual behaviour patterns. Rather, it was intended to deal with emotional problems, and was very much concerned with the way people interpret experiences that affect the way they look at the world. There is a great emphasis on encouraging people to test out their ideas to see if their perceptions are correct (often very difficult in prison, which is inherently an artificial environment). Given the fact that the evidence does not favour current offending behaviour programmes, and that some of them have been found to make some individuals worse, asking whether anything else might be tried seems extremely pertinent. Of course, 'anything else' covers a multitude of possibilities.

One clear lesson to be learned from the research is that many people in prisons are suffering from mental health problems, sometimes very serious ones.[11] Yet mental health care in prisons throughout the Western world is generally accepted as being substandard, despite the large number of such problems among offenders. These mental disorders are not always directly related to their offending, although recent evidence has linked depression with a substantially increased risk of violent offending.[12] However, it is known that many offenders with mental disorders have embarked upon illegal drug use as a means of 'self-medication' because they believe (rightly or wrongly) that these drugs help to alleviate their symptoms.[13] For many offenders, this leads on to committing offences in

---

11   See, amongst others, Abracen et al. (2014) for a study of Canadian parolees, Coid (2003) for a study of UK prisoners and Kingston et al. (2011) for a study of elderly UK prisoners.

12   See Fazel et al. (2015).

13   Several studies have shown this (Ruiz et al. 2012; Værøy 2011; Yee 2005).

order to sustain the drug use. Thus, the offending is an indirect consequence of their mental health problems. There is good evidence that diverting such prisoners into drug treatment rather than prison can alleviate their problems, and the risk that they pose, and save public money into the bargain.[14] It is not simple to calculate how much wasted effort and money could be saved by treating mental health problems in offenders, but it would certainly be substantial.

It was mentioned earlier that so-called 'operant conditioning' or behaviour modification techniques can be effective in changing behaviour, but that we do not usually have control of the 'reinforcers' which are necessary to strengthen more acceptable behaviour. However, there is an exception to this: if we are concerned with institutional behaviour then we usually have considerable control of the reinforcers. It is perfectly possible to create programmes in which acceptable institutional behaviour is encouraged. In some cases this may be directly beneficial (for example, where prisoners assault staff or otherwise make their jobs more difficult) but it could also indirectly benefit other rehabilitation efforts. A stable and calm environment is one in which prisoners are more likely to cooperate with rehabilitation efforts, and less likely to discourage other prisoners from doing so. In the early days of behaviourism so-called 'token economy regimes' were suggested. In these, prisoners or psychiatric patients could earn tokens for good behaviour which they could later spend in a shop run by the institution. I have seen this used to great effect in a long-stay psychiatric ward, but some inmates see this as a manipulative technique which treats them like children. It certainly does remind one of those infant school schemes which award gold stars or 'smiley face' stickers for good behaviour. More subtle behaviour modification schemes are possible. These may use verbal praise for good behaviour and

14   For example, Carey *et al.* (2006) and Anglin *et al.* (2013).

encourage the offender in the direction of earning something that he wants (extra visits, home leave, extra privileges, etc.) by stressing how his behaviour is helping him reach it.[15]

A more innovative approach to treatment is developing out of our increasing knowledge of how the brain works. In describing how we might be 'hardwired' for poor judgement I mentioned the amygdala, a structure in the brain which is particularly important in classifying situations as threatening (or not). It has been found that in individuals with a history of severe emotional trauma the amygdala is enlarged. Given the often abusive backgrounds from which many offenders come, it is probably not surprising that many of them also have enlarged amygdalae. However, one disadvantage of having an enlarged, and therefore highly active, amygdala is that one is too ready to interpret situations as threatening when in fact they are not. Treatments for this problem could include systematic relaxation training, meditation and mindfulness training. All of these have been shown to be helpful in mitigating some of the effects of an abused background. This is consistent with our modern neurobiological knowledge, according to which the brain is not fixed and immutable at birth, as used to be thought. Rather, it generates new brain cells as they are needed by its various different structures, and so the development of the brain through life reflects the life experience of the individual. Reversing these changes might not be easy, which might partly explain why changing criminal patterns of behaviour is also not easy. However, recognition that our behaviour reflects changes in brain development over the lifespan offers the possibility that 'treatment' could be adapted to the individual. Instead of the

---

15 A presentation on the use of this technique in 'approved premises' (probation hostel) was given at the 2016 Conference of the Forensic Division of the British Psychological Society (Newman 2016). Training in this system, called RAID®, is provided by a private company, but there is no 'off the shelf' offending behaviour package.

current vogue for 'one size fits all' treatments we could begin to think in terms of treatment for a particular set of structures in the brain.[16]

But treatment in any formal sense is not the only thing that may help. It has long been known that educational attainment is poor in prisoners, and many are illiterate. A recent report suggested that rates of illiteracy are three times what they are in the general population.[17] No one would suggest that education is an automatic barrier to further crime, but there is no doubt that for many offenders poor educational attainment has barred them from employment opportunities. Since work is the socially acceptable way of gaining money, it follows that barriers to work are also barriers to normal law-abiding living. More than that, many offenders have never achieved much by leading a conventional lifestyle, and education can give them the confidence to try to achieve it.

So what is the evidence that education may help offenders keep out of trouble in future? The short answer is that the evidence is mixed. As early as 1995 one American study concluded that education could have a big impact on recidivism rates and pleaded for prisoners' education grants, which were then being withdrawn, to be reinstated.[18] Another study conducted in three American states concluded that there was clear evidence for a significant reduction in both arrests and convictions following education in prison.[19] The reductions in recidivism which the study quoted (as high as 30% in some cases) exceed those generally claimed for cognitive-behavioural treatment programmes, and certainly indicated high cost-effectiveness. Similar figures were claimed in a study of Australian prisoners,

---

16   See Beech *et al.* (in press).

17   See Prisoners' Education Trust (2015).

18   See Karpowitz and Kenner (1995).

19   See Steurer and Smith (2003).

although the vocational education and training which they investigated was more explicitly employment related.[20] Another study suggested that it was much more effective to help prisoners obtain a college education, as opposed to improving the educational goals they had not achieved at school.[21] On the basis of these studies one can certainly say that education as an aid to reducing recidivism looks promising, although it is certainly not the whole answer, and further strictly controlled research could help to decide what works best and for whom. Randomised controlled trials are likely to be difficult in this field, because conducting such a trial would mean refusing education to some people who requested it. This poses difficult ethical and probably legal problems, but that is no reason not to try. What is clear is that educational achievement has made a great deal of difference to some individual offenders, and a more systematic approach to it would probably help many.[22] The potential benefits are considerable, and compared with having to prosecute and imprison people, so are the savings.

In the last few years the idea of 'restorative justice' (RJ) has gained momentum. The basic principle behind RJ is that offenders are not only punished for their offence, but also given the opportunity to atone for it in some way. In some cases this may involve meeting their victims face to face, making an apology, or perhaps performing some kind of work which would help make good what they have done wrong. It will be obvious that not every offender is suitable for this kind of scheme. At the very least, they must accept responsibility for their offence and recognise that it was wrong. Since RJ schemes normally require some kind of input from the victim it is clear also that not every victim is going to be suitable. Because there

---

20   See Callan and Gardner (2005).

21   See Batiuk *et al.* (2005).

22   For a readable real-life account of how education helped a life sentence prisoner turn his life around, see James (2016).

are so many factors involved, it is difficult to evaluate RJ schemes and randomised controlled trials are virtually the only way to make sure that these factors are balanced out in groups of people who do and do not undertake the scheme. Fortunately, the highly respected Campbell Collaboration database includes a systematic review of ten randomised controlled trials which were conducted in several different countries.[23] The researchers found a substantially lower reconviction rate amongst those who had undergone RJ schemes than amongst those who had not. Reconvictions mean expensive court proceedings, and possibly even more expensive imprisonment. The researchers estimated that because of the lower reconviction rate the RJ schemes paid for themselves eight times over. That was not the only finding: victims also liked the RJ schemes. Compared with those whose cases had been handled through the regular criminal justice system, they expressed much higher levels of satisfaction. With the modern emphasis on putting victims at the heart of criminal justice policy, this ought to be a relevant consideration. Why would victims prefer RJ? The review was not able to answer this entirely, as some of the individual studies did not record much information about it. However, those that did found that victims in RJ groups were much more likely to have received an apology from the offender, and much more likely to rate it as sincere. They also had greater confidence (correctly) that the offender would not repeat the offence. These findings were particularly true for female victims. As with education, few would suggest that restorative justice schemes are suitable for every case. But where they are suitable, there is already evidence that they do better than the traditional handling of both offenders and victims by the criminal justice system.

It should be obvious that there are a number of genuinely promising possibilities. Although there is still a need for research

---

23   See Strang et al. (2013).

and development of these areas, an end to cognitive-behavioural programmes need not mean an end to constructive interventions designed to encourage offenders to lead better lives and create fewer victims. What is clear is that the present fixation with cognitive-behavioural programmes is consuming the lion's share of increasingly scarce resources and thereby stifling the development of other, possibly more effective, interventions.

EVALUATION AND RESEARCH

Evaluation of our professional practices should go hand in hand with the practices themselves. For example, evaluation should be built into any treatment programme, which currently is not the case. Not only have many current UK programmes not been evaluated, but in most cases no plans have been announced to evaluate them in future. Indeed, in some cases it has been specifically announced that they will *not* be evaluated. This is seriously bad practice, equivalent to medical authorities deciding that a particular medication will be issued, regardless of any side-effects it might have and regardless of whether it works. Not only interventions, but also assessments (including risk assessments) should be subject to continuous evaluation.

This principle is actually pretty fundamental. Other professionals may have some excuse for not recognising it, but psychologists have none, as it is built into their basic training. Nevertheless, in examining the research literature on offending behaviour programmes they have not practised what they were taught. This has been repeatedly pointed out by critics from inside and outside the profession over the years, but criminal justice system practitioners have steadfastly ignored the message. This is what led an exasperated Professor Margaret Hagen to refer to their behaviour as a 'scam'. Whatever one thinks of the description, she was certainly right to draw attention to the fact

(20 years ago now) that most of the programmes hailed in the so-called 'what works?' literature had produced no proof that they worked at all. Two decades on the position looks no better, although lots of very poor evaluations have been published which really do not prove anything at all. To rectify this situation:

- *We should ensure that no new programme is put forward by psychologists unless it includes a built-in evaluation of its effectiveness.* Evaluation should be conducted by means of a randomised controlled trial.

- *Plans for evaluations should be published in advance and strict adherence to the announced methods maintained, in the manner of the much-respected Campbell Collaboration database.* This would give the opportunity for colleagues to suggest improvements to the methods before they are finally implemented. It would also make it much more difficult to 'tweak' the data after it has been collected. This is not to suggest that anyone in this field practises wholesale cheating, but it is notoriously easy for researchers to persuade themselves that an unwelcome result is invalid because it defies their expectations.

- *Given the proven tendency for people to find results that suit their prejudices (confirmation bias), the evaluation should not be undertaken by those conducting the programme.*

- *All programme evaluations should be published, no matter what the outcome.* If they are not accepted for publication in a reputable journal, they should be published on a website with suitable announcements to let people know they are there. This would overcome the 'bound for publication' bias, whereby unsuccessful trials tend to remain unpublished, making the published results look artificially good by comparison.

COMMUNICATION

As noted earlier, communication is a necessary part of professional life. It is essential if we are to report properly on the work that we do, including reporting on the individuals whom we assess. It is also essential that we inform decision-makers properly (that is, fully and honestly) about what we can and cannot do, as well as what we recommend in any individual case. Communication with fellow professionals is equally essential, as we should be discussing work and its problems and outcomes with them, in order to give and receive information which will help us maintain high professional standards. It has already been suggested that many criminal justice psychologists do not communicate well with those outside of their service. It has also been suggested that they do not welcome input from fellow professionals, and that this may extend to failing to keep up to date with developments in their field. In theory, that should make them open to charges of professional misconduct, but trying to prove that can be very difficult indeed. Practitioners in the private sector may be more aware of this, because they are legally required to have professional indemnity insurance which may not be valid if they do not keep themselves up to date. In the public sector, practitioners are normally covered by whatever arrangements their employer makes, and the regulator accepts these as an alternative. But, misconduct or not, the worst thing about this isolation is probably that it encourages a silo mentality which becomes impervious to external comment or criticism.

This is a serious professional issue. Whilst it is undesirable to pit one section of the profession against another, the best chance of achieving satisfactory professional standards amongst criminal justice psychologists is for the wider profession to examine what they are doing, and help them to improve standards. This brings us back to professional regulation.

PROFESSIONAL REGULATION

Professional regulation of psychologists in the UK and most other Western countries is carried out by means of a register of suitably qualified people. Typically, registrants have to demonstrate their compliance with registration standards in some way. In the United States it is usual that they have to undertake training and further education courses, and be able to produce certificates proving that they have done so. In the UK it is compulsory for practitioners to maintain a record of their training and professional development activities. A certain percentage (generally around 2% for each professional group registered) are selected each year to have their professional development records examined in detail. This is more than simply counting attendance certificates from training courses: less formal activities such as reading books and articles can be included, but they must be backed up by written evidence of study and reflection. In theory, therefore, practitioners who do not keep up to date are at risk of being discovered by a random check. In addition, anyone who is made the subject of a misconduct complaint could also be asked to show that they are complying.

The difficulty that all such registration schemes have is that it is very difficult to define exactly what constitutes 'keeping up to date'. No one can keep up-to-date with everything in a fast developing field such as psychology. Therefore, practitioners must be selective, and responsible practitioners will naturally seek to keep up to date with developments most relevant to the field in which they practise. For example, someone carrying out treatment programmes might reasonably be expected to keep up to date with developments in that field, but might not need to keep up to date with developments in fields of assessment mainly used by practitioners specialising in criminal trial work.

There is another difficulty: policing breaches of the code of conduct can be very expensive. In particular, serious complaints are generally referred to a hearing, which is conducted rather like a criminal trial. At such hearings, both the registration authority and the defendant may be legally represented. Holding such hearings also incurs overheads and staff costs. Registration bodies are understandably unwilling to enter into these proceedings unless they are very sure of their ground, and it is difficult to be that certain. Typically, matters regarding one's level of training and professional development are very much matters of opinion. What one practitioner thinks is adequate may not be accepted by another, and lengthy legal arguments can result. Consequently, certainly in the UK, and according to my colleagues also in the United States, it is difficult to ensure that practitioners really are up to date. It is much easier to concentrate on dealing with gross breaches of conduct, such as fraud or sexual impropriety committed against clients or patients. In any case, these will often involve criminal conviction, which would generally be grounds for removal from the register anyway. Such cases are relatively clear-cut and policing them is both cheap and easy.

In my opinion, this is one of the reasons why the present situation has arisen. Practitioners know that, whatever the rules may say, in practice they can report on people as they please and run whatever programmes they like, and there will be no professional consequences as long as they meet the requirements of their employer. The only way to correct this is to police more strictly. Registration authorities must do more than pay lip service to the idea of upholding professional standards. It is frankly absurd that practitioners can use techniques that are known to be ineffective, or scientifically inadequate, or interview and 'assess' non-English speakers without an interpreter, and that nothing can be done about it. Very important decisions may be taken about individuals as a result of these professional actions, and as long as their employer is happy there seems to be no way of halting the abuse. If 'abuse' seems a strong word, then one should bear in mind that arbitrary treatment by government authorities is an abuse of human rights. Western governments have signed up to various international treaties and declarations agreeing to maintain these rights. They did not do this in order to be undermined by members of the criminal justice system. Therefore I suggest that:

- *Regulating authorities should give basic professional standards (such as keeping up to date) a much higher priority than they currently do.* Psychologists ought to be asking for this already, but very few of them are. If tighter policing is expensive, then it would probably be possible to expand the numbers of people involved on a voluntary basis. For example, in the UK the British Psychological Society used to regulate the profession before 2009, and used volunteer psychologists, as well as representatives of other professions, to do this. Otherwise, higher registration fees may be the only option.

- *Where psychologists have clearly been giving advice or professional opinions not supported by the research literature, this should be regarded as misconduct.* Currently, at least in the UK, it is very difficult to get the regulating authority to take a decision on such matters. The reason given is normally that they do not get involved in differences of professional opinion between practitioners. The problem with this is that sometimes practitioners are unequivocally wrong. If they are not held to account for this, they will carry on with the same bad practice.

- *Ideally public money might be provided for prisoners who wish to take legal cases to challenge lack of progress through the prison system.* There is a logic to doing so, even if proposed cases were filtered by a judge in order to weed out the frivolous ones, because wasteful practices waste public money and should be challenged. Those most entitled to do the challenging are those most directly affected – that is, offenders themselves – yet very few of them have enough money to take cases at their own expense.

MENTAL HEALTH PROBLEMS

It was mentioned earlier that mental health problems are rife in the prison population. In the UK this has been reflected in a recent surge in the figures for prison suicides. This has been attributed to a variety of factors, including such things as overcrowding and reductions in staff who can organise meaningful activity – currently many prisoners are spending up to 23 hours a day in their cells. Prison may not have helped these people, but there is no doubt that many of those who harm themselves had mental health problems before they entered prison.[24] The fact remains that it is quite difficult to obtain treatment for mental health problems in prison. Indeed, it is generally recognised as a problem everywhere in the UK and other Western countries, where mental health services are often last in the queue when resources are being allocated. Inside prison it is worse; it is a matter of common experience that getting prison authorities (including their psychologists) to take prisoners' mental health problems seriously, even when related to their offending, is often uphill work. Yet there are clearly cases where a mental health problem is strongly related to a prisoner's offending.

A dramatic example of this occurred in the UK recently, where a life sentence prisoner had been transferred to open prison and was on home leave. It is usual that such prisoners undertake several home leaves, usually of a few days at a time,

---

24   See Stubbs and Durcan (2016).

before being finally released. This man received his life sentence for murdering his partner, whom he had discovered to be a child abuser. This was particularly threatening to him because he had been abused himself as a child, and it had left lasting psychological damage. Unfortunately, whatever offending behaviour courses he may have undertaken during his sentence, no one seems to have thought that treatment for his abuse-related trauma was a priority. While on home leave he learned that an elderly man living nearby had been convicted of child abuse in the past. He went to attack this person, who was defended by another neighbour. In the resulting affray the neighbour was killed. In this case, timely treatment for the prisoner's abuse-related trauma might not only have relieved his distress, but also saved an innocent life.

In a less dramatic case with which I was involved, a man who was quite clearly suffering from post-traumatic stress disorder, as a result of a serious assault, overreacted to an aggressive approach by a neighbour. When the neighbour took refuge behind his front door, the man attacked the front door in an apparent attempt to gain entry. He ended up damaging the front door quite extensively and being charged with that offence. What both these cases have in common is that those affected by trauma have overreacted very seriously to a perceived threat. The problem for the cognitive-behavioural kind of programme is that it is aimed at altering attitudes (whether successfully or not is irrelevant for the moment) rather than dealing with extreme emotional reactions. People suffering from this kind of trauma do not stop to consider their attitudes and reason things through before acting. Their response is extreme and unthinking, something akin to the proverbial 'red mist'. Treatments may be available for such problems, but they do not consist of essentially rational, verbal processes taking place amongst a group of people in a classroom who have not had a similar traumatic experience. Furthermore, they should only be carried out by practitioners trained in the appropriate clinical techniques, which most forensic practitioners are not.

Drug problems are also rife amongst the offender population, both inside and outside prison. Many petty crimes are committed in order to obtain money for drugs. Far from curing this problem, prison makes it worse, and drugs are plentiful. Indeed, I knew one man without previous drug problems who actually became a heroin addict inside prison. Since the so-called 'war on drugs' began, the problems have multiplied rather than decreased. However, taking a militaristic approach is not the only way of tackling this problem. Several countries have now decided to treat drug abuse primarily as a health problem and reduced or eliminated criminal penalties. In particular, Portugal has now been using a different approach for 15 years. The results have included a drop in drug use, a drop in drug-related crime and several well-documented public health benefits, such as a reduction in HIV and hepatitis C infections.[25] Deaths from drug overdoses have also reduced dramatically. Drug use has not been legalised, but downgraded from a criminal offence to an administrative one, similar to motoring offences like speeding or parking illegally. Offenders are directed to drug counselling services and may have to pay a small fine, but there is no criminal record and no imprisonment. Of course, as with other mental health problems, drug addiction cannot be tackled without resources. However, the evidence seems to be that treating drug use as a health problem rather than a criminal problem achieves better results and therefore saves money, as well as reducing the adverse impact on the wider community.

To be fair, the current policy (or lack of one) regarding the mental health needs of offenders is not the fault of psychologists alone. However, there has been almost no recognition of the problem amongst criminal justice psychologists, who have

---

25   See Transform (2014).

preferred to continue on their current path of targeting alleged 'criminogenic needs'. Drugs and alcohol are considered merely to be 'disinhibitors', and attitudes and beliefs remain the primary targets for intervention. Similarly, forensic psychologists appear to have put little or no pressure on policymakers to provide mental health facilities for offenders. At least in UK prisons, that has been regarded as a matter for health services, which are generally bought in from external providers, with the result that prison psychologists can wash their hands of the matter. Whether or not a facility is available depends upon the service specification. External services regularly decline to provide treatment on the grounds that it is not covered by their contract. It may reasonably be argued that this is a problem of bad policy, rather than bad psychological practice, but no criminal justice professionals are better placed than psychologists (even those who are not fully qualified) to draw attention to prisoners' mental health problems. At the very least, psychologists could create some pressure for better policy. They could:

- *Recognise when a person has identifiable mental health problems*, and draw attention to this in the reports that they write.

- *Recognise that mental health problems and any required treatment may have implications for risk*, and should therefore be a factor in risk assessment reports.

- *Acknowledge that the treatment needs of offenders may not simply require the targeting of criminogenic needs*, but that mental health needs may also need to be treated.

- *Where adequate mental health facilities are not available, make this fact plain in risk assessment reports*, so that decision-making bodies will be faced with the unmet need and may be held accountable if they fail to meet it.

REVIEW TRAINING AND QUALIFICATIONS

It will be clear by now that I think the training and qualifications of many forensic psychologists are not adequate. Many of them have had a very narrow training in just those techniques that they are required to use by their employers. This inevitably gives rise to inadequate practice, because many of them are ignorant not only of other branches of psychology but also of other areas of forensic practice which may be relevant to cases that they deal with. I have given some examples earlier in this book: the 'manipulative' prisoner who turned out to be very suggestible and therefore gave different answers to different interviewers; the elderly prisoner who thought his memory was too poor to benefit from a cognitive-behavioural programme, but whose views were dismissed without any memory testing; the sexual abuse victim who was re-traumatised by being forced to undergo a sex offender treatment programme. The practitioners who dealt with these people might not have made these mistakes if their professional training had been broader based, including more study of how forensic psychology links into other fields, and a more holistic approach, rather than seeing offenders as a collection of criminogenic needs.

Another problem is clearly that trainees, who are not fully qualified psychologists, are doing so much of the psychological work in criminal justice systems, both in the UK and other jurisdictions. Not only do trainees conduct psychological assessments, risk assessments and treatment programmes, but (at least in the UK) they also appear in front of parole panels and give 'expert' evidence. In fact, trainees are barred by the rules of their profession from giving expert psychological evidence in courts, but it is done on a daily basis: parole hearings are courts. Expert status is very important, because in most legal systems, including those of the UK, expert witnesses are not confined to giving factual evidence: they may also give professional *opinions* as evidence.

When I was a member of the British Psychological Society's Investigatory Committee we received a query from a parole panel psychologist. She was, quite rightly, concerned that panels were receiving 'expert' evidence from trainees. The Committee consulted the chair of the BPS's Forensic Division, who explained that these trainees were not acting as expert witnesses, but were attending as 'professional' witnesses. It was pointed out that as they were not qualified professionals they could hardly be professional witnesses either, but the fact that all trainees are supervised by qualified psychologists was held to be good enough.

Supervisors are supposed to read their trainees' reports and countersign them before they are submitted, to confirm that they reach a suitable standard. Unfortunately, the experience of people who have worked in or observed this system is that it is *not* good enough. It is clear that supervisors often have very little time allotted for supervision purposes, and that sometimes they may countersign trainees' reports after only cursory examination. This may be partly due to a very high ratio of trainees to supervisors: when I enquired in one prison I was told that the ratio there at that time was ten to one. I have no idea how typical that was, but in one case that I knew of, a trainee countersigned a report herself, because she was not able to get hold of her supervisor. The misdemeanour was obvious, because both signatures were next to each other at the bottom of the last page. This borders upon illegality, because it is illegal to practise as a psychologist if one is not legally registered, and trainees are not. Supervisors are, which is one reason why they are required to countersign reports; it is only the supervision that gives legitimacy to the trainees' work. In spite of this, every example of poor practice given in this book was approved by one or more supervisors. If we cannot trust the supervisors we are in trouble.

Much of this book has been a plea for evidence-based practice, and so is this. Training should be evidence based, and not manualised. In the UK, for example, treatment programmes are thought of by the criminal justice system as a proven technology, and consequently practitioners must adhere strictly to a manual of rules about how treatment should progress. Some treatment sessions are even videoed and inspected to make sure that treatment is done by the book. It is doubtful whether such a rigid system would be therapeutic even if the treatment rationale were basically sound. Certainly, it leaves little room for treating people as complex individuals with complex needs. Rather, it requires prisoners to be shoehorned into a one-size-fits-all treatment which may or may not be suitable. But, as we have seen, the treatment rationale is *not* basically sound, and continuing to train future practitioners in these techniques is therefore not sound either. There is a pressing need for training to be both evidence based and more holistic. Currently it is neither. Good training is not the answer to every problem, but without it the kind of problem I have identified is inevitable.

LEAVING THE SCIENCE BEHIND

Tenzin Gyatso, the 14th and current Dalai Lama, has had many quotations attributed to him. One of them is, 'If scientific analysis were conclusively to demonstrate certain claims in Buddhism to be false, then we must accept the findings of science and abandon those claims.'[1] Interestingly, Pope Francis has also made statements accepting the scientific reality of evolution and the so-called 'big bang' theory of the origin of the universe.[2] Why bring religious leaders into this discussion? Simply because religions tend to have very strict systems of belief, and religious leaders are often very reluctant to accept scientific evidence which may contradict them. If some of the world's great religious leaders can accept that scientific evidence provides the factual basis for our understanding of the world, then scientists themselves should have no problem with it.

Plenty of evidence has been presented to show that many of the flaws known to exist in human judgement are present in all humans, and not just those who lack specific training. Indeed, there is no evidence that any form of training can remove these biases, and good reason to think that it cannot even in principle do so. This is certainly the view of the Nobel laureate who identified many of these flaws.[3] One piece of research which has not so far been described is one of the classic psychological

---

1   See Barash (2014).

2   See Tharoor (2014).

3   See Kahneman (2011), especially the final section, 'Conclusions'.

experiments and is, or should be, familiar to every psychologist. This was conducted by a group of psychologists in America, under the leadership of David Rosenhan, who were concerned about the accuracy of psychiatric diagnosis.[4]

Rosenhan and a group of students ('pseudopatients') presented themselves at different psychiatric hospitals, complaining of hearing voices. When asked what these voices were saying, they replied that they were not very clear, but they often heard the words 'empty', 'hollow' and 'thud'. The admitting authorities almost invariably diagnosed schizophrenia,[5] a mental disorder that is often characterised by auditory hallucinations, and admitted the pseudopatients for treatment. Once admitted, the pseudopatients would *immediately* stop complaining of symptoms and tell the doctors they felt they were okay now. Despite a lack of reported symptoms, it took some of them many weeks to be discharged. One of the interesting findings of this research was that perfectly ordinary everyday behaviour was often interpreted by hospital staff as abnormal, just because the people doing it were 'patients'. Rosenhan reported his research, which was greeted with outrage by the psychiatric establishment, as it clearly showed they were unable to tell the difference between genuine and fake patients. But Rosenhan went further. He announced that a new experiment was to take place, in which further pseudopatients would approach hospitals in a particular area. During the period in question, these hospitals diagnosed far fewer cases of schizophrenia and identified a large number of people as Rosenhan's pseudopatients. None of them in fact were, because this time none had actually

---

4   See Rosenhan (1975). This paper is also widely available on the Internet as a download in PDF format.

5   In one case, the diagnosis was manic depressive psychosis. Some have suggested that Rosenhan's conclusions were unduly harsh, as all the patients were eventually discharged and their illnesses judged to be in remission, but the fact remains that perfectly well people were all diagnosed with very serious mental illnesses.

presented themselves, despite Rosenhan's announcement. This caused further outrage. As with criminal justice authorities, the response of the psychiatric establishment was not to examine its own mistakes, but to shoot the messenger.[6]

Indeed, although Rosenhan's research concerned psychiatric hospital admissions, there are many parallels with other institutions, especially prisons. It is a regular occurrence that many prisoners' actions are regarded as sinister when they would not be so regarded in the outside world. For example, any expression of anger (a normal, everyday emotion) tends to be treated as abnormal, and evidence of dangerousness. Purely verbal impulsiveness, as evidenced by joking and perhaps off-colour remarks, is seen as evidence of behavioural impulsiveness, although the two are quite different. In fact, I have often seen examples of men who were dangerously impulsive in their youth, but who have not been violent for years, although they still make impulsive remarks that others would find distasteful (I stress *distasteful*: I am not referring to threats or aggressive remarks). Yet these off-colour remarks are taken as evidence of dangerousness, despite the complete absence of any physical threat. Issues of social class and culture can also complicate 'professional' perception. I once remarked to a parole panel in exasperation that no matter what we did with the parole applicant he was not going to turn into a nice well-brought-up middle-class boy. They appeared to have quite unrealistic ideas of what to expect from him. None of these ideas were genuinely related to risk.

Of course, it is not only psychologists and psychiatrists who get things wrong. Similar processes have been documented in teachers in the United States, especially with regard to ethnicity.

---

6   More recently, Slater (2004) repeated the experiment on a solo basis and found it was just as easy to be diagnosed as schizophrenic on the basis of fake symptoms. However, she found psychiatrists much less likely to recommend institutionalisation, and felt that she was treated with much more respect than Rosenhan had reported. Some things apparently do get better.

For example, white children of a given level of ability are more than three times as likely as black children of the same level to be recommended for 'gifted children' programmes.[7] Similarly, black children are more likely than white children to be suspended or expelled, for misbehaviour that is no worse. Research has also shown both that coaching can overcome these biases, and that they are not related to racial attitudes expressed by the teachers concerned. That is, they do not support or approve of discriminatory practices, but their decision-making is affected anyway. As with other research, the decision-makers are not always aware of why they take the decisions they do.

It is inconceivable that such biases do not affect psychologists and other criminal justice professionals when they quite clearly affect everybody else, but I do not know of any programme intended to measure such biases, let alone correct them. The irony of this is that it is psychologists themselves who have demonstrated the existence of these flaws in judgement. We have also demonstrated that there is a neurobiological basis for these errors, and as we all have the same neurobiology these errors must be universal. We cannot now turn around to our critics and say, 'Oh, but we didn't mean *us*; it's just the rest of you.' These biases in judgement affect all human beings, and if we are to maintain any credibility as a profession – and especially as a science – we must face up to the fact that this includes us. Some people may doubt that psychology can ever be a science, and certainly in everyday discussions I often hear that point of view. But it is a weak argument. Science is not a collection of dogma in the manner of some religious or political beliefs. Science is essentially a set of methods for determining facts. The division of science into different subject areas, like physics, chemistry, etc., is an artificial division which we impose on scientific knowledge for our own convenience. In other words,

---

7   See Weir (2016). This did not happen if the teacher was black as well.

scientific methods may be used to study anything at all, including the behaviour of human beings.

As I have been at some pains to point out in this book, there are well-established evidence-based conclusions that we can draw from some of the scientific work that has been done on human behaviour. Inevitably, some of this work will challenge those who have very fixed ideas about behaviour. As the work of Kahneman and Ariely shows, even qualified professionals will defend their entrenched ideas against a challenge, however weak these ideas are. In many cases these ideas have become entrenched for reasons that are nothing to do with the evidence. They represent the vested financial and career interests of those involved, and challenging the ideas means challenging the individuals who cling to them. This is not new. At the end of the 19th century physicists mostly believed that an invisible and undetectable substance called 'ether' permeated all matter and all space. At least one science-fiction story was written speculating on what might happen if the earth passed through a band of the ether which had poisonous properties (a novella, *The Poison Belt*, by Arthur Conan Doyle, published in 1913). When Einstein first advanced his theory of relativity most physicists argued against it, and defended the concept of the ether. This may have been partly because Einstein was a humble clerk in the Swiss patent office, and partly because they found his work difficult to understand. However, almost certainly it was partly because they had worked with these ideas all their professional lives and turning their entire worldview upside down was too much for them to accept.

Forensic psychology today is in a similar position, and to some extent so is the whole of psychology. There is a fixation on cognitive-behavioural treatment which threatens to exclude almost everything else. There has also been a fixation on risk assessment which has aspired to the level of accuracy desired by politicians and policymakers, rather than to a level consistent with the evidence about what is actually possible. We have seen a proliferation of plausible-sounding but not evidence-based schemes, which generally do no good and some of which are actually harmful. The 'Scared Straight' and 'Greenlight' schemes are good examples of this. Another is the 'Broken Windows' policing scheme, sometimes referred to as 'zero tolerance'. In fact, 'zero tolerance' is a stricter version, but the basic principle is the same: the idea is that vigorously policing minor offences prevents more serious ones from arising. The evidence now suggests that it does not.[8]

What all of these schemes have in common is that they were not based on a proper theoretical understanding of how crime arises or how behaviour may be changed. They arose simply because somebody thought they were a good idea and persuaded policymakers to provide the funding. Frankly, a lot of ideas about crime suffer from the same problem, whether dreamed up in academia or in government circles. There is lots of hypothesising, and lots of politically motivated thinking, but very little true science. Science normally starts with a theoretical understanding of the problem at issue, and only when this has been tested and elaborated upon through experimentation do we move, tentatively, to practical interventions. This model does not always get things right, but other models pretty much always get things wrong. If there is one message I would like you to take away from this book it is that the practical usefulness of psychology falls off very rapidly as it drifts away from scientific method. Much of what I have said has been a plea for a psychology based on the science that it *claims* to be based on. Our practice should be firmly based on evidence from truly scientific research. Then we might not have to ask, as Professors Ward and Gannon did, 'Where has all the psychology gone?'[9]

---

8   This is the scheme popularly (though somewhat erroneously) associated with the former New York Mayor Rudi Giuliani, and practised widely in the US (Childress 2016).

9   See Gannon and Ward (2014).

POSTSCRIPT

In Chapter 7, in the section entitled 'The offending behaviour industry', I mentioned that two sex offender programmes had been abruptly closed down by the UK Ministry of Justice in early 2017. At the time of writing that chapter it was not clear why this had happened, and I speculated that the Ministry of Justice was belatedly responding to some of the scientific evidence which had long been published. It now appears that this was wrong. The real story was much more sinister.

On 24 June 2017 the Daily Mail Online published an article by an investigative journalist called David Rose[1]. Coincidentally, on 14 June I had met Rose at a conference at which he was an after-dinner speaker. We had discussed the abrupt cessation of the sex offender programmes, and I had mentioned the criticisms made of them by myself and others. He was very well-informed already, but I was able to refer him to some scientific papers which he had not come across. He mentioned that he was going to be publishing an article on this topic shortly, and that he had been talking about the sudden policy change to people within the Ministry of Justice. So had I, but they had evidently told him more than they had told me! I had also spoken to colleagues in North America, who seemed quite perplexed at the news; some of them had previously been employed in the UK Ministry of Justice and had helped to set up the programmes in the first place. They were now running them over there, as were many of their colleagues.

According to Rose, the reason for the sudden abandonment of these sex offender programmes was that the Ministry of Justice

---

1   See Rose (2017).

had been conducting its own scientific evaluation of them, and the results were startling. You may recall that I explained how some psychological interventions appear to cause a 'rebound' effect, so that they made the targeted behaviour *more* likely rather than less. Rose's informants told him that the internal Ministry of Justice evaluations had found just such an effect, and it was very powerful. Their results indicated a 25% *higher* reconviction rate amongst those who had undergone a programme compared with those who had not. I had been criticising these programmes for 15 years, but even to me this seemed an extraordinarily bad result. It could have been an extreme finding, resulting from a small sample size, and not very significant in absolute terms. However, Ministry of Justice researchers are perfectly capable of designing quality evaluations. This was confirmed when the Ministry of Justice called in an outside expert to review the research. This was Friedrich Lösel, a university-based researcher with considerable experience in this area, and author or co-author of many well-known papers, some of which have been referred to in this book[2]. He confirmed that in his opinion the research was valid and should be accepted.

The sinister aspect of the story is that, having established that the research was valid, Liz Truss, then Minister of Justice, decided it should be kept secret. Lösel was also instructed not to reveal its contents. Just think about that for a minute: in a democratic society a politician took the decision not to reveal the results of state-funded research, not because there was anything wrong with it, but because it was true but embarrassing. Given that there was a general election pending at the time, it may simply have been that Truss was hoping to delay breaking the news until after the election, in which her party was hoping to achieve a large parliamentary majority. This interpretation gained credibility when the report was quietly published on the

---

2   For example, Lösel and Schmucker (2005) and Schmucker and Lösel (2015).

Ministry of Justice website on 30 June 2017[3]. This was heavily criticized in the British press, especially by the Times newspaper, which published a two-page spread on both the programmes and the secrecy[4]. It also published a leader article which was very critical of the repeated refusals by the Ministry of Justice to heed the warnings raised by myself and others.

However, it had already attracted agitated responses from North America. I had posted news of the article on an Internet discussion group called the International Discussion on Psychology and Law. Within minutes there were responses from American colleagues, mostly expressing disbelief. Perhaps the study was methodologically sloppy, they suggested. Perhaps the effects were really very small and therefore unimportant. I replied that, given the reactions of both Prof Lösel and the Ministry, this was really unlikely. One colleague based in the Wisconsin Department of Corrections, which runs a lot of these programmes, protested vigorously (and repeatedly, in several emails) that there could be all kinds of things wrong with such a study. In theory there could; it would not be the first time. But the validation of the research by an outside expert like Lösel still suggested that this was unlikely. Furthermore, it is the first time that the UK Ministry of Justice has ever reacted to any new research with such a rapid U-turn in policy. Nonetheless, North American colleagues who did not want to accept the news were already joining the dots up to make the picture less threatening than it had appeared at first.

Now that the report was finally published, it became apparent that the research project was indeed of high quality. It was not a randomized controlled trial, which would be the best way of evaluating the treatment. However, it was a matched design, in which those undergoing treatment were matched on a number

---

3   See Mews, Di Bella and Purver (2017).

4   See Hamilton (2017). The Times operates a pay wall, so online access may be restricted for those who are unwilling to take out a subscription.

of risk factors with those who were not. Indeed, the matching was far superior to that of most studies in this field. The sample size was also large, comparing 2,562 treated men with 13,219 untreated men. This makes it one of the largest scale studies ever attempted in this field. As pointed out earlier, small sample sizes are prone to statistical fluke effects, and are the bane of research in this field. Over an average period of 8.2 years, all of the men were followed up to see whether they reconvicted. The reconviction rates were approximately 8% for untreated men, and 10% for treated men. The treated men therefore reconvicted at a higher rate, although both rates are actually very low, which (contrary to popular belief) is typical of sex offenders. One American colleague pointed out that the difference is very small in absolute terms, but it does represent 20 new offences for every 1,000 men who have been through the 'treatment' programme. To put the best possible interpretation on it, the treatment failed. The worst interpretation is that it made offenders somewhat more risky than they were before. This is not the first time this has happened: as discussed earlier, both the Scared Straight and the Greenlight programmes resulted in higher reconviction rates, not lower.

It seems to me that this affair amply vindicates the stance that this book has taken with reference to sex offender programmes. Not only have the results been poor, and possibly counter-productive, but there has been a great unwillingness on the part of government authorities all over the Western world to admit this. Considerations which are essentially political can perpetuate the vested interests of the offending behaviour industry and try to conceal the truth about failed policy. As I have repeatedly stated in this book, the evidence was already there to be seen. The experts advising government authorities, both in the UK and around the world, cannot say that they did not know. The truth is, they did not *want* to know.

In their articles the journalists speculated that the Ministry of Justice could now find itself on the receiving end of a number of lawsuits. They suggested that victims of sex offenders, who had been released after treatment on the basis that risk was reduced, might sue for the damage they had suffered. On the other hand, indeterminate-sentenced men whose imprisonment was unnecessarily prolonged in order for them to undertake such programmes may also have a case, as that prolonged imprisonment may have been unlawful. Again, this is an issue that could involve both victims and offenders in other countries besides the UK, particularly in the United States and Canada where many of these programmes originated. That is for the lawyers to decide, but I know that some are interested.

Finally, this scandal only refers to sex offender programmes. We do not have any comparable evaluation of the programmes which target offending behaviour of other types, particularly violence. Nor as yet is there any evaluation of the new UK programmes, 'Kaizen' and 'Horizon', which are intended to replace the existing ones for sexual and violent offenders. As they are based on the same cognitive-behavioural principles, there is reason to doubt whether they will be any more effective, and whether release decisions should be related to them in any way. Indeed, they could turn out to be as counter-productive as the programmes that they replace.

The sex offender programmes have been shown to be dramatically lacking in effectiveness. Although this research was conducted in the UK, the programmes it evaluated are very similar to those run throughout the Western world. The implications for offending behaviour programmes run far and wide. What is now needed is a thorough evaluation of other programmes, and an examination of other practices such as risk assessment.

REFERENCES

Abracen, J., Langton, C.M., Looman, J., Gallo, A., *et al.* (2014) Mental health diagnoses and recidivism in paroled offenders. *International Journal of Offender Therapy and Comparative Criminology 58*(7), 765–779.

American Physical Society (2005) *Power line fields and public health.* Available at www.aps.org/policy/statements/95_2.cfm, accessed on 25 May 2017.

Andrews, D.A., and Bonta, J. (2016) *The Psychology of Criminal Conduct* (6th edn). Abingdon, Oxfordshire: Routledge.

Anglin, M.D., Nosyk, B., Jaffe, A., Urada, D. and Evans, E. (2013) Offender diversion into substance use disorder treatment: The economic impact of California's Proposition 36. *American Journal of Public Health 103*(6), 1096–1102.

Ariely, D. (2012) *The (Honest) Truth about Dishonesty: How We Lie to Everyone – Especially Ourselves.* New York: HarperCollins.

Atir, S., Rosenzweig, E. and Dunning, D. (2015) When knowledge knows no bounds. *Psychological Science 26*(8), 1295–1303.

Austin, J., Coleman, C., Peyton, J., and Johnson, K.D. (2003) Reliability and validity study of the LSI-R risk assessment instrument, final report. Available at www.researchgate.net/publication/266891710_RELIABILITY_AND_VALIDITY_STUDY_OF_THE_LSI-R_RISK_ASSESSMENT_INSTRUMENT_ACKNOWLEDGMENTS, accessed on 25 May 2017.

Babiak, P. and Hare, R.D. (2007) *Snakes in Suits: When Psychopaths Go to Work.* London: HarperCollins.

Baddeley, A., Eysenck, M.W. and Anderson, M.C. (2014) *Memory* (2nd edn). London: Psychology Press.

Barash, D. (2014) *Is Buddhism the most science-friendly religion?* Available at https://blogs.scientificamerican.com/guest-blog/is-buddhism-the-most-science-friendly-religion/, accessed on 19 June 2017.

Barbaree, H.E., Blanchard, R. and Langton, C.M. (2003) The development of sexual aggression through the lifespan: The effect of age on sexual arousal and recidivism among sex offenders. *Annals of the New York Academy of Sciences 989*, 59–71.

Bartlett, F.C. (1932) *Remembering: A Study in Experimental and Social Psychology.* Cambridge: Cambridge University Press.

Batiuk, M.E., Lahm, K.F., Mckeever, M., Wilcox, N. and Wilcox, P. (2005) Disentangling the effects of correctional education: Are current policies misguided? An event history analysis. *Criminal Justice* 5(1), 55–74.

BBC (2014) *Family hears judge say victim statements make 'no difference'*. Available at www.bbc.co.uk/news/uk-28644799, accessed on 8 August 2016.

Beck, J.S. and Beck, A. (2011) *Cognitive Behaviour Therapy* (2nd edn). New York: The Guilford Press.

Beech, A.R. (2016) *The neurobiological basis of offending indicating innovative approaches to treatment for offenders*. Paper presented at the British Psychological Society's Division of Forensic Psychology Annual Conference, Brighton.

Beech, A.R., Carter, A., Mann, R.E. and Rotstein, P. (in press) *Handbook of Forensic Neuroscience*. Oxford: Wiley.

Benforado, A. (2015) *Unfair: The New Science of Criminal Injustice*. New York: Broadway Books.

Blasko, B. (2013) *The uncharted influence of prison staff decision-making*. PhD thesis, Temple University, Philadelphia. Available at http://cdm16002.contentdm. oclc.org/cdm/ref/collection/p245801coll10/id/218401, accessed on 18 March 2017.

Boer, D.P., Hart, S.D., Kropp, P.R. and Webster, C.D. (1997) *Manual for the Sexual Violence Risk-20: Professional Guidelines for Assessing Risk of Sexual Violence*. Vancouver, BC: The British Columbia Institute Against Family Violence.

Bonham, G., Janeksela, G. and Bardo, J. (1986) Predicting parole decision in Kansas via discriminant analysis. *Journal of Criminal Justice* 14(2), 123–133.

Bradford, S. and Cowell, P. (2012) *The decision-making process at parole interviews (indeterminate imprisonment for public protection sentences)*. Research summary 1/12. Available at www.justice.gov.uk/downloads/publications/research-and-analysis/moj-research/decision-making-process-parole-reviews-ipp. pdf, accessed on 5 September 2016.

Bransford, J.D., Brown, A.L. and Cocking, R.R. (2004) *How People Learn: Brain, Mind, Experience, and School*. Washington, DC: National Academy Press. Available at www.csun.edu/~SB4310/How%20People%20Learn.pdf, accessed on 25 May 2017.

Cahill, K., Lancaster, T. and Green, N. (2010) Stage-based interventions for smoking cessation. *Cochrane Database of Systematic Reviews* November 10(11), CD004492.

Callan, V. and Gardner, J. (2005) *Vocational Education and Training Provision and Recidivism in Queensland Correctional Institutions*. Adelaide, South Australia: National Centre for Vocational Educational Research.

Campbell, T.W. (2004) *Assessing Sex Offenders: Problems and Pitfalls*. Springfield, IL: Charles C. Thomas.

Campbell, T.W. and DeClue, G. (2010) Flying blind with naked factors: Problems and pitfalls in adjusted-actuarial sex-offender risk assessment. *Open Access Journal of Forensic Psychology 2*, 75–101.

Cann, J. (2006) *Cognitive Skills Programmes: Impact on Reducing Reconviction among a Sample of Female Prisoners.* (276). London: Home Office. Available at http://webarchive.nationalarchives.gov.uk/20090121164757/http://www.homeoffice.gov.uk/rds/pdfs06/r276.pdf, accessed on 25 May 2017.

Carey, S.M., Finigan, M., Crumpton, D. and Waller, M. (2006) California drug courts: Outcomes, costs and promising practices: An overview of Phase II in a statewide study. *Journal of Psychoactive Drugs* SARC Supplement 3, November, 345–356.

Childress, S. (2016) The problem with 'broken windows' policing. *Frontline* 28 June. Available at www.pbs.org/wgbh/frontline/article/the-problem-with-broken-windows-policing, accessed on 26 January 2017.

Clarke, R. and Cornish, D. (1972) *The Controlled Trial in Institutional Research: Paradigms or Pitfall?* London: HMSO.

Cleckley, H. (1976) *The Mask of Sanity* (5th edn). St Louis, MO: Mosby.

Coid, J.W. (2003) The co-morbidity of personality disorder and lifetime clinical syndromes in dangerous offenders. *Journal of Forensic Psychiatry and Psychology 14*(2), 341–366. doi: 10.1080/1478994031000116381

Coid, J., Petruckevitch, A., Bebbington, P., Jenkins, *et al.* (2003) Psychiatric morbidity in prisoners and solitary cellular confinement, II: Special ('strip') cells. *Journal of Forensic Psychiatry and Psychology 14*(2), 320–340. doi: 10.1080/1478994031000095501

Coid, J., Yang, M., Ullrich, S., Zhang, T., *et al.* (2007) Predicting and understanding risk of re-offending: The prisoner cohort study. Ministry of Justice *Research Summary* 6. Available at www.crim.cam.ac.uk/people/academic_research/david_farrington/priscomoj.pdf, accessed on 25 May 2017.

Coid, J., Yang, M., Ullrich, S., Zhang, T., *et al.* (2011) Most items in structured risk assessment instruments do not predict violence. *Journal of Forensic Psychiatry and Psychology 22*(1), 3–21.

Condon, R. (2004) *The Manchurian Candidate.* London: Orion Books.

Copas, J. and Jackson, D. (2004) A bound for publication bias based on the fraction of unpublished studies. *Biometrics 60*(1), 146–153.

CPP Inc. (2009) from www.cpp.com/products/mbti/index.aspx, accessed on 25 May 2017.

Craig, L. (2008) How should we understand the effect of age on sexual recidivism? *Journal of Sexual Aggression 14*, 185–198.

Creeden, K. (2009) How trauma and attachment can impact neurodevelopment: Informing our understanding and treatment of sexual behaviour problems. *Journal of Sexual Aggression 15*(3), 261–273.

Creeden, K. (2013) Taking a developmental approach to treating juvenile sexual behavior problems. *International Journal of Behavioral Consultation and Therapy 8*(3–4), 12–16.

Dalgard, O.S. and Kringlen, E. (1976) A Norwegian twin study of criminality. *British Journal of Criminology 16*, 213–232.

Danziger, S., Levav, J. and Avnaim-Pesso, L. (2011) Extraneous factors in judicial decisions. *Proceedings of the National Academy of Sciences USA 108*(17), 6889–6892.

Dearden, E. (2014) Family's heartache as judge claims victim impact statements make 'no difference'. *Independent*, 5 August. Available at www.independent. co.uk/news/uk/crime/familys-heartache-as-judge-claims-victim-impact-statements-make-no-difference-9648329.html, accessed on 25 May 2017.

DeClue, G. (2013) Years of predicting dangerously. *Open Access Journal of Forensic Psychology 5*, 16–28. Available at www.oajfp.com/blank-5, accessed on 18 July 2016.

Dennis, J.A., Khan, O., Ferriter, M., Huband, N., Powney, M.J. and Duggan, C. (2012) Psychological interventions for adults who have sexually offended or are at risk of offending. Cochrane, 12 December. Available at http:// onlinelibrary.wiley.com/doi/10.1002/14651858.CD007507.pub2/full, accessed on 25 May 2017.

Dernevik, M. (2004) Structured clinical assessment and management of risk of violent recidivism in mentally disordered offenders. Unpublished PhD thesis, Karolinska Institutet, Stockholm. Available from http://publications. ki.se/xmlui/bitstream/handle/10616/39264/thesis.pdf?sequence=1, accessed on 25 May 2017.

Dietrich, A. (1994) Assessing risk of violence in mentally disordered offenders with the HCR-20. Unpublished MA thesis, Simon Fraser University.

Dineen, T. (2004) *Manufacturing Victims: What the Psychology Industry Is Doing to People* (3rd edn). London: Constable and Robinson.

Dror, I. (2016). A hierarchy of expert performance. *Journal of Applied Research in Memory and Cognition, 5*, 121–127.

Dror, I, and Murrie, D. (2017). A hierarchy of expert performance applied to forensic psychological assessments. *Psychology, public policy and law,* (in press).

Dror, I., and Rosenthal, R. (2008). Meta-analytically quantifying the reliability and biasability of forensic experts. *Journal of Forensic Science, 53 (4)*, 900-903.

Dreger, A. (2015) *Galileo's Middle Finger: Heretics, Activists, and the Search for Justice in Science*. New York: Penguin Press.

D'Silva, K., Duggan, C. and McCarthy, L. (2004) Does treatment really make psychopaths worse? A review of the evidence. *Journal of Personality Disorders* 18(2), 163–177.

Elliott, I.A., Beech, A.R., Mandeville-Norden, R. and Hayes, E. (2009) Psychological profiles of Internet sexual offenders: Comparisons with contact sexual offenders. *Sexual Abuse: A Journal of Research and Treatment* 21(1), 76–92.

Englich, B., Mussweiler, T. and Strack, F. (2006) Playing dice with criminal sentences: The influence of irrelevant anchors on experts' judicial decision making. *Personality and Social Psychology Bulletin 32(2)*, 188.

Eysenck, H.J. (2004) *Decline and Fall of the Freudian Empire* (2nd edn). Harmondsworth: Penguin Books.

Falshaw, L., Friendship, C., Travers, R. and Nugent, F. (2003) Searching for 'What Works': An evaluation of cognitive skills programmes. Home Office Research, *Findings 206*. Available at http://webarchive.nationalarchives.gov.uk/20110218135832/rds.homeoffice.gov.uk/rds/pdfs2/r206.pdf, accessed on 25 May 2017.

Fazel, S. and Danesh, J. (2002) Serious mental disorder in 23,000 prisoners: A systematic review of 62 surveys. *The Lancet 359*(9306), 545–550. doi: 10.1016/s0140-6736(02)07740-1

Fazel, S., Wolf, A., Chang, Z., Larsson, H., Goodwin, G. and Lichtenstein, P. (2015) Depression and violence: A Swedish population study. *Lancet Psychiatry 2*(3), 224–232.

Forde, R.A. (1978) Twin studies, inheritance and criminality. *The British Journal of Criminology 18*(1), 71–74.

Forde, R.A. (2003) Defending the indefensible. *The Psychologist 16*(7), 348–349.

Forde, R.A. (2014) Risk assessment in parole decisions: A study of life sentence prisoners in England and Wales. Doctoral thesis, University of Birmingham. Available at http://etheses.bham.ac.uk/5476, accessed on 25 May 2017.

Forde, R.A. (2017) When profit comes in the door, does science go out the window? In B. Cripps (ed.) *Psychometric Testing: Critical Perspectives*. London: Wiley.

Friendship, C., Blud, L., Erikson, M. and Travers, R. (2002) *An evaluation of cognitive behavioural treatment for prisoners*. Home Office Research, *Findings 161*. Available at library.college.police.uk/docs/hofindings/r161.pdf, accessed on 18 August 2016.

Furby, L., Blackshaw, L. and Weinrott, M.R. (1989) Sex offender recidivism: A review. *Psychological Bulletin 105(1)*, 3–30.

Gannon, T.A., and Ward, T. (2014) Where has all the psychology gone? A critical review of evidence-based psychological practice in correctional settings. *Aggression and Violent Behavior 19*(4), 435–446.

Goldacre, B. (2008) *Bad Science*. London: Fourth Estate.

Goldacre, B. (2012) *Bad Pharma*. London: Fourth Estate.

Gore, K.S. (2007) Adjusted actuarial assessment of sex offenders: The impact of clinical overrides on predictive accuracy. PhD, Iowa State University. Unpublished.

Grubin, D. (2011) A large-scale evaluation of Risk Matrix 2000 in Scotland. *Sexual Abuse: A Journal of Research and Treatment 23*(4), 419–433.

Gudjonsson, G. (1997) *The Gudjonsson Suggestibility Scales Manual*. Hove, East Sussex: Psychology Press.

Gudjonsson, G. (2003) *The Psychology of Interrogations and Confessions: A Handbook*. Chichester: John Wiley and Sons.

Guy, L.S., Kusaj, C., Packer, I.K. and Douglas, K.S. (2015) Influence of the HCR-20, LS/CMI, and PCL-R on decisions about parole suitability among lifers. *Law and Human Behavior 39*(3), 232–243.

Hagen, M. (1997) *Whores of the Court: The Fraud of Psychiatric Testimony and the Rape of American Justice*. New York, NY: HarperCollins.

Hamilton, F. (2017). Expert warnings over failure of rehab for rapists were ignored. *The Times, 1 July 2017*. Available at https://www.thetimes.co.uk/edition/news/expert-warnings-over-failure-of-sexual-offenders-treatment-programme-were-ignored-b78n05ng7, accessed on 3 July 2017.

Hanson, R.K. (2001) Age and sexual recidivism: A comparison of rapists and child molesters. *Public Safety Canada*. Available at www.publicsafety.gc.ca/cnt/rsrcs/pblctns/sxl-rcdvsm-cmprsn/index-en.aspx, accessed on 25 May 2017.

Hanson, R. K., and Bussière, M. T. (1998) Predicting relapse: A meta-analysis of sexual offender recidivism studies. *Journal of Consulting and Clinical Psychology 66*(2), 348–362.

Hanson, R.K., and Morton-Bourgon, K.E. (2004) *Predictors of sexual recidivism: An updated meta-analysis*. Toronto, Ontario: Public Works and Government Services Canada.

Hanson, R.K., and Morton-Bourgon, K.E. (2005) The characteristics of persistent sexual offenders: A meta-analysis of recidivism studies. *Journal of Consulting and Clinical Psychology 73*(6), 1154–1163.

Hanson, R.K., and Morton-Bourgon, K.E. (2009) The accuracy of recidivism risk assessments for sexual offenders: A meta-analysis of 118 prediction studies. *Psychological Assessment 21*(1), 1–21.

Hanson, R.K., Bourgon, G., Helmus, L., and Hodgson, S. (2009) A meta-analysis of the effectiveness of treatment for sexual offenders: Risk, need, and responsivity. *Public Safety Canada*. Available at www.publicsafety.gc.ca/cnt/rsrcs/pblctns/2009-01-trt/2009-01-trt-eng.pdf, accessed on 25 May 2017.

Hanson, R.K., Gordon, A., Harris, A.J.R., Marques, J. K., *et al.* (2002) First report of the Collaborative Outcome Data Project on the effectiveness of psychological treatment for sex offenders. *Sexual Abuse: A Journal of Research and Treatment 14*(2), 169–194.

Hanson, R.K., Harris, A.J.R., Scott, T.-L. and Helmus, L. (2007) *Assessing the risk of sexual offenders on community supervision: The Dynamic Supervision Project.* Ottawa, Ontario: Public Safety Canada. Available at www.static99.org/pdfdocs/hansonharrisscottandhelmus2007.pdf, accessed on 25 May 2017.

Hare, R.D. (1998) The Hare PCL-R: Some issues concerning its use and misuse. *Legal and Criminological Psychology, 3*(1), 99–119.

Hare, R.D. (1999) *Without Conscience: The Disturbing World of the Psychopaths among Us.* New York, NY: Guilford Press.

Hare, R.D. (2003) *Hare PCL-R Technical Manual* (2nd edn). Toronto, ON: Multi-Health Systems.

Harkins, L., Beech, R. and Goodwill, A. (2010) Examining the influence of denial, motivation, and risk on sexual recidivism. *Sexual Abuse: A Journal of Research and Treatment 22*(1), 78–94.

Harkins, L., Howard, P., Barnett, G., Wakeling, H.C. and Miles, C. (2014) Relationships between denial, risk, and recidivism in sexual offenders. *Archives of Sexual Behavior 44*(1), 157–166.

Harris, J.R. (1995) Where is the child's environment? A group socialization theory of development. *Psychological Review 102*(3), 458–489.

Hart, S.D. (2005) The 'state of the art' in risk assessment. Paper presented at the International Conference on the Management and Treatment of Dangerous Offenders, York, England.

Hart, S.D., Michie, C. and Cooke, D.J. (2007) Precision of actuarial risk assessment instruments: Evaluating the 'margins of error' of group v. individual predictions of violence. *British Journal of Psychiatry 190*(suppl.49), 60–65.

Heinz, A.M., Heinz, J.P., Senderowitz, S.J., and Vance, M.A. (1976) Sentencing by parole board: An evaluation. *The Journal of Criminal Law and Criminology 67*(1), 1–31.

Helmus, L., Hanson, R.K., Thornton, D., Babchishin, K.M. and Harris, A.J.R. (2012) Absolute recidivism rates predicted by Static-99R and Static-2002R sex offender risk assessment tools vary across samples: A meta-analysis. *Criminal Justice and Behavior 39*(9), 1148–1171.

Henning, K.R. and Frueh, B.C. (1996) Cognitive-behavioral treatment of incarcerated offenders: An evaluation of the Vermont Department of Corrections' cognitive self-change program. *Criminal Justice and Behavior 23*, 523–541.

Hewson, B. (2014) The cult of victimhood and the limits of the law, part 1. *The Barrister*. Available at www.barristermagazine.com/barrister/index. php?id=544, accessed on 18 March 2017.

HM Inspectorate of Probation (2006) *An independent review of a serious further offence case: Anthony Rice*. London, England: HM Inspectorate of Probation. Available at www.justiceinspectorates.gov.uk/probation/wp-content/uploads/sites/5/2014/03/anthonyricereport-rps.pdf, accessed on 25 May 2017.

Hoffman, D.H. (2015) *Report to the Special Committee of the Board of Directors of the American Psychological Association: Independent Review Relating to APA Ethics Guidelines, National Security Interrogations, and Torture*. Washington, DC: American Psychological Association.

Hood, R. and Shute, S. (1999) Parole decision making: Weighing the risk to the public. *Home Office Research Findings 114*. Available at http://webarchive. nationalarchives.gov.uk/20110218135832/http://rds.homeoffice.gov.uk/rds/pdfs/r114.pdf, accessed on 25 May 2017.

Hood, R. and Shute, S. (2000) The parole system at work: A study of risk-based decision-making. *Home Office Research Study 202*. Available at http://rds. homeoffice.gov.uk/rds/pdfs/hors202.pdf, accessed on 25 May 2017.

Hutchings, B. and Mednick, S.A. (1974) Registered criminality in the adoptive and biological parents of registered male adoptees. In S.A. Mednick, F. Schulsinger, J. Higgins and B. Bell (eds), *Genetics, Environment, and Psychopathology*. Amsterdam: North Holland.

James, E. (2016) *Redeemable: A Memoir of Darkness and Hope*. London: Bloomsbury Circus.

Jolliffe, D. and Farrington, D. (2007) *A Systematic Review of the National and International Evidence on the Effectiveness of Interventions with Violent Offenders*. (16/07). London: Ministry of Justice Available at www.crim.cam.ac.uk/people/academic_research/david_farrington/violmoj.pdf, accessed on 25 May 2017.

Kahneman, D. (2011) *Thinking, Fast and Slow*. London: Allen Lane.

Kakoullis, A., Le Mesurier, N. and Kingston, P. (2010) The mental health of older prisoners. [Review]. *International Psychogeriatrics 22*(5), 693–701.

Karpowitz, D. and Kenner, M. (1995) *Education as Crime Prevention: The Case for Reinstating Pell Grant Eligibility for the Incarcerated*. Annandale-on-Hudson, NY: Bard College.

Kenworthy, T., Adams, C.E., Bilby, C.A.L., Brooks-Gordon, B. and Fenton, M. (2003) Psychological interventions for those who have sexually offended or are at risk of offending. *The Cochrane Collaboration*. doi: 10.1002/14651858. CD004858

Kingston, D.A., Olver, M.E., Harris, M., Wong, S.C.P. and Bradford, J.M. (2015) The relationship between mental disorder and recidivism in sexual offenders. *International Journal of Forensic Mental Health 14*(1), 10–22.

Kingston, P., Le Mesurier, N., Yorston, G., Wardle, S. and Heath, L. (2011) Psychiatric morbidity in older prisoners: Unrecognized and undertreated. *International Psychogeriatrics 23*(8), 1354–1360.

Kline, P. (2000) *A Psychometrics Primer.* London: Free Association Books.

Krauss, D.A. (2004) Adjusting risk of recidivism: Do judicial departures worsen or improve recidivism prediction under the federal sentencing guidelines? *Behavioral Sciences and the Law 22*, 731–750.

Kroner, D.G., Mills, J.F. and Reddon, J.R. (2005) A coffee can, factor analysis, and prediction of antisocial behaviour: The structure of criminal risk. *International Journal of Law and Psychiatry 28*, 360–374.

Krznarik, R. (2013) Have we all been duped by the Myers-Briggs test? *Fortune*, 15 May. Available at http://fortune.com/2013/05/15/have-we-all-been-duped-by-the-myers-briggs-test, accessed on 25 May 2017.

Lifton, R.J. (1989) *Thought Reform and the Psychology of Totalism: A Study of 'Brainwashing' in China.* Chapel Hill, NC: University of North Carolina Press.

Livesley, W.J. (2012) Integrated treatment: A conceptual framework for an evidence-based approach to the treatment of personality disorder. *Journal of Personality Disorders 26*(1), 17–42.

Loftus, E.F. (1997) Creating false memories. *Scientific American 277*, 70–75.

Loranger, A.W. (1997) *Assessment and Diagnosis of Personality Disorders: International Personality Disorder Examination (IPDE).* New York: Cambridge.

Lösel, F. and Schmucker, M. (2005) The effectiveness of treatment for sexual offenders: A comprehensive meta-analysis. *Journal of Experimental Criminology 1*, 117–146.

Marques, J.K., Wiederanders, M., Day, D.M., Nelson, C. and van Ommeren, A. (2005) Effects of a relapse prevention program on sexual recidivism: Final results from California's sex offender treatment and evaluation project (SOTEP). *Sexual Abuse: A Journal of Research and Treatment 17*(1), 79–107.

McCord, W. and McCord, J. (1964) *The Psychopath: An Essay on the Criminal Mind.* Princeton, NJ: Van Nostrand.

McDougall, C., Perry, A.E., Clarbour, J., Bowles, R. and Worthy, G. (2009) *Evaluation of HM Prison Service Enhanced Thinking Skills Programme: Report on the Outcomes from a Randomised Controlled Trial.* (3/09). London: Ministry of Justice. Available at www.reclassering.nl/documents/Rapport%20ETS.pdf, accessed on 19 August 2016.

McGinnies, E. (1949) Emotionality and perceptual defense. *Psychological Review* 56(5), 244–251.

McNaughton Nicholls, C., Callanan, M., Lagard, R., Tomaszewski, W., Purdon, S. and Webster, S.D. (2010) *Examining Implementation of the Stable and Acute Dynamic Risk Assessment Tool Pilot in England and Wales.* (4/10). London: Ministry of Justice. Available at www.publicsafety.gc.ca/cnt/rsrcs/pblctns/2009-01-trt/2009-01-trt-eng.pdf, accessed on 26 May 2017.

McNeil, B., Pauker, S.G., Sox, H.C.J. and Tversky, A. (1982) On the elicitation of preferences for alternative therapies. *New England Journal of Medicine 306,* 1259–1262.

Meehl, P. (1954) *Clinical versus Statistical Prediction: A Theoretical Analysis and a Review of the Evidence.* Minneapolis, MN: University of Minnesota Press.

Meehl, P. (1973) Why I do not attend case conferences. In P. Meehl (ed.) *Psychodiagnosis: Selected Papers.* Minneapolis, MN: University of Minnesota Press.

Mews, A., Di Bella, L., and Purver, M. (2017). *Impact evaluation of the prison-based Core Sex Offender Treatment Programme.* London: Ministry of Justice. Available at https://www.gov.uk/government/uploads/system/uploads/attachment_data/file/623876/sotp-report-web-.pdf, accessed on 3 July 2017.

Miller, A.K., Rufino, K.A., Boccaccini, M.T., Jackson, R.L. and Murrie, D.C. (2011) Differences in person perception: Raters' personality traits relate to their Psychopathy Checklist-Revised scoring tendencies. *Assessment 18(2),* 253–260.

Miller, G.A. (1956) The magical number seven, plus or minus two: Some limits on our capacity for processing information. *Psychological Review 63,* 81–93.

Ministry of Justice (2013) *Story of the Prison Population 1993–2013 England and Wales.* London: Ministry of Justice. Available at www.gov.uk/government/uploads/system/uploads/attachment_data/file/218185/story-prison-population.pdf, accessed on 25 May 2017.

Minkel, J.R. (2010) Fear review: Critique of forensic psychopathy scale delayed 3 years by threat of lawsuit. *Scientific American,* 17 June.

Mitchison, S., Rix, K. J., Renvoize, E. B. and Schweiger, M. (1994) Recorded psychiatric morbidity in a large prison for male remanded and sentenced prisoners. *Medicine, Science and the Law 34(4),* 324–330.

Mlodinow, L. (2009) *The Drunkard's Walk: How Randomness Rules Our Lives.* London: Allen Lane.

Mokros, A., Stadtland, C., Osterheider, M. and Nedopil, N. (2010) Assessment of risk for violent recidivism through multivariate Bayesian classification. *Psychology, Public Policy, and Law 16,* 418–450.

Mooney, J.L. and Daffern, M. (2011) Institutional aggression as a predictor of violent recidivism: Implications for parole decision making. *The International Journal of Forensic Mental Health 10,* 52–63.

Morgan, K. and Smith, B. (2005a) Parole release decisions revisited: An analysis of parole release decisions for violent inmates in a southeastern state. *Journal of Criminal Justice 33*(3), 277–287.

Morgan, K. and Smith, B. (2005b) Victims, punishment, and parole: The effect of victim participation on parole hearings. *Criminology and Public Policy 4*(2), 333–360.

Morgan, R.D., Kroner, D.G., Mills, J.F., Serna, C. and McDonald, B. (2013) Dynamic risk assessment: A validation study. *Journal of Criminal Justice 41*(2), 115–124.

Morton, S. (2009) Can OASys deliver consistent assessments of offenders? Results from the inter-rater reliability study. Ministry of Justice *Research Summary 1/09*. Available at http://webarchive.nationalarchives.gov. uk/20100505212400/http://www.justice.gov.uk/publications/docs/oasys-research-summary-01-09.pdf, accessed on 14 July 2016.

Murrie, D.C., Boccaccini, M.T., Caperton, J. and Rufino, K.A. (2012) Field validity of the Psychopathy Checklist-Revised in sex offender risk assessment. *Psychological Assessment 24*(2), 524–529.

Murrie, D.C., Boccaccini, M.T., Guarnera, L.A. and Rufino, K.A. (2013) Are forensic experts biased by the side that retained them? *Psychological Science 24*(10), 1889–1897.

Murrie, D.C., Boccaccini, M.T., Johnson, J.T. and Janke, C. (2009) Does interrater (dis)agreement on Psychopathy Checklist scores in sexually violent predator trials suggest partisan allegiance in forensic evaluations? *Law and Human Behavior 32*(4), 352–362.

Neal, T.M.S. and Grisso, T. (2014) The cognitive underpinnings of bias in forensic mental health evaluations. *Psychology, Public Policy, and Law* (preprint publication online). doi: http://dx.doi.org/10.1037/a0035824

Newman, A. (2016) Psychologists working with approved premises. Paper presented at the BPS Division of Forensic Psychology Annual Conference 2016, Brighton.

Northcraft, G.B. and Neale, M.A. (1987) Experts, amateurs and real estate. An anchoring-and-adjustment perspective on property pricing decisions. *Organisational Behavior and Human Decision Processes 39*, 84–97.

Nugent, P. and Zamble, E. (2001) Affecting detention referrals through proper selection. *Forum on Corrections Research 13*(1), 27–30.

O'Toole, M. (2010) Interview: Jo Bailey, NOMS head of forensic psychology. *Civil Service World*. Available at www.civilserviceworld.com/psychologists, accessed on 18 July 2017.

Office of Justice Programs (2014) *Sex Offender Management Assessment and Planning Initiative*. Available at www.smart.gov/SOMAPI/pfv.html, accessed on 27 October 2016.

Oskamp, S. (1965) Overconfidence in case-study judgments. *Journal of Consulting Psychology 29*(3), 261–265.

Padfield, N. and Liebling, A. (2000) An exploration of decision-making at discretionary lifer panels. *Home Office Research Study 213*. Available at www.researchgate.net/publication/268259295_An_exploration_of_decision-making_at_discretionary_lifer_panels, accessed on 26 May 2017.

Park, R. L. (2000) *Voodoo Science: The Road from Foolishness to Fraud*. New York: Oxford University Press.

Parris, M. (2015) We're all victims of the victimhood industry. *The Times*, 17 October.

Perry, J.C., Banon, E. and Ianni, F. (1999) Effectiveness of psychotherapy for personality disorders. *American Journal of Psychiatry 156*(9), 1312–1321.

Petrosino, A., Turpin-Petrosino, C. and Buehler, J. (2009) 'Scared straight' and other juvenile awareness programs for preventing juvenile delinquency [review]. *The Cochrane Library* (1). Available at http://onlinelibrary.wiley.com/doi/10.1002/14651858.CD002796.pub2/full, accessed on 26 May 2017.

Philipse, M.W., Koeter, M.W., van der Staak, C.P. and van den Brink, W. (2006) Static and dynamic patient characteristics as predictors of criminal recidivism: A prospective study in a Dutch forensic psychiatric sample. *Law and Human Behavior 30*(3), 309–327.

Porter, S., Birt, A.R. and Boer, D.P. (2001) Investigation of the criminal and conditional release profiles of Canadian federal offenders as a function of psychopathy and age. *Law and Human Behavior 25*(6), 647–661.

Porter, S., ten Brinke, L. and Wilson, K. (2009) Crime profiles and conditional release performance of psychopathic and non-psychopathic sexual offenders. *Legal and Criminological Psychology 14*(1), 109–118.

Postman, L., Bronson, W.C., and Gropper, G.L. (1953) Is there a mechanism of perceptual defense? *The Journal of Abnormal and Social Psychology 48*(2), 215–224.

Prisoners' Education Trust (2015) New government data on English and maths skills of prisoners. Available at www.prisonerseducation.org.uk/media-press/new-government-data-on-english-and-maths-skills-of-prisoners, accessed on 17 November 2016.

Prochaska, J.O. and DiClemente, C.C. (1982) Transtheoretical therapy: Towards a more integrative of model of change. *Psychotherapy: Theory, Research and Practice 20*, 161–173.

Pulakos, E.D. (2005) Selection Assessment Methods: A guide to implementing formal assessments to build a high-quality workforce. Available at www.shrm.org/hr-today/trends-and-forecasting/special-reports-and-expert-views/documents/selection-assessment-methods.pdf, accessed on 26 May 2017.

Quinsey, V.L. and Maguire, A. (1986) Maximum security psychiatric patients: Actuarial and clinical prediction of dangerousness. *Journal of Interpersonal Violence* 1(2), 143–171.

Quinsey, V.L., Harris, G.T., Rice, M.E. and Cormier, C.A. (2006) *Violent Offenders: Appraising and Managing Risk* (2nd edn). Washington DC: American Psychological Association.

Reason, J. (1990) *Human Error*. Cambridge: Cambridge University Press.

Rice, A.K., Boccaccini, M.T., Harris, P.B. and Hawes, S.W. (2014) Does field reliability for Static-99 scores decrease as scores increase? *Psychological Assessment.* doi: 10.1037/pas0000009

Rice, M.E. and Harris, G.T. (2003) The size and sign of treatment effects in sex offender therapy. *Annals of the New York Academy of Sciences 989*, 428–440.

Robertson, I., Bartram, D. and Callinan, M. (2002) Personnel selection and assessment. In P. Warr (ed.) *Psychology at Work* (5th edn). London: Penguin.

Rose, D. (2017). The scandal of the sex crime 'cure' hubs: How minister buried report into £100 million prison programme to treat paedophiles and rapists that INCREASED reoffending rates. *Mail Online*. Available at www. dailymail.co.uk/news/article-4635876/Scandal-100million-sex-crime-cure-hubs.html, accessed on 27 June 2017.

Rosenhan, D.L. (1975) On being sane in insane places. In T.J. Scheff (ed.) *Labeling Madness*. Oxford: Prentice-Hall.

Rufino, K.A., Boccaccini, M.T. and Guy, L.S. (2011) Scoring subjectivity and item performance on measures used to assess violence risk: The PCL-R and HCR-20 as exemplars. *Assessment 18*(4), 453–463.

Ruiz, M. A., Douglas, K.S., Edens, J.F., Nikolova, N.L. and Lilienfeld, S.O. (2012) Co-occurring mental health and substance use problems in offenders: Implications for risk assessment. *Psychological Assessment 24*(1), 77–87.

Sadlier, G. (2010) *Evaluation of the Impact of the HM Prison Service Enhanced Thinking Skills Programme on Reoffending Outcomes of the Surveying Prisoner Crime Reduction (SPCR) Sample.* (19/10). London: Ministry of Justice. Available at www.gov.uk/government/uploads/system/uploads/attachment_data/file/193641/eval-enhanced-thinking-skills-prog.pdf, accessed on 26 May 2017.

Sampson, A. (1973) *The Sovereign State: The Secret History of ITT*. London: Hodder and Stoughton.

Sampson, R.J. and Laub, J.H. (2003) Life-course desisters? Trajectories of crime among delinquent boys followed to age 70. *Criminology 41*(3), 301–339.

Schmucker, M. and Lösel, F. (2015) The effects of sexual offender treatment on recidivism: An international meta-analysis of sound quality evaluations. *Journal of Experimental Criminology.* doi: 10.1007/s11292-015-9241-z

Serin, R. and Preston, D.L. (2000) Programming for violent offenders. *Forum on Corrections Research* 12(2), 45–48. Available at www.csc-scc.gc.ca/research/forum/e122/122k_e.pdf, accessed on 18 August 2016.

Serin, R.C., Gobeil, R. and Preston, D.L. (2009) Evaluation of the persistently violent offender treatment program. *International Journal of Offender Therapy and Comparative Criminology* 53(1), 57–73.

Sheldon, K. and Howitt, D. (2008) Sexual fantasy in paedophile offenders: Can any model explain satisfactorily new findings from a study of Internet and contact sexual offenders? *Legal and Criminological Psychology* 13, 137–158.

Shepherd, S.M., and Lewis-Fernandez, R. (2016) Forensic risk assessment and cultural diversity: Contemporary challenges and future directions. *Psychology, Public Policy, and Law* 22(4), 427–438.

Shine, J. and Hobson, J. (1997) Construct validity of the Hare Psychopathy Checklist, Revised, on a UK prison population. *Journal of Forensic Psychiatry* 8(3), 546–561.

Skeem, J.L. and Cooke, D.J. (2010) Is criminal behavior a central component of psychopathy? Conceptual directions for resolving the debate. *Psychological Assessment* 22(2), 433–445.

Skeem, J.L., Polaschek, D.L.L., Patrick, C.J. and Lilienfeld, S.O. (2011) Psychopathic personality: Bridging the gap between scientific evidence and public policy. *Psychological Science in the Public Interest* 12(3), 95–162.

Skinner, B.F. (1965) *Science and Human Behaviour*. New York: The Free Press.

Skinner, B.F. (2014) *Verbal Behaviour*. Cambridge, MA: B.F. Skinner Foundation. Available at www.bfskinner.org/wp-content/uploads/2014/05/Verbal-Behavior.pdf, accessed on 1 August 2016.

Slater, L. (2004) *Opening Skinner's Box: Great Psychological Experiments of the Twentieth Century*. London: Bloomsbury Publishing.

Slovic, P., Monaghan, J. and MacGregor, D.G. (2000) Violence risk assessment and risk communication. *Law and Human Behavior* 24(3), 271–296.

Smith, B., Watkins, E. and Morgan, K. (1997) The effect of victim participation on parole decisions: Results from a south-eastern state. *Criminal Justice Policy Review* 8(1), 57–74.

Sterbenz, C. (2014) Why Norway's prison system is so successful. *Business Insider UK*, 11 December. Available at http://uk.businessinsider.com/why-norways-prison-system-is-so-successful-2014-12, accessed on 20 January 2017.

Steurer, S.J. and Smith, L.G. (2003) *Education Reduces Crime: Three-state Recidivism Study (Executive Summary)*. Lanham, MD: Correctional Education Association.

Stewart, A., Dennison, S. and Waterson, E. (2002) Pathways from child maltreatment to juvenile offending. *Trends and Issues in Criminal Justice* (241). Available at www.aic.gov.au/media_library/publications/tandi_pdf/tandi241.pdf, accessed on 18 July 2017.

Strang, H., Sherman, L.W., Mayo-Wilson, E., Woods, D. and Ariel, B. (2013) Restorative Justice Conferencing (RJC) Using Face-to-face Meetings of Offenders and Victims: Effects on Offender Recidivism and Victim Satisfaction. A Systematic Review. *Campbell Systematic Reviews* 2013: 12. Available at www.restorativejustice.org.uk/resources/restorative-justice-conferencing-using-face-face-meetings-offenders-and-victims-effects, accessed on 26 May 2017.

Stubbs, J. and Durcan, G. (2016) Preventing prison suicide: Perspectives from the inside. *Centre for Mental Health*, 24 May. Available at www.centreformentalhealth.org.uk/preventing-prison-suicide, accessed on 18 March 2017.

Sutherland, S. (2009) *Irrationality*. London: Pinter and Martin.

Sutton, H. (1971) *Vector*. New York: Dell Books.

Svenson, O. (1981) Are we all less risky and more skilful than our fellow drivers? *Acta Psychologica* 47, 143–148.

Tharoor, I. (2014) Pope Francis says evolution is real and God is no wizard, *The Washington Post*, 28 October. Available at www.washingtonpost.com/news/worldviews/wp/2014/10/28/pope-francis-backs-theory-of-evolution-says-god-is-no-wizard/?utm_term=.a22e8fa8ce40, accessed on 26 May 2017.

The Parole Board for England and Wales (2015) Parole Board Constitutional Document. London: The Parole Board. Available at www.gov.uk/government/organisations/parole-board/about/our-governance, accessed on 8 August 2016.

Thomas, M. and Jackson, S. (2003) Cognitive-skills group work. In G.J. Towl (ed.) *Psychology in Prisons*. Oxford: Blackwell.

Thomas-Peter, B. (2006) The modern context of psychology in corrections: Influences, limitations and values of 'What Works'. In G.J. Towl (ed.) *Psychological Research in Prisons*. Oxford: BPS Blackwell.

Thomas-Peter, B. (2015) Structural violence in forensic psychiatry. In D.A. Crichton and G.J. Towl (eds) *Forensic Psychology* (2nd edn). London: Wiley.

Thomas-Peter, B. and Jones, J. (2006) High-risk inferences in assessing high risk: Outstanding concerns in the clinical use of the PCL-R. *The British Journal of Forensic Practice* 8(4), 3–18.

Towl, G.J. and Crichton, D.A. (1996) *The Handbook of Psychology for Forensic Practitioners*. London: Routledge.

Towl, G.J. and Crichton, D.A. (2016) The emperor's new clothes? *The Psychologist* 29(3), 188–191.

Transform (2014) Drug decriminalisation in Portugal: Setting the record straight. *Transform*, 11 June. Available at www.tdpf.org.uk/blog/drug-decriminalisation-portugal-setting-record-straight, accessed on 17 January 2017.

Tully, R.J., Browne, K.D. and Craig, L.A. (2014) An examination of the predictive validity of the Structured Assessment of Risk and Need – Treatment Needs Analysis (SARN-TNA) in England and Wales. *Criminal Justice and Behaviour* 42(5), 509–528.

Turpin-Petrosino, C. (1999) Are limiting enactments effective? An experimental test of decision making in a presumptive parole state. *Journal of Criminal Justice* 27(4), 321–332.

Tversky, A. and Kahneman, D. (1974) Judgement under uncertainty: Heuristics and biases. *Science 185*, 1124–1131.

Twardosz, S. and Lutzker, J.R. (2010) Child maltreatment and the developing brain: A review of neuroscience perspectives. *Aggression and Violent Behavior* 15(1), 59–68.

Værøy, H. (2011) Depression, anxiety, and history of substance abuse among Norwegian inmates in preventive detention: Reasons to worry? *BMC Psychiatry.* doi: 10.1186/1471-244X-11-40

Varela, J.G., Boccaccini, M.T., Murrie, D.C., Caperton, J.D. and Gonzalez Jr, E. (2013) Do the Static-99 and Static-99R perform similarly for White, Black, and Latino sexual offenders? *The International Journal of Forensic Mental Health 12*(4), 231–243.

Vitacco, M.J., Neumann, C.S., and Jackson, R.L. (2005) Testing a Four-Factor Model of Psychopathy and Its Association with Ethnicity, Gender, Intelligence, and Violence. *Journal of Consulting and Clinical Psychology 73*(3), 466–476.

Wakeling, H.C., Freemantle, N., Beech, A.R., and Elliott, I.A. (2011) Identifying predictors of recidivism in a large sample of United Kingdom sexual offenders: A prognostic model. *Psychological Services 8*(4), 307–318.

Walsh, T. and Walsh, Z. (2006) The evidentiary introduction of psychopathy checklist-revised assessed psychopathy in US courts: Extent and appropriateness. *Law and Human Behavior 30*(4), 493–507.

Walters, G.D., and Lowenkamp, C.T. (2016) Predicting recidivism with the Psychological Inventory of Criminal Thinking Styles (PICTS) in community-supervised male and female federal offenders. *Psychological Assessment 28*(6), 652–659.

Webster, S.D., Mann, R.E., Carter, A.J., Long, J., *et al.* (2006) Inter-rater reliability of dynamic risk assessment with sexual offenders. *Psychology, Crime and Law 12*(4), 439–452.

Wegner, D.M. (1994) *White Bears and Other Unwanted Thoughts: Suppression, Obsession, and the Psychology of Mental Control.* New York, NY: Guilford Press.

Wegner, D.M. (2002) *The Illusion of Conscious Will.* Cambridge, MA: Massachusetts Institute of Technology.

Weir, K. (2016) Inequality at school. *Monitor on Psychology* 47(10), 42–47.

Weisburd, D. (2003) Ethical practice and evaluations of interventions in crime and justice: The moral imperative for randomized trials. *Evaluation Review,* 27, 336-354.

Welsh, A. and Ogloff, J. (2000) Full parole and the aboriginal experience: Accounting for the racial discrepancies in release rates. *Canadian Journal of Criminology* 42(4), 469–491.

Wilkinson, R. and Pickett, K. (2009) *The Spirit Level: Why Equality is Better for Everyone.* London: Penguin Books.

Wilson, J. A. (2007) Habilitation or harm: Project Greenlight and the potential consequences of correctional programming. *National Institute of Justice Journal (257)*, 2–7.

Wood, J.M., Nezworski, M.T., Lilienfeld, S.O. and Garb, H.N. (2003) *What's Wrong with the Rorschach? Science Confronts the Controversial Inkblot Test.* San Francisco: Wiley.

Yee, A.G. (2004). *Medical and mental illness in the ageing jail population.* Unpublished Ph.D. thesis. George Fox University, Oregon.

Zinger, I. and Forth, A.E. (1998) Psychopathy and Canadian criminal proceedings: The potential for human rights abuses. *Canadian Journal of Criminology* 40(3), 237–276.

SUBJECT INDEX

AUTHOR INDEX